yoga is THE ALL

an invitation to <u>sensational</u> life

reflections & invitations by

Brian J. Shircliff & the Companions of VITALITY Cincinnati

Helen Buswinka • Penny Costilla • Mike Eck • Kristen Iker
Crystal Judge • Leann Kane • Nikki Leonard • Tina Nelson
Aprilann Pandora • Logan Probst • CJ Pierce • Amanda Sanders
Liz Smith • Tonia Smith • Jean Marie Stross • Val Vogel
Patricia Williams • Linsay Wilson • Carol T. Yeazell

VITALITY

buzz & books

(re)discovering roots

vitalitycincinnati.org

yoga is THE ALL: an invitation to sensational life

Published by VITALITY buzz & books Cincinnati, OH (U.S.A.)

vitalitycincinnati.org

This book has been published to raise funds for VITALITY Cincinnati, a 501(c)3 education-based nonprofit. All proceeds from sales of this book benefit the mission of VITALITY Cincinnati: sharing holistic self-care from neighborhood to neighborhood, person to person, and breath by breath since 2010.

The opinions and ideas expressed herein are those of the authors and do not necessarily represent the opinions of the Board of Trustees of VITALITY Cincinnati. Any errors, of course, are solely the authors'.

Every effort has been made to give credit to other people's original ideas through the text itself and the recommended resources that follow this text. If you feel something should be credited to someone and is not, please get in touch through vitalitycincinnati. org and every effort will be made to correct this text for future printings. Thank you!

We invite you to honor your mind, your body, your whole self. Do only what you know to be right for you. While the invitations offered here in this book, on VITALITY's website and social media, and in our classes are geared to be gentle and easily modified by the participant to fit the participants's needs, please consult your medical doctor or health professional before undertaking any practices shared by VITALITY, its staff or volunteers.

These artists contributed their work to this edition—thank you! Parrish Monk created the beautiful painting on the front cover as a fundraiser for his INKAA Education Program. Julie Lucas of withinwonder.com created VITALITY Cincinnati's inspiring logos and the insightful interior artwork on the pages that follow. Diana Avergon created the beautiful print on the back cover of this book. Tom Payne graciously and wonderfully photographed the cover paintings.

Feldenkrais®, Feldenkrais Method®, Functional Integration®, and Awareness Through Movement® are service marks of the Feldenkrais Guild® of North America. Movement Intelligence® & Bones for Life® are the intellectual property of Ruthy Alon. And honoring all of these special programs lifted up as helpful in this book: The Bengston Energy Healing Method®, Healing Touch Program®, Body-Mind Centering®, EmbodiYoga®, SoulCollage®, Esalen®

First published by Dog Ear Publishing
8888 Keystone Crossing
Suite 1300
Indianapolis, IN 46240
www.dogearpublishing.net

ISBN: 978-145756-944-9

Library of Congress Control Number: _____

This book is dedicated to all
who have come to know the heartbeat of the earth

and who are discovering
that yoga, then, is more a question
of 'how' we do and are
than 'what' we do and try to become...

may one's personal experience guide
all we do and all we teach as 'yoga'

may we appreciate the wisdom
of the tangled mess and the brilliance
coexisting in the yoga 'traditions'
which have always been permeable

may we appreciate the wisdom
of the tangled mess and the brilliance
coexisting within every creature —
you, me, ALL —
and, with such wisdom, love even more.

**In gratitude to our VATRONS
who seek with us all a new way forward &
who have helped bring forward this new book
by contributing $25 or more
to make this publication possible**

we thank you!

Anonymous, Cynthia Allen & Larry Wells, Davi Brown,
Helen Buswinka, Joyce & Tom Choquette, Michael Conway,
Mary & Tim Cronin, Erin Crowley, Joyce Dicks, Mary Duennes,
Andy Fraley, James Gaunt, Brian Geeding, Ed Hausfeld,
Amelia Herold, Kristen Iker, Gary Johnson, Alex Jones,
Rachel & Matt Kemper, Maggie & Russ King, Mary Laymon,
Allie & George Maggini, Melissa Maxwell, Melissa McNeill,
Mary Ann Meyer, Alice Michels, Parrish Monk, Melanie Moon,
Becky Morrissey, Ellen Noonan, Aprilann Pandora, Bob Reineke,
Alli Shircliff & Rafael Gallardo, Brian Shircliff, Dan Smith, Tonia Smith,
Jean Marie Stross & Daniel Price, Joy & Bob Thaler, Howard Thoresen,
Tricia Watts, Tiffany West, Amy & Steve Whitlatch, John Williams,
Elizabeth J. Winters Waite, Carol T. & Bruce Yeazell

CONTENTS

why? 1

INVITATIONS TO THE ALL...
PATANJALI's EIGHT LIMBS:

an image of THE ALL 94-95

Encountering THE ALL...reflections from VITAL-friends

CONTENTS

why?

I like to begin all of my writings with 'why?' to lay out where I'm inviting us to go on this co-writing journey . . . if you'd rather skip to the invitations to experience THE ALL and come back to this later, of course, the choice is yours. Those experiences begin on page 27.

Well, of course you don't need me to tell you that you have known yoga your whole life. Maybe even in the womb. Maybe especially in the womb.

And maybe, like the most of the rest of us, you've forgotten.

Perhaps this little book might be a way to help you and all of us remember. THE ALL.

Sure, we all get little glimpses of it.

THE ALL . . . the bliss-rich experience of life that comes seemingly out of nowhere. And everywhere.

THE ALL . . . the way the sunlight glimmers on that leaf, the way a friend's voice soothes you, the incredible sensation of a beloved's touch, the first taste in the morning that explodes your mouth, the smell of the dank earth in Spring.

THE ALL . . . our place in this infinite universe, even more infinite within us, the whole world of a cell, even more infinite in our dreams—as if 'more infinite' were possible. But I think you get the idea.

Anyway, I hope you get glimpses of it. This 'ALL.' Every day.

Sadly though, the last place many of us find it is in yoga studios. For a lot of reasons. And I've been guilty of that too in the past as a leader of yoga-practice.

The big umbrella under which yoga-practice—as in moving and breathing and resting—has been called in our modern world is 'hatha yoga.' Hatha is a Sanskrit word, something having to do with hitting or striking, something involving effort or force. Later, people perhaps realizing that this was harsh came up with another interpretation of 'hatha' as having to do with the coming together of sun and moon . . . what Carl Jung much later called 'the divine marriage,' the coming together of complements, realizing THE ALL.

While I think remembering the divine marriage of seeming 'complements' is valuable—as you'll soon discover—I think it's very important to be with this more rooted, ancient explanation of 'hatha' as having to do with 'force' (as Sanskrit scholar Jason Birch has researched very thoroughly in "The Meaning of 'hatha' in Early Hathayoga") or 'striking' or violent efforting . . . or as I would like to suggest, doing something that effects change.

And as you'll soon see, hopefully very gently. With as little effort as possible.

In the same article, Birch points out that the great debate in the world of yoga—for centuries!—is whether or not effort should be needed to know enlightenment.

And Birch even leaves Gautama, the human being people called the Buddha, out of the argument. And Gautama, who is said to have practiced the yoga of his day 2500 years ago and did not find enlightenment through yoga, surely does find enlightenment in his own clever way, in a way that is gentle and without force . . . though with great attention!

I'm grateful for scholars like Jason Birch who enlighten those of us who do not—yet—know Sanskrit and who are not afraid to turn over all the words related to a word like 'hatha'—throughout the centuries! —to discover a word's glimmering meaning. Linguists like Birch help us to know how ancient words were used through the centuries—and how they weren't. The Sanskrit glossary I have used often in the past is still touting that sun-moon thing which is nice but which doesn't get to the roots—not the roots of the yoga tradition, not the roots of ourselves and our experience, at least in ALL that we can be.

Sometimes our beliefs get in the way of actually having an experience. That's much of the 'why?' for this book . . . to invite us to peel away layers of what grew to become the 'yoga' we inherited in the 20th & 21st centuries so that we might get a glimmer—a personal experience, perhaps—of what the more ancient yogins might have known.

So . . . this book here in your hands is an invitation to EXPERIENCE, not so much one of philosophical or philological debate.

Our hope at VITALITY is that the EXPERIENCES we invite might participate in what heals our world, in what helps us to remember the whole of it, THE ALL. Perhaps such experiences awaken in us something that helps us to understand the roots of yoga as well . . . of just what the most ancient yogins sitting on the edge the Indus River discovered 3000-5000 years ago.

You might wonder why a white gay guy, born in suburban 'America' (with wonderful Pakistani neighbors on both sides of his family-home—the smells of their gardens and of their kitchens still delight me 30+ years later), who has not yet been to India, who has not yet studied Sanskrit (but has a pretty good touch on ancient languages, (con)textual-analysis, and value-coding in ancient-languages via Greek and Hebrew, biblical studies on my own and at university)—how can someone like this have anything helpful to say about yoga, and enough helpfulness to write a book about it?

Very fair. And yet 25+ years of meditation in a variety of forms on a more than daily basis and very significant holistic studies might give me a pass to say something. Not to mention my personal experience! And yours!

And my ability to analyze texts—especially ancient ones—for their wisdom and their problems seems to have been helpful for a lot of students in a variety of classrooms. Such analysis is really exegesis . . . leading a meaning out of an old text that might have something to say to our world however many centuries later, leading a meaning out of an old text that might expose our assumptions about our own current world and help us to grow as sensible human creatures moving forward.

Just as Birch has done with his study of 'hatha' and its meanings through the centuries, exegesis of ancient texts can help us to peel back the layers of the onion—of that ancient world and of our own 21st century self—to discover the rich smell of the center of the onion . . . and ourselves.

DISCOVERING OUR ASSUMPTIONS...

A friend of mine said something quite profound about these yoga texts that everyone turns to for wisdom, including myself. He grew up in India, and not in the highest caste or class. He and a number of family members have the highest degrees available in their chosen fields and have been very helpful to the modernization and growth of India in ways that humans need: clean water, housing, bridges, etc. And with all this good work, much respected work, he and his family will never be seen for all they are in India because they are not from the highest caste or class.

This should trouble anyone. It troubles me. How some of the trappings of the past hold us down from freedom in the present moment—all too often without even noticing them!

Before I had met this Indian friend for dinner one night, I had been preparing for the next day's class at a nearby coffee shop. When he saw me carrying my copy of *The Bhagavad Gita*—one of the key texts to understanding some of the roots of yoga—he said something that has stayed with me forever, "You know, people of our caste in India often doubt the wisdom of a text like this because its very assumptions are that the caste-system is wise and good. Says it right there in the text, check it out for yourself."

Eek. He's right. *The Bhagavad Gita* does indeed say it multiple times, and even right out of the mouth of the incarnation of God.

I went home that night thinking about the same problems in the Bible. That sometimes the story is about the lower-classes finding clever ways toward liberation—and that sometimes the text was created to deny the lower-classes equality as human beings. All of this is within the same 'book' that is the Bible, this massive book being more of a collection of over 1000 years of writers trying to make sense of life, of THE ALL, all with very different questions beckoning them in each generation.

Ancient world or modern world, life is quite different—right?—when you're on the top of the pyramid of power or when you are being oppressed.

Texts invite us to ponder, to not be so quick to decide on anything.

We must be smart and careful and wise when putting our whole 'yes' on any text—no matter how 'sacred' and 'infallible' people tell us the text is. True of the Bible. True of *The Bhagavad Gita*. True of the words ascribed to Gautama, the Buddha, in *The Dhammapada* or the Pali canon. True of any text.

We must be wise to realize the helpful in any text, and also the problematic.

SWEET LADY J . . . SLOW WISDOM THAT CATCHES YA!

In 2017, I published 3+ years of work on what is considered one of the first voices of the biblical tradition: *Sweet Lady J*. I don't go too far out on the limb to say that this first voice is a woman—other scholars have noted that too. Sweet Lady J (as I call her) or J/Yahwist (as scholars call this biblical 'writer') tells stories that eventually become most of the book of Genesis—and her stories are bawdy, funny, punny, crazy, wild, and very sexy.

More than likely, her stories were told around campfires for centuries. They are fun, memorable—I can imagine the laughs her stories created around those campfires . . . bed-time stories to put things right before a deep night of rest. Her stories do something within the hearer, they unfurl themselves—even 3000 years later, today.

And more than likely, her stories ruffled so many feathers that people began changing them, softening them, cutting out the sexiness and the fun of them.

Some campfires preserved her tales, others changed them. Others took her characters and created new, less sexy plots. In biblical scholarship, we have called these campfire-authors who changed Sweet Lady J's stories and characters E/Elohist. These campfires can't even come to grips with the sexy name for THE ALL that Sweet Lady J uses: Yahweh. E/Elohist calls THE ALL 'Elohim' which gets translated through the tradition as the generic name 'God.' I'll have more to say later about the sexy name that is Yahweh. Yahweh—THE ALL—is quite sexy in Sweet Lady J's stories!

As I worked with Genesis, as I leaned into the diverse voices that are there in that book, I found that some central whole, some very similar imagination exists there—and that's what I played with in the book *Sweet Lady J* . . . attempting to tease out that original voice that is hers from the editorial concrete and other campfires' voices surrounding Sweet Lady J's voice.

When all of these different campfires and peoples were later rounded up and enslaved by the great powers of Assyria and then Babylon in 722 and 597 BCE—this was CENTURIES after Sweet Lady J most likely composed her tales—all of thee campfires with different stories and all of these campfires having to deal with the terrible pains of exile and slavery and losing freedom, it was then that these different versions of stories collided very intimately.

A band of priests tried to be peacemakers between the different campfires and let these multiple versions of stories exist—quite wise! Though how they did that created a soupy mess of a text—Genesis, the first book of the Bible—that is a compilation of all of these differing versions, and even some clever 'glue' to connect them all together in the beginnings of a tradition that soon became Judaism, though it wasn't called that at first. The remaining four books of these priestly editors' masterpiece—Exodus, Leviticus, Numbers, and Deuteronomy—try to cement that tradition together.

As a result, what we have today are the first five books of the Bible—the Torah to Jewish-minded people or the Pentateuch to Christian-minded people or large swaths of The Book to Muslim-minded people.

These five books of the Bible are riddled with contradictions—do this, don't do this. One story glorifies a character who has sex out of wedlock, another area of the text poo-poos such a possibility with death by stoning. Such contradictions happen over and over and over again in the Bible.

I argue that there are plenty of times when Sweet Lady J's writing gets overly softened by men, by the priests who acted as editors to craft those first five books . . . just one more instance of men tamping down a woman's wisdom, even by verb choice.

Read the classics of the yoga tradition—especially Patanjali's Sutras and *The Bhagavad Gita* just to name two key texts—and you'll witness similar problems emerging as there are in the Bible. The Indian friend I mentioned earlier certainly notes one very important problem.

THE SOUPY MESS OF THE YOGA TRADITION(S)

Pick one of the yoga/meditation classics out of India—Patanjali's Sutras or *The Bhagavad Gita* or even *The Dhammapada*—and you'll discover quickly that like the Bible each one of these texts has 'seams'—places where there are contradictions, places where it teaches this way and then later a very different way, places where generation after generation of yoga/meditation practitioners is trying to figure something out by writing/composing.

And these three texts—and many others—even seem to be having conversations with one another as they plod along through the centuries—as their devotees try to take an idea from another group/text and mesh it into their own text's/group's ways of understanding life and the world.

Perhaps a human person is much like a text—what I said ten years ago will (hopefully) be far different from what I say and believe today. I continue to work it out, and am influenced in so many ways through such wise permeability. And I am gift and clarity and brilliance and contradiction and confusion and problem, all rolled into one human person. I venture to say every person is.

So what are we to do? What are we to do with the tangled mess of each human person, each text composed by them? Throw the baby out with the bathwater?

Should we all never again listen to the wisdom of some human-teacher or the Bible, of *The Bhagavad Gita* and Patanjali, of any ancient text that has a dose of caste/class repression in it? or that was written with contradictions or with problematic assumptions?

Friends, there would be nothing to read.

For that matter, should we stop people from talking or stop listening to the ideas espoused by someone who once said something awful or posted something mean-spirited or did something wrong in their life—even if what they have to say today might help people?

Friends, not a single person would be able to speak.

We all have gifts. We all have problems. We're all a tangled, beautiful mess. And we're all trying to figure out how to live this life—and the wise ones try to figure out how to live in such a way that recognizes that each creature is vital to life, that we all participate in THE ALL.

WHAT TO DO ABOUT BABIES & THE DIRTY BATHWATER?

So what are we to do about yoga, if it was propagated by people who believed and lived in such a way that considered some creatures were more valuable than others—indeed that some creatures are better than others (the caste-system) and even that some people—the untouchables—didn't even fit into the hierarchy and are expendable and worth nothing?

I'll lay down my cards here on the table for you to see very clearly my take on the dirty bathwater and what to do about it . . . about 'hatha,' about yoga, about life.

I've been trying for years to live in such a way that respects every creature, that recognizes the life and THE ALL in every creature. And every day I fail. And every morning I wake up and try again. I try to grow. I be with my growth. I love myself in the midst of my failures because it seems to be the only thing that changes anything in a helpful way—no matter how many 'self improvement plans' and resolutions I make. And yoga has helped me on that journey, with this growth—even though yoga was propagated by men and sometimes women who did not have a view toward equality, of the full scope of THE ALL.

So regarding the metaphor of the baby and the bathwater . . . I'm holding the baby and loving it and nurturing it as best I can and know this baby will grow in ways that I won't even be able to fathom. And as for the bathwater that's now dirty and not fit for drinking—bathwater used to wash this precious baby—I know the earth has its way of cleaning it. The earth has cleaned dirty bathwater for millennia! Gratefully modern technology helps clean dirty water too! We've been drinking other creatures' urine and shit and waste for millennia, right? There is only so much water on this planet, and the planet has its ways of keeping us alive, especially when we tend it and nurture it gently and lovingly, as I am the baby.

As for 'hatha yoga' and its many interpretations and recommendations through the centuries, many of them involving force within oneself to achieve enlightenment, often at a cost . . . I've left behind the 'violent force' camp and find the 'no effort at all' camp not entirely helpful for me or the people who have come to VITALITY classes for their own glimpses of enlightenment, of THE ALL.

Perhaps to know 'yoga,'

perhaps to know or remember THE ALL,
all we need
is a nudge,
a hint . . .
something gentle
to nudge us from our usual perch of comfort
forward
into a (re)new(ed) way of sensing and experiencing life.

But that's for you to decide, of course, what's most helpful for you.

SO MUCH YOGA TODAY...

How not-so-gentle most yoga-practice has become, though! And I've been guilty in years past of that not-so-gentle move as well.

What kinds of things have you heard from people who don't practice yoga? What are people's assumptions about yoga-practice today? What are your own assumptions?

Perhaps sit with a cup of tea or coffee and consider these assumptions . . . whether they are your assumptions or someone else's.

I'll lay out a few of mine here to nudge the conversation along . . .

How many people have told me that they can't do yoga because they can't touch their toes? That they're not strong enough? That they don't like to sweat? That it moves too fast?

How many people have told me that they can't meditate because their mind goes every which way? That their mind monkeys around with them? That they have too many thoughts? That they'd never be able to slow them all down?

How many people have told me that they can't do yoga because they don't look good in yoga-tights or don't have a body fit for a magazine cover? (I don't either. Yet.)

If touching your own toes and having no thoughts or having a maga-zine-body are the pre-requisites of doing 'yoga,' then we're all lost.

You had better be having thoughts!

'Thoughts' or impulses running through your nerves and collagen-rich connective tissue are what are keeping you sitting up to read this page — and not just your eyes are moving to read this page. These 'thoughts' within you to read the page direct not only your eyes to focus with those beautiful tiny little eye muscles that aim your eyes to follow words — these muscles that aim and direct and organize the entire musculature of your whole body, from eye muscles down to your toes —

not to mention how those 'thoughts' then do something to interpret the words into some meaning within you! —

and to do all of this at the same time as something within you breathes and beats your heart and digests food and turns it into something useable and swallows germ-predators and digests them too and recycles water and gets waste or what's no longer needed to move on out of your body and on and on and on and on —

not to mention what ideas and thoughts form within you every second about what you're reading here and that cookie you want in the kitchen and how your Aunt Sally is doing and how cute that barista was yes-terday and what you need to pick up at the grocery later and why that kid said that awful thing to you on the playground decades ago and that fantasy you have to do whatever and on and on and on and on.

These are all thoughts.

And the pre-supposed goal is to want to have none of them, according to some yoga-practitioners?

Well, then you'd be dead.

You need 'thoughts' to stay alive . . . at least the ones involving heart-beating and breathing and such. Some 'guru' yoga-practitioners once boasted to have stopped their hearts and breaths for hours or days or weeks or longer. William J Broad's excellent *The Science of Yoga* (2012) very calmly and wisely points out that the scientific evidence of 'gurus' tested through this heart-and-breath-stopping is not exactly accurate. Even my much-loved Krishnamacharya's heart-beat slowed down a great deal during scientific tests but his heart never stopped. Gratefully.

We need thoughts.

Now nudging yourself with some 'technique' in some way to be with yourself and your thoughts and to appreciate them with as little judgment or attachment as possible because these thoughts and everything— how quickly they all change from second to second!—is another matter entirely.

How often do these slowing-down 'techniques,' such ways of knowing yoga, THE ALL, how often do these even get discussed in yoga classes today?

How have we lost our way with what 'yoga' really is?

Are we hopping around so much or sleeping so much that we've lost the invitation that surrounds and includes us, THE ALL?

LARRY SCHULTZ WAS RIGHT…STUDENTS TEACH US BEST!

The need for a book like this was born through the important challenges some of my earlier students made to me a few years ago as I was waking up to the 'workout' I was running seemed to have less and less to do with what I knew of 'yoga.' At the same time as these students were challenging me, the ashtanga-vinyasa practice I had been engaging twice a day, six days a week for a handful of years was wearing down my own body. Such a regimen was what some of teachers of the lineage had told me was necessary, what could be important for knowing THE ALL, though they didn't call it that—they often called it samadhi.

And more on that later. When I visited my older teachers and read stories about ashtanga-vinyasa co-creator Pattabhi Jois and his personal yoga-practice, I noticed that my teachers and the 'guru' himself didn't practice every day, twice a day, six days a week—and for good reason. Ashtanga-vinyasa practice was wearing them down too.

And not only that, many of the people who had joined our training at VITALITY reported back that most of the people coming to their classes loved their long guided meditations but couldn't engage well with the yoga-shapes of the ashtanga-vinyasa practice. Ashtanga—even the 'modified primary' version created by my much-loved teacher Larry Schultz was too much for some people. It was way more than the nudge (hatha) that they needed to remember again THE ALL.

I knew that something different—a much different kind of yoga-practice—was needed. Maybe even something that was more similar to the tai chi and qigong-styled practices that I had been teaching even before yoga. Indeed, is there really any difference between yoga-shapes and tai-chi-shapes, I wondered?

So I began offering slower, gentler ways to explore, to discover, to notice 'yoga' . . . . something that didn't involve sun salutations or standing shapes, something that didn't involve a million handstands or abs, something that was slower with the invitation to savor just a few shapes, something that did involve long meditative pauses, that invited an awareness of THE ALL with movement and rest. My students told me after a few weeks of this, "We didn't do this at the studio I studied at in California or Portland (or anywhere cooler than Cincinnati). This is not yoga you're teaching us. We want the real yoga!"

"These shapes have Sanskrit names," I offered. "They've been around for many years, some say even thousands of years, even if Patanjali didn't name any shapes. And what would it matter if these shapes didn't have Sanskrit names? Krishnamacharya invented shapes and sequences on the spot with his students as he saw the need."

"No, this is not yoga." They were so sure of themselves. And I loved them in that moment—though I have to say that I was surprised by their insistence that what we were doing was not also yoga. "We'll get to a vinyasa-flow sequence in a few weeks, the flow you know and for which you're craving so much—but for now, can you entertain the possibility that yoga is not a specific series of movements as it is about a special awareness?"

They looked sullen. They tried to lead a rebellion, within and without.

When I invited even gentler versions of yoga-shapes they knew, they brought in all the pictures they'd seen in magazines and in BKS Iyengar's *Light on Yoga* (1966 & many versions) and the poster with Pattabhi Jois' primary series and even Swami Vishnu-devenanda's *The Complete Illustrated Book of Yoga* (1960 & 1988). "Here," my students said, "This is the way we're supposed to look in yoga. We do these asanas like this and we get bliss!"

I flipped through their picture books and posters. I had studied most of them, of course, in my own trainings and personal studies. "You do things like this and you won't be able to walk," I offered.

"Not if you follow this book step-by-step," they pushed Iyengar's *Light on Yoga* at me, "he's alignment-based. So it's safe! See, all his pictures, right? There're like hundreds of pictures in here."

I pointed out a few alignment-based pictures in Iyengar's book that many of us yoga teachers had been using at the direction of our teachers—and these alignment-based teachers had required shoulder-replacements and knee-replacements and hip-replacements. From yoga!

As I stared at the front cover of *Light on Yoga*, and noticed the title's tagline 'The Bible of Modern Yoga,' I offered, "I'm amazed Iyengar let that be put on the cover of his book." I flipped through it again. "Surely, Mr. Iyengar is wise and has much to offer us. Any yoga teacher does who invites us to EXPERIENCE something in our own skin, on our own terms. But do you really think it was wise for him to write a book with all these pictures and descriptions of these exceedingly complex shapes (asanas) and let any fool—like me!—then try to attempt them just based off mimicking him in these pictures? And possibly hurt myself. And not just a little!"

"Nah-uh," they said.

The shapes in Iyengar and Vishnu-devenanda's books and the books and posters about Jois's primary series—not to mention the multiple highly-complex series he created to follow primary series—they are exceedingly complicated! Just a glance at the pictures, the photos, and it's not a stretch to say they look dangerously complex. I asked my students, "Would you want your friends—your teenage kids—picking up a book like one of these and thinking that this is what yoga is about? Or even worse TRYING some of these ridiculously complex shapes?"

"Nah-uh. It's fine. They're doing it, and so can we. Teach us headstand, come on!" they demanded.

"Have you read what William J Broad reported in *The Science of Yoga* about what has happened to people in headstand? All the hospital visits, the major injuries —"

"It's in a book—it must be okay!" they said, "and these books are written by gurus! Surely they know things that you don't know and that William J Broad doesn't know, you're not a guru! It's not on your business card!"

Darned right. I'm a human—just like Krishnamacharya.

Now what the heck was I going to do with these people who had come to me to learn something of yoga, something to teach others? And safely! What was I going to do, especially now that the ashtanga-vinyasa yoga that I had slowed down in my teaching and my personal practice to be more alignment-focused was still hurting me. My hips ached. My shoulders felt like rocks—very strong for sure but also very inflexible. From yoga!

THE GIFT OF TELEVISION MEMORIES

I sat in meditation awhile, something my wise teachers suggested I do if I ever came to a difficulty in my life.

I sat there on and off for many days.

I remembered a slower, gentler yoga-practice . . . I had seen it hundreds of times as a kid on TV . . . Lilias Follan (even from our own city!) offered a style of yoga-practice too many of us had forgotten. She showed up in my living room, on my family's TV, every day before *Sesame Street* on PBS when I was just a kid.

As I took the hop-around style of ashtanga-vinyasa yoga—even the slower, softer version I had created for myself and my students—out of the mix of my life for a few weeks and added in a gentler style I had seen on TV with Lilias and then in Becky Morrissey's classes in Cincinnati, I found that much of my hip and shoulder pain disappeared—must have been exacerbated by what I was doing hopping around with ashtanga-vinyasa yoga!

And I came to fall in love with this quieter practice of moving and breathing and resting . . . and the wild sensations that arose within me as I practiced yoga in this gentler way. In moving more slowly, I seemed to catch things that I must have missed moving so quickly in my ashtanga-styled practice.

My hip pain definitely was lessened by this practice. My shoulders softened a bit by leaving behind for awhile the ashtanga-vinyasa style I had been taught.

But not completely. It would take things outside the yoga 'tradition' to help me entirely. And more on that later.

I wondered about this ashtanga-vinyasa yoga and its popularity today. How did all this come about?

Not only was the style of ashtanga-vinyasa yoga injuring my body—even with THE BEST alignment cues offered by THE BEST alignment-guided teachers—it really bothered me that its biggest fans no longer practiced it every day. Pattabhi Jois, the biggest proponent of ashtanga-vinyasa yoga and co-creator of it with Krishnamacharya, did not practice the yoga-movements of his own series in the latter half of his life—though it is said that he did meditate every day, and he was limber enough to walk every day. He could have created some different yoga-shapes or sequences for his body, like things I was discovering in my new and gentler practice. But he didn't do that, as far as we know, because he was so committed to growing his version, his brand of yoga. It seems that in the books about him—*Guruji* (2010), for example—very few of his students ever saw him practice. Sadly, with the encouraging and much needed #metoo movement, it has come to light that Pattabhi Jois was also known to use his hands and full body with his students in violent, harmful, trauma-inducing ways for some of his students.

I'll have much to say about Pattabhi near the end of the book, and about what we could do about his legacy and significant teaching that he's left us in light of the present-day knowledge brought forward by some of his students about some of Pattabhi's inappropriateness, his indecency, his violence, the tangled mess of life that he is—perhaps that every human being is, though of course to different degrees.

None of this violent, hands-on work is the 'hatha,' the violent force, to which the ancient and medieval yoga texts seemed to point. For sure.

KRISHNAMACHARYA...THE WISER NON-GURU

If Pattabhi had stayed with his teacher, Krishnamacharya, just a little bit longer! Maybe a lot longer.

If BKS Iyengar had stayed with Krishnamacharya longer too—for even more asana alignment instruction and the all-important tailoring yoga to the individual that was Krishnamacharya's hallmark-teaching and to know what Krishnamacharya was unearthing about yoga in the second-half of his 101 years of life!

But Jois and Iyengar did not stay with Krishnamacharya. Not for very long at all.

The 'gurus'—Jois and Iyengar—knew a great deal, yes. And I'm grateful for all they offered us in ushering yoga to all that it is today. These two men helped spread yoga around the world. We have much to be grateful about for their enthusiasm, for all that yoga did for each of them to want to share it so, so much as they did. Iyengar credits yoga with rescuing him from significant disease as a young man. But these 'gurus' didn't seem to know what their incredible teacher Krishnamacharya was doing, how he was inventing way more than ashtanga-vinyasa yoga in which Jois and Iyengar were steeped.

And so here we are, all three of them now dead after long lives of teaching and discovering all that they did, all that they could in their lifetimes. Here we are with what we know about yoga—its helps and its hurts—through the three of them (and many more people) and through our own personal experiences of helps and hurts and hopes and dreams. What are we to do?

I sat in meditation some more.

And then I went back to the roots, the very things Krishnamacharya spent his century (1888 - 1989) studying and experiencing, toying with the ancient wisdom. I went back hundreds and (perhaps) thousands of years. I sought out 'new' things for my students and me to consider from the treasure-trove of yoga writings.

I offered that Patanjali, in his yoga sutras, says that yoga-movements and yoga-shapes (asana, in Sanskrit) are only one-eighth of a yoga practice. One-eighth! I said, "Most of yoga is meditation, a way of noticing. Do you know Patanjali only says a few lines of his Sutras about asana, about yoga-shapes? And what he does say makes it seem there are no particular shapes, not as we know them."

My students continued their protest. "Meditation has nothing to do with yoga. You're wrong. Yoga is beautiful movement—like a dance! And it makes me look better in the mirror!"

"What do you do with Yogananda? or with Vivekananda and his 1893 speech about yoga in Chicago? His yoga was very focused on meditation, and the ecstasy that can come from it."

"Who is that?"

"He, uh, he's a student of Ramakrishna. Vivekanada got a standing ovation—for two whole minutes—before he even spoke! Seven thousand people! That's what people saw in him, in his eyes! From HIS practice, much of it meditation."

"But it's not yoga if you don't move!"

I offered that *The Bhagavad Gita*, another of the primal texts of yoga, was actually a story about finding one's way, one's duty in life. And that yoga-shapes (asana) had very little to do with the path of yoga in this text either. In fact, the main character finds 'yoga'—THE ALL—in this text through a conversation on the edge of the battlefield where he's deciding whether to fight or not.

"Stop this!" my students said. "Teach us yoga!"

I asked how they felt after these gentler and slower movements I had begun teaching and inviting in classes, how they felt after a long span of seated or reclining meditation, of rest. "Good, I feel good—but it's not yoga! I signed up to learn to teach yoga!"

I'm not proud to say that my blood was boiling—and it would take the wisdom of another ancient 'yoga' teacher to heal some of this inner turmoil. (More on him later.)

How did we get here? Not just my students and me in this argument—but much of the world thinking that yoga was wearing skinny pants (if that) and sweating profusely and looking good and 'finding your edge' and reading trendy yoga magazines with well-shaped yoga-practitioners that are nice on the eyes and having a designer yoga mat and the right water-bottle and a nifty carrier for your yoga-gear and, ultimately, fitting in—how did we get here?

I've read and heard stories of modern-era Indian yogins too embarrassed to tell their families they were going to dedicate their lives to yoga. Far cry from today! How did we get to where we are with yoga being a $16 billion industry in the United States (reported by *Forbes*, 15 March 2016), where yoga has much to do with belonging and certainly—at least in most circles—far from embarrassing?

I continued wondering, really, more and more, how different the tai chi I had learned for about seven years before studying yoga was any different from these yoga-shapes. If I brought awareness to my body moving and resting in each place, in each shape I allowed my body to inhabit—what did it matter if it was called 'yoga' or 'tai chi' or whatever name. Truthfully, as I read the yoga classics, I wondered if I might be right—that yoga has less to do with what we do with our bodies than with how we tune into our bodies. That 'yoga' was more about sensation, about sensing ourselves in every way possible. And then some.

I noticed that the vinyasa-flow that A.G. Mohan learned from Krishnamacharya was far from sun salutations and a million plank-up-dog-downdogs, the vinyasa-combination said to be created by Krishnamacharya. I passed around Mohan's book *Krishnamacharya* (2010) and showed my students Krishnamacharya's vinyasa-flow created in the second half of his life, so very different from the plank-up-dog-downdog vinyasa.

My students protested all the more.

I asked my classes, "Have you read Patanjali? Did your studios in California or Portland or whatever cool places you studied talk about Patanjali? Or *The Bhagavad Gita*? Do you know who Krishnamacharya is, 'the father of modern yoga'? Have you even <u>tried</u> the 'vinyasa' practice in Mohan's book? Have you noticed that there is no updog or downdog in his vinyasa? You do know that Pattabhi Jois was Krishnamacharya's student, right?"

"No. I don't know who any of these people are—and I really don't care. Yoga is about getting stronger and flexible and, and, that's what you're supposed to be teaching us —"

I couldn't argue with that. But the path to getting there . . . .

GRATITUDE FOR CHALLENGES

Today, I am grateful to those students who challenged me to think through what I knew about yoga through my own experience, to be able to put into words and questions and invitations what could be through 'yoga'. To be fair to all my challenging students . . . what is quoted above did not come from a single person in a single class . . . I've hammed it up (a little) . . . I hear these questions all the time, even among people I'd say are wise and enlightened in many ways. I'm grateful for you all!

Sure, there are millions of writings and videos and all about yoga—even about these roots of yoga that I was offering my students as evidence of non-ashtanga-vinyasa yoga-practice. But most of these resources are inaccessible, in my opinion. Sure, they've been written in English, translated into English. Sure, they try to bring forward a little bit of what is there in the ancient & medieval writings we have about yoga—but they seem to have so little to do with life in the 21st century that their value as 'translations' is very limited. They miss the EXPERIENCE that could connect an ancient-inviter with a modern-curious-one.

I wonder often about how to bring these ancient teachings forward for the 21st century.

And my hope is that this little book can become a bridge between the 21st century yoga 'beginner' and the vast studies of yoga, ancient and medieval and modern—especially since the teachings in these texts rarely agree with one another. How could a beginner even make sense of the tangled mess of the yoga tradition without first having some experience of THE ALL themselves . . . of being reminded that they've known THE ALL their whole lives . . . long before they stepped on a designer yoga mat?

Who are 'beginners'? Krishnamacharya was said to think of himself as a student of yoga, even when he could have easily considered himself the most learned yogin of the modern era, a guru and even more than that. But he didn't—he knew the depth of EXPERIENCE. He knew the depth of the yoga-tradition. He knew how much there was to learn . . . that we all are and will always be beginners.

A NEW WAY FORWARD

I recently taught some yoga classes at a local high school and at a nursing school, classes more akin to what Krishnamacharya was offering in the second-half of his life and much less like what most people are used to of what Krishnamacharya taught Pattabhi Jois, ashtanga-vinyasa yoga. The students' comments are illuminating:

"I found it very relaxing and was not pressured like I am when doing yoga at the studio I usually go to where I am subtly invited to be the strongest or the most flexible."

"I didn't feel forced to do anything. I was able to relax, and that helped a lot."

"I suddenly realized I loved everybody in the room."

"I didn't feel forced to do these deep and extremely painful stretches that are usually asked of me."

I was overjoyed that young people were finding value in such a gentler practice of moving and breathing and resting. But the question came up within me again: what have we become? what have we yoga-teachers offered to the world these past few generations that makes people think yoga needs to be painful, that people need to put their bodies in painful contortions to achieve 'yoga'?

Have we lost the roots of who we are?

I was once with them, trying to sweat it out, pain being the edge, the gain. And sure, bizarre body-contortions can be fun. But if they cause us a lot of pain, then are we really doing ourselves any favors? Aren't we imprinting pain into our body-awareness during a time when we are hoping to relax, care for oneself? And wouldn't such an imprint then link relaxation & self-care with pain in ourselves?

Yikes.

GYM CULTURE

I've wondered that about my own gym workouts too. I used to lift very heavy and often and was quite proud of my efforts and my results. I liked hanging with the 'cool kids' and being strong and hitting personal bests with big lifts. But then I started noticing the toll on my body . . . and watched my much younger friends grunting and crying and thinking the pain would somehow give them some incredible gain. Sure, if I were trying to escape harm, I'd grunt and do whatever I needed to do to get away from harm—even if it would make me crazy sore the next day. And maybe sensible 'training' is indeed to exceed where you've ever been before—at least every once in a while. But to purposely create big doses of soreness and pain EVERY DAY or multiple times a week that would make my friends or me need to take tons of ibuprofen or need real self-care just to get through the next tough workout a couple days from now—is this really smart? Is this really knowing your body, knowing yourself through and through? Could there be other ways to achieve great leaps and personal bests?

The perspective in our country—maybe the world—maybe we're missing something . . . ? Maybe we've missed the forest and the trees . . . THE ALL.

LISTEN TO THE BREEZE . . .

There's something you know . . . feel whatever it is you feel . . . stay here awhile, in your knowing, your feeling, your sensing . . .

I know a renewed way toward yoga. And so do you.

It's perhaps what the first yoga practitioners knew in the Indus River Valley way back when, 3000 - 5000 years ago. Before the yoga-shapes had names, before they were even particular or special shapes to be taught, before the ayurvedic-types knew what was best for each 'type' of us to eat, before the multi-billion dollar industry knew what props and water-bottles and clothes and mats and magazines you needed to buy to find enlightenment, before there was a registry of who was certified to teach yoga with 200 or 500 hours of training. As if that were truly enough! Hundreds of hours are certainly a beginning! A beginning! For sure! For sure!

You know it too, what these ancient yogis and yoginis and yogins knew. You've known it forever, though perhaps you didn't call it 'yoga.' Perhaps we'd all be wise to begin calling THE ALL and your glimpses of it and my glimpses of it 'yoga'—no matter where or when we find those glimpses.

Let's discover what we might find together!

Your EXPERIENCE is worth way more than knowing a bunch of things.

It's your experience that has brought you this far on your path, how you've listened to your experience, wondered about it, toyed with it, played with it, let it unfurl for how many years . . .

and sure, those contortions of a 'traditional' yoga practice might be possible, yes, and might be pain-free, yes, before and after, yes . . . if and when we sense ourselves in them with all that we are and choose what's best for oneself.

This, my friends, my fellow-human creatures, this sensing, this feeling every bit of everything inside and out . . . this is 'yoga' . . . knowing THE ALL. Yoga invites, maybe even requires sensing, feeling your experience, in its so, so many ways. On a mat and off. And all it takes to <u>sense</u>

something is the most gentle nudge, the smallest stimulus, right, your <u>experience</u> of the smallest stimulus, right?

And it's your experience that might save the world—not any guru or hero or teacher or authority figure or anyone else . . .

toward a (re)new(ed) way forward for our world on this amazing planet!

absolute bliss
samadhi

When have you known bliss?

When have you had so much fun, so much pure joy that you could barely stand it? When you could not contain the joy? When it burst out of you like a little kid?

Perhaps take some time today—in your favorite chair, outside, in a coffee shop, on your yoga mat, resting against a wall, anywhere you'd like—and ask yourself when you've known bliss.

See if you can re-live it a bit, feel it, notice the sensations in your body as the memory of this experience comes back home to you, within you, as you remember it.

Stay with it, be with it awhile.

Consider doodling, drawing, singing, dancing, playing with these sensations in any way that feels right for you.

Bask in that feeling of bliss —

no matter how you've experienced it in the past . . . even if it somehow 'embarrasses' you or you wouldn't want to share how it happened for you.

Maybe you can find bliss in this very moment . . . with whatever you're experiencing right now.

When we know bliss, when we taste it and experience it so palpably even years after it first happened, we know 'yoga' . . . we know THE ALL of life.

deepening rest
dhyana

Consider taking a nice walk.

Yes. That might seem a strange invitation when you just read 'deepening rest' just a second ago.

Perhaps this is an actual walk outside, where the wind blows. Or if that's not possible for some reason, maybe in your imagination.

Perhaps in your walking today, there's no place to go, no place to get to . . . just simply walk along and discover what happens for you . . . .

Notice if you can walk so slowly as to become curious about and tune into every step . . . and then walk at your normal pace and see how that feels.

What do you discover as you walk?

What things, what people do you see as you walk?

What sounds, what voices do you hear?

What does the air feel like on your skin?

Maybe you can even touch a leaf from a tree . . . and what does that feel like?

What does the air smell or even taste like?

What stirs in your guts as you walk?

Take some time simply walking in the garden of the universe . . . even if it's a concrete jungle in which you walk, what life do you notice here?

What immense life is below your feet—one, two feet below you in the deeper dirt . . . all the way to the lava-core of the earth?

Savor every sensation with every step, with every breath . . . .

And then as you're ready, take a rest. Maybe on a bench, maybe on the ground, maybe back home inside.

Take some time to have nowhere to go for awhile.

Allow your body to take whatever shape it would like in these moments, and of course ask yourself if there's something you might do for yourself to make yourself even one tiny fraction more comfortable. Bring along whomever or whatever might help you to rest awhile.

What bliss do you know about life in movement and in rest?

being with
dharana

Consider taking some time in the evening or just as the day is moving into night . . . perhaps with a candle, perhaps a beeswax candle.

See if you can be present with the noise of the match, with how the wick catches the flame, with how the candlewax responds to the new flame . . . second by second by second. And the smells, of burning, of change.

You'll, of course, want to sit close by but far enough away from the flame to be safe, as well as keep flammables away from the flame. Fire is powerful—fire within us and this flame burning before you!

And sit here awhile and watch and listen and smell and feel and notice. Stay here as long as you can. Be with yourself and this flame for awhile.

What happens for you?

Yoga is a Sanskrit word from the root 'to yoke' or to join or to unite . . . union. Scholars tells us that it was a word used when a person hitched the cart to the land-animal, a horse or ox. In a sense, connecting something to something else.

And that might be a helpful image. And yet, as the ancient yogins of the Indus River Valley came to know, ultimately, there is no 'connecting' anything as we begin to observe, as we practice yoga . . . because how can anyone connect what is already whole, one, limitless, infinite, indivisible except to know that it's all—THE ALL—already connected

. . . especially as we know in our day on a subatomic level, the realizations of quantum physics, that there truly is no separation. That what is 'you' is well beyond the bounds of your skin—that quarks dart this way and that, appear and disappear to who-knows-where, inside 'you,' outside 'you.'

Ultimately, to 'connect'
with God or the Universe or Nature
or whatever name you have for it, THE ALL,
to 'connect' with anyone or anything is impossible,
for those who know.
How can you connect with what you already are?

So be here. Rest here. Wonder. Know.

Let the candle-flame teach you. Within and without.

Amazing how it all came to be...

This story takes place about 100 years ago, when yoga was already almost a lost art in India. (Yes, you read that right.)

A young man had a father who instructed him in yoga-movements (asana), in nudging one's breath into a new rhythm (pranayama), and in Sanskrit, the ancient language of yoga and religious ritual in what we call 'India' today.

When the young man was ten, his father died.

But the boy had an insatiable appetite for learning yoga and yoga-philosophy and healing through ayurveda, the ancient study of medicine of which yoga is a part. He studied with family members, at monasteries, at universities.

And he had some wild experiences of life—of THE ALL—through his yoga-practice that encouraged him to want to learn and know more. He was after 'the more' of all he had found so far. Some of these wild experiences even helped him to craft poetry about yoga-study—poetry that one day would guide his whole personal pursuit and teaching/ sharing of yoga.

As all yoga students did in those days, he begged for his food—just some wheat to mix with water to make himself little cakes. He eventually earned the maximum number of university-certificates available in these yoga studies but got a notion that there was still more to learn. One of his teachers told him that he would have to leave India to find 'the more' of yoga—that he would have to go to Tibet, that there was a teacher there who knew the other yogic ways, the deeper roots.

The young man, now almost thirty, discovered he needed special government papers to cross over into Tibet. And lo and behold, the viceroy who could help the young man to get the papers he needed was very ill. The young man reached out to the viceroy and gave him a specific regimen of yoga-movements and a specific diet tailored for the man and the viceroy was cured. The viceroy made the passage to Tibet easy for the young man—as long as he promised to come back for three months every year to help the viceroy's health and his family's health.

YOGA—THE ALL—CANNOT BE CONTAINED BY ONE NATION

So the young man made his way into Tibet—200 miles of walking in three weeks to get to the ashram where this master was said to teach. Perhaps it would be some fancy place high up in the mountains . . . . you know, the images of beautiful monasteries we see in movies, even in dreams.

He came to a cave and found the master he was seeking, a man and his wife and three children who lived in the cave with him.

This was no fancy monastery! This was no ashram! This was a cave!

This was no celibate wise-man! This master had a family! And this master shared his knowledge with his wife and children!

This was all quite startling! Nothing like he had experienced in India!

This master spoke of 8.4 million asanas, yoga-movements that his ancient teachers knew . . . 8.4 million yoga-shapes to account for as many living beings on the earth. This cave-dweller said he knew 7,000 of them himself, 7,000 of these asanas. The young man was able to learn 700 asanas over the seven years he lived with his master.

But most of his study was learning and studying and eventually memorizing the yoga classics and helping to care for the 'house' in which they all lived together. And as for these 'texts' . . . much of it was simply learning by ear, not so much by eye, by reading . . . Patanjali's Sutras, the story of *The Bhagavad Gita*, many other texts that we all might recognize, some that are more obscure.

Imagine day upon day of this life . . . making yoga-shapes, studying them deeply, meditating and playing with one's breath for hours on end, learning ancient teachings by meditatively repeating them out loud after his teacher, living with this family in a cave, assisting with house-holder-life, caring for the children. For years! With very little distraction of city life—the only distractions being the ones he put before himself. With the only 'get-away' a hike up the mountain to even cooler temperatures and sights, all in a thin robe—high on a mountain, a new perch upon which to meditate and practice what would become his life-long love of pranayama and wonder.

Imagine the life.

The things he learned! So deeply.

When he knew it was time to return home, his master's only charge, his only request for 'payment' was for his student to marry, have children, and share this yoga wisdom with others . . . to be a 'house-holder' and family-man, not a celibate monk. This was a radical request! At this time, most yoga teachers were unmarried monks or hermits, men who had chosen the path of yoga-study without romantic-relationship, the life Patanjali advocated and for whom he had written his sutras.

SHARE THE WISDOM OF THE CAVE!

When the young man finally returned home, now no longer a young man and now probably the most studied yogin of India—at less than 40 years of age!—he married and had children and lived a simple life, as his teacher requested. (Imagine it—his debt to his teacher was TO LIVE!) He taught people yoga one-on-one, for the most part, and when his students had money to offer him, he humbly asked them to place it on the altar to God, the altar he had in his home, for he felt he was only doing his duty to offer the teachings that had been so generously offered to him. This yogi knew that this practice and his life were all much bigger than him.

When he wasn't teaching or being with his family or tending his vegetable garden, he spent most of his hours every day meditating and playing with his breath, this 'pranayama.' And he continued studying and memorizing ancient texts, penetrating their depths, opening himself up to what might be possible through them, through this deeper wisdom, even when the texts contradicted themselves. He tested out their wisdom. He sought the best ways to live and grow that he could possibly know, and he seemed to be open to the reality that what he thought he knew last year paled in comparison to what he was discovering today . . . that there was no final answer.

He took on great challenges that led to great opportunities, like taking on the yoga-teaching at a palace where yoga-instruction and various forms of athletics and meditation had been ongoing for generations.

And it was there that he received requests to teach interesting groups of people—even a large group of twelve-year-old boys. What was he going to do with these wild ones, he must have imagined. The slower and gentler sequences he had devised for his older students probably would not work with all the rambunctious energy of these twelve-year-old boys!

So he devised for this group a more playful, more fast-paced series, a series hallmarked by linking one's breath with the movement. He met these rambunctious kids where they were—he knew himself many, many shapes and he noticed these boys knew British gymnastics. (thanks N.E. Sjoman!) So being the good teacher he was, he melded the two. This yoga-practice that later came to be called ashtanga-vinyasa yoga by his student Pattabhi Jois who felt this style of yoga-practice most reflected the teachings of Patanjali. 'Ashtanga' was coined by Patanjali—ashtanga is a Sanskrit word meaning eight limbs or eight branches. (More on this very soon.)

This series of fast-paced yoga-movements was carried around the world by Pattabhi and others. Even BKS Iyengar's early teachings look pretty similar. I once saw a video online of Iyengar teaching and the flow of the class very much resembled ashtanga-vinyasa yoga. One of the Iyengar classes I attended in Ireland was indeed the same basic sequence.

Pattabhi Jois and BKS Iyengar—two of the more well-known spreaders of yoga-practice around the world in the 20th century—were students of this same teacher, after all.

How important it is to remember that this ashtanga-vinyasa series was designed for twelve-year-old boys! It later became the yoga that most of the world knew—that most adults of all ages practice in the United States & Europe today (though I hope this book invites some change with that)—in health clubs and gyms and hot yoga and regular-temperature yoga studios, in parks, nearly in every neighborhood of most mid-level and larger cities. But we all too often forget that this master-teacher taught this jump-around-yoga class to twelve-year-old boys every day and then went and taught one-on-one, individual classes to others that looked NOTHING like these jump-around ashtanga-vinyasa classes. This master-teacher knew that he had to tailor his yoga-teaching to the individual—with different breath combinations (pranayama) and different sequences of yoga-movements (asana), with different styles of meditation and different dietary suggestions. What works for one might be poison for another!

THE WORLD EVENTUALLY SEEKS WISDOM

People from all over the world came to him, came to this master-teacher. Even a famous actress! When she knocked on his door and asked to learn yoga, to teach yoga, this master-teacher said no. He said women were not to learn yoga—except maybe within their own families, as his wife and daughters learned yoga from him.

Credit this woman for showing up the next day and asking again. And credit this man for examining his assumptions that prior evening and realizing there was no good reason in the yoga tradition to exclude women from learning and teaching yoga. Indeed, some of the most ancient poems of the yoga tradition—the *Rig Veda*—were said to be composed by rishikas, by women-sages.

This 20th century woman who knocked on the door was Eugenie Peterson, and this man took her on as his student. She later took the name Indra Devi, and she taught yoga all over the world during her 102 years of life! And her yoga-practice probably—and wisely—looks much different from the practices being shared by Pattabhi Jois and BKS Iyengar and their families.

All of this master-teacher's students took their learnings all over the world . . . all the great and famous names of yoga that we still talk about today . . . in addition to Indra Devi, Pattabhi Jois and his ashtanga-vinyasa yoga, BKS Iyengar who watched his teacher devise props to make yoga-movement and meditation easier and who eventually left behind ashtanga-vinyasa yoga for a more 'aligned' approach to yoga . . . a few more greats: Desikachar, A.G. Mohan and his son Ganesh, and many more. Desikachar was this master-teacher's son—and what a credit to the master-teacher that he did not force his son to follow in his own footsteps. Desikachar's story of following his father is quite moving.

Rarely did this master-teacher leave his hometown in his later years, rarely did he teach more than one or two students at a time unless it was his weekly lecture on the ancient texts. If you were late to your appointment with him, he just looked at the clock and at you until you got the point and were never late again. And if he thought you had not practiced your yoga-movements since the last time he saw you, he would send you home to come back next week after you had had plenty of practice. No one learned a new series of yoga-movements until mastering the first set he had given you.

GRATITUDE FOR A MODEL OF A NEW WAY FORWARD

It is because of this little, powerful man who owned next to nothing, who lived in economic poverty to gain the abundance of THE ALL as most yogins did in India during the time and before, who let nature be the music-playlist for his yoga classes, who accepted only donations for his classes, who did not get flustered when the political climate changed and his yoga school had to close or move, who wore the same piece of cloth every day until it wore out, who dared to allow women to be his students (unheard of at the time in India), who lived to be 101 years of age and a student throughout, who did not want to be called guru because he knew he was still learning, even after 100 years . . . it is because of him that we are here today. Without his having the courage to go to the cave and study the deeper roots of yoga and learn even more about how to tailor classes for all his diverse students—especially those 12-year-old boys!—yoga would not have reached us all the way to Cincinnati where I write this . . . at least not with a deeper look at the roots of the practice that we are being invited to practice here through his ever-expanding insights.

This master and 'father of modern yoga' was, of course, Tirumalai Krishnamacharya, though he never felt he was a master or a guru.

Maybe he was wise to the debilitating effects of putting any human being above another, though he knew from his own experience just how important it is to learn with people as he did with his teacher in the Tibetan cave, the great yogi Ramamohana Brahmachari.

Perhaps the hallmark of his teaching yoga-movements (asana), the hundreds upon hundreds of shapes that Krishnamacharya learned from his teacher and then the hundreds or even thousands he created as he felt need, the hallmark for him was moving with awareness . . . of sensing deeply what you feel in each shape, in each moment.

A.G. Mohan began his studies with Krishnamacharya around 1970, near the end of Krishnamacharya's life (1888 - 1989). His son Ganesh Mohan, an avid student of yoga and a medical-physician, often comes to Cincinnati to share these teachings and the style of asana is simple, gentle, soft . . . all about listening to your body, listening with a subtle awareness to each very slow movement so that your ever-wise nervous system can interpret every bit of every movement and slow down and then use pieces of those slow movements in your everyday life.

In many ways, this style of yoga practice has a similar strategy to the movement practice Moshe Feldenkrais (Awareness Through Movement® / Feldenkrais Method® / Functional Integration®) and his famed student Ruthy Alon (Movement Intelligence® / Bones for Life®) invite through their movement studies. We'll soon hear about each of their stories, their contributions to movement with awareness that is, in my opinion, the true hallmark of yoga . . . that it is internal-sensation we are invited to notice, to be with, perhaps to play with. Indeed, it's about the only thing Patanjali has to say about asana—do less, relax, and feel! And with such gentle awareness, something begins to happen in your body, things can change rapidly as your body remembers its wholeness, as things unwind and find release and new ways of being because something within you—some deep, primal intelligence—realizes that you don't have to effort as much as you once did.

Do you have the courage to move slowly with deep listening and awareness and see what happens for you—whether that's on a yoga-mat or in many of the daily moves of your life? Do you?

Of course, there are times to move quickly too. Perhaps there's a beauty in even noticing the different speeds that life demands of us.

What the Desikachars and the Mohans and many students of Krishnamacharya's later years learned and now share is gentler, wiser, slower, more like an inquiry, sometimes with very different alignment cues than the ones that have become too often concretized (and all too often problematic) in the past couple generations. Theirs is an alignment very much based on sensation. Indeed, many of us practicing the alignment cues of Pattabhi Jois and BKS Iyengar for years and years have found some of them brilliant and some of them very problematic. My own shoulder and hip issues of the past are Exhibit A. Perhaps a deeper wisdom is needed, a wisdom cultivated by Krishnamacharya in his later years, a wisdom that Pattabhi Jois and BKS Iyengar both might have missed out on, as brilliant as they are. Do less . . . listen more.

Deep listening, deep sensing of oneself is needed if we are to know yoga, if we are to remember THE ALL—even for a second. It's not so much the shape as it is the sensation in the shape.

And surely ashtanga-vinyasa yoga can be done this way too, with attention to sensation, with a deep listening awareness that aligns us wisely from the inside-out. And such is the yoga-movement style we now practice and share at VITALITY, a practice that grows every day as we need it to, as we tailor the practice to each person in that particular moment, tailoring everything in the spirit of Krishnamacharya's yoga-wisdom!

sensation appreciation pratyhara

Just what were they doing in the Indus Valley 3000 - 5000 years ago?

This is where yoga was said to have begun, with the rishis and rishikas of lore.

The rishis and rishikas of this long-ago era were part of the roots of the meditative and yogic traditions, a small slice of which we know today in the West. Rishi / Rishika is Sanskrit, and it's not an easy word to pin down. (Ha!) Most Sanskrit-English glossaries call them sages or poets, some note their affinities for discovering new dimensions, some note that 'rishi' might have something to do with movement, with being able to flow . . . and some link it with a Sanskrit-relative that has to do with ecstasy, bliss. (I hope Jason Birch does some careful research on this for us, as he did with 'hatha'!)

Imagine that —
that cultivating wisdom and meditation and movement has to do with bliss, with ecstasy!

Have you ever known that?

We could spend a lot of time learning Sanskrit and pouring over the massive Vedas, the writings of the later rishis (masculine form) and rishikas (feminine form) who recorded what had happened to their great . . . great-grandparents. And we might find some benefit from such an inquiry.

Or you could continue in your own moving-with-awareness practice and begin to discover in your own body, in your own time, in your own way just what the rishis and rishikas were discovering in their own moving and breathing and resting. And perhaps that is these first-practitioners' invitation from the edge of that Indus River . . . to know yoga, union, THE ALL, in your own skin and beyond.

Ultimately, is there any separation between you, me, the earth, the air we breathe, the life we share?

Writing much later than the legends of the rishis and rishikas of the *Rig Veda*, Patanjali offers a simple roadmap—the eight limbs—to such a discovery of yoga, of THE ALL, and we will explore those limbs more deeply in a bit. In fact, we already are. But you might be able to figure out the roadmap yourself . . . through your own daily practice of moving and breathing and resting, of tailoring this 'practice,' this life, so gently and easily, to your own creation.

What might you discover today
as you allow your senses to lead you...
and then after some time
with each sense getting sharper
and clearer and more cooperative with the others —
notice how something begins to happen?

What is it?

What was that taste or smell or sight or sound or touch that positively, ecstatically, exploded your sensations today?

Tune into sensation and discover for yourself.

breath rhythming
pranayama

Pranayama invites you to become aware of and change your natural breathing pattern to have an overall effect of creating change in your body and in your life.

Your breathing has had its own natural rhythms all day—from sleep early this morning to beginning to stretch out and get up from bed to walking to sitting to climbing stairs or a hill to this moment reading this right now and all the different things you've done all day—without you probably purposefully changing anything. You have an intelligence to which you probably rarely pay much attention . . . something within you that knows when and how to breathe.

Before you begin nudging your breathing pattern into a new rhythm with any of these invitations here or with anyone else's, perhaps there's some wisdom in simply observing your natural breathing pattern and how it changes through the day and night.

Your natural breathing pattern is different if you're sitting and reading this than if you stare out the window and think about whatever is on your mind. Right? See if you can notice the change.

Your natural breathing pattern is different if you're walking on flat ground than if you're walking uphill, right?

Your natural breathing pattern changes depending on what you're feeling as you and a friend talk, right? And your natural breathing pattern fluctuates depending on what you talk about, right?

Your natural breathing pattern at times is very deep and full and at other times faster, right?

Your natural breathing pattern at times is very small and slow, right? Like when you're in your deepest sleep or trying to fall asleep.

Notice too that in simply observing your natural breathing pattern in any moment actually changes it . . .

perhaps that observation is all that is needed to nudge us into change, into changing one's life . . . ?

Thankfully, if you forget to observe your breathing, something within you takes care of it yourself to keep you alive as long as you need to live!

And as with all things, the simplest 'technique' is perhaps the most profound.

With most pranayama, you're invited to do your best to breathe through your nose . . . both your inhale and your exhale.

As you can probably remember from your high school health or biology class, your nose is a natural filtration system . . . the mucous-covered little hairs catch particles and the mucous-lining of your nose helps to warm the air that comes through you.

Some days, you might find that you are stuffed up and unable (for now) to breathe through your nose. We of course never want to force our breathing, never want to make it conform to something or some shape or technique that might harm us. Maybe on these stuffed up days, you just need to rest and let your body find its rhythm again.

Some times in the day, you might notice that one nostril allows airflow more easily than the other. And later in the day it might even switch. And later, maybe I need to breathe through my mouth to reset the internal pressures that allow breathing to happen in its own wise way.

For me, half the fun of pranayama is simply noticing what Nature has given me in each moment . . . Nature's wisdom to keep me alive.

When you mindfully breathe, when you gently pay some attention to your breathing, things can begin to slow down too . . . .

What happens as you breathe? See if you can observe it.

Of course, you can shape your breath—or maybe more importantly you can allow your breath to shape you in that mysterious way it does when you allow it.

Discover what happens for you as you breathe . . . .

shape making
asana

You might have noticed, as you've been reading this book, at least if you're an intelligent creature, that you have shifted the way you sit.

When one seat becomes uncomfortable, you shift, you move, even the slightest bit.

This is smart, this is intelligent, right?

You rest in a place, enjoy all you can in that place, in that particular shape and arrangement of your body, and then you move. Movement and rest. Movement and rest. And sensation, of course, is your guide.

This is asana, literally to find one's seat through which to observe the world, to observe one's self. Swami Yogakanti tells us that asana means 'seat' in Sanskrit in her *Sanskrit Glossary of Yogic Terms* (2007).

There will be a day, on this path, when perhaps you will no longer need to move at all, or at least as often, during the course of your rest, your meditation, your awareness of the moving sensation in rest.

Of course even then, as long as you're alive and breathing, you're moving. Your breath is a full-body experience. Have you noticed that even the very bottoms of your feet move as you breathe?

So when we say that, one day on this path, you might know stillness, you might be finding a very different 'comfort' where you don't need to move as often . . . that you might one day find a way to be—to be 'still' (and yet moving so much with breathing+), to know such a 'dynamic stillness' that is meditation—without moving a leg to bring relief or readjusting the blanket or chair you sit upon or whatever.

There will be a day, as Gautama knew, when you can rest in your seat (in your asana) without purposefully moving. Without pain.

That day will simply arrive. No need to make anything happen. No need to cause yourself any grief or any pain.

SENSING OFFERS YOU CHOICES...HEALTH!

For now, be intelligent! Move as you need to! Rest as you need to! Sense yourself! Decide for yourself what you need! When we sense ourselves, we realize we have a choice—to stay as we are or to move in an infinite number of pleasing ways. You're the only one who knows what you need, after all, to know THE ALL.

The ancient yogins seemed to think they could have more of these glimpses in seated meditation, in the dynamic stillness that happens when we rest here awhile.

Maybe that's in a chair, maybe that's on the ground.

Can you sense the power of your own 'dynamic stillness'?

Your breath moves your whole body, even in that short 1 - 2 second pause between exhaling or inhaling.

Your heart beats and each beat reverberates through you, even down to your toes!

And then there are all those electrical impulses running through you in what we call the nervous system, impulses rippling through all kinds of collagen-rich tissue.

And your breath—take a little more time to notice it. It's incredible, yes? What an amazing creature you are!

Each breath ripples through every cell of your body, your whole body changes shape—even so slightly—with each inhale, each exhale.

Of course, you don't need me to tell you, to invite you to stay here as long as you wish, as long as it's interesting . . . <u>you know</u>!

Our practice of sitting and noticing and responding as needed, our life becomes a dance, then, between resting in stillness and moving freely, in loving ways for oneself. Movement and rest, movement and rest.

Ecstasy. Bliss. It's right there waiting for you to notice it, to have that experience for yourself.

And no it's not waiting for you to make yourself 'perfect' . . . whatever that means. The experience of ecstasy or bliss is not waiting for you to be the weight you think you should or the body-shape you hope to be or working the job of your dreams or thinking you need to finish working through that trauma from eons ago or taking the vacation that you long for or having sex with the person of your fantasies.

Ecstasy and bliss wait for you to know them in every second of every day. Right here. Right now.

CATCH A FEW SECONDS OF ECSTASY OR BLISS TODAY?

Maybe you're tired of sitting like this? Maybe you need to change it up a little. Do it! And move slowly, and notice the feeling of relief that comes with the smallest change.

Get up and move, or choose a similar way to being seated, something that resembles a little the way you were seated before but just slightly differently, just slight enough to give you complete relief from whatever slight discomfort you might have felt to make you want to change it up a bit.

Give yourself such love in this constant flow, this constant moving-stillness that is life.

Movement and rest. Movement and rest.

Something is constantly moving within you,
some very deep intelligence,
to keep you not only comfortable but ALIVE
in and with THE ALL!

Moshe Feldenkrais

healing it all
with Awareness Through Movement®

Amazing how it all came to be again, at about the same time in the history of the world as Krishnamacharya, though in a very different place thousands of miles apart from each other . . . as if it were an idea in the breeze, in the air, for all to welcome.

I marvel at Moshe Feldenkrais' life.

He was a man who knew trauma—in all too many ways.

And he was a man who found a way out,
a way through trauma—in some very surprising ways.

He left home, Ukraine, when he was fourteen, in 1918. For a lot of reasons. Fear of the Russian government rounding up the adolescent boys in a pogrom, one more show of strength to put down the Jewish families so that they never became too powerful. Fear of another power persecuting Jews (soon to come). Moshe's fear of his own pretty severe father.

So off he went, on a 2,000 mile journey toward a place about which Jewish folks had high hopes: British-Mandate Palestine. The old Israel. The hoped-for new Israel.

Much of that journey was alone. In sub-zero temperatures. Through lands where the threat of death was more than a suspicion.

But before he knew it—and probably a testimony to his personality—Moshe attracted another 200 people to join him. They eventually arrived in Tel Aviv, more than six months after he began walking.

Tel Aviv is now one of the world's great cities. But in 1919, it was a field of dust.

Moshe and his friends lived in tents and built the first buildings of this now-great city. Moshe was known for his strength, his ability to haul concrete up stairs all day long—not easy work!

It must have been quite the life—hard manual work by day, no parental supervision by night. In their teenage years. Imagine!

Except for the danger involved. Jewish settlers in the area were forbidden to carry weapons. Moshe and his friends were easy targets for robbery, even for violent-play.

So Moshe and his friends studied jujitsu, martial arts—something to help them stave off the attacks.

But all that training and practice—years' worth!—proved futile. They still got attacked. And they still were not able to defend themselves quickly enough. Moshe observed that his first reaction to being jumped—despite all of that self-defense training, years of it in fact—was reflex-like, to put up his hands in front of his face and body in fear or surprise or self-protection. And in that split-second of fear and fear's reflex, the aggressor could have his way with Moshe and his friends. And did, all too often.

So Moshe wondered . . . why not include that reflex-like move with hands to one's own face as part of the self-defense move? Throw your hands up and then bear down on the aggressor. Train that way. Include that first move as part of training in self-defense. And he found it worked!

Soon, he devised a way to disarm an opponent with a knife—the common weapon of choice for these robberies—using jujitsu-like, clever thinking in the face of danger, by using the opponents' attack against them.

CLEVER JUJITSU WORKS...BUT THAT KNEE!

Meanwhile, Moshe kept injuring his knee. On the football (soccer) field. Sometimes laying him up for months. No matter, he thought, I'll just read and write.

Later he completed his own high school studies—much later than he would have back home. He was hired as a tutor to help students and discovered just how important the relationship between tutor and student is. A strategy that works with one person might not work with another . . . that to be helpful we need to join the student in their struggles and in their gifts . . . that we need to tailor our teaching to the individual and meet the student where the student is . . . that the relationship is key.

Soon after, he left Tel Aviv to study physics in Paris. He went from the bottom of the class to the top as he learned to work in new ways for himself. Later, he had grown so much as a student that he was admitted to the world-famous Sorbonne to begin his doctoral studies. While he was in Paris, he helped found a judo club, studied more martial arts with some of the best in the world who were amazed at his creative skills, and worked in the labs of the Curies on radium. He married Yona, a pediatrician.

Typical life! (ha)

As World War 2 broke out and the Nazis were invading France, Moshe escaped with his wife and other Jewish scientists on the last boat out of France before the Germans secured the borders. He was probably very high on the Nazi 'find' list as a Jewish scientist who knew something about radium—and he even carted some radium out of France with him!

Once he arrived in Great Britain, with a name like Feldenkrais, he was detained as a spy until a fellow scientist recognized him and secured his release. Moshe was immediately whisked away to Scotland with the other European intelligentsia to develop helpful things for the war effort. Moshe's job was to develop SONAR for the submarine portion of the war.

By day, Moshe and others would work on the war effort. By night, the brightest minds of Europe got to play, to share with one another their passions and other discoveries. Moshe, of course, shared his judo skill and created a new judo club in Scotland.

THAT KNEE AGAIN...!

But something was getting in the way. He repeatedly injured his knee, and soon could no longer walk on it. He tried everything, consulted a doctor who told him he'd never be able to walk on that knee again unless he had surgery. Moshe asked what the success rate of the surgery was—in the 1940's let's remember! The surgeon proudly announced, "50-50!"

Moshe had had another surgery on his arm a few years back—and his arm was never quite the same. Regarding the possibility of knee surgery, Moshe said no way. The doctor probably smiled and said that Moshe would never be able to walk on that knee. But Moshe promised that he would. He would find a way.

And through his own injuries to his knee, Moshe figured out something that science is just beginning to understand. The nervous system rules all. We can massage the musculature and connective tissue all we want. And that can feel quite nice and get fluids moving and all and take our stress levels down significantly. But it might not improve much the function of someone's knee in the long run.

With his three snapped ligaments in his knee—which never grew back, of course—he found that he could stand and walk and eventually even squat and continue to practice judo and even do some pretty significant strength moves!

This was of course impossible. The doctors and surgeons had told him so. He had very little holding his knee together. They told him he'd have no chance of walking again without surgery.

But he walked. He walked.

How?

MAKING THE IMPOSSIBLE POSSIBLE

When he was at his worst with his knee, he rested his body on the ground. Completely flat on his back. And he noticed that he was pain-free in that arrangement, with gravity bearing down on him in a very different way than when standing. But there was something strange about his shoulder on the same side as his knee injury. It was firmer, tougher—probably all that concrete-hauling back in Tel Aviv when he was younger.

In a lecture many years later, we can hear Moshe wondering about some 'friend' of his—his indirect way of probably talking about himself. He says something like, I wonder if when I went up against that brute on the football field if my firmer shoulder had anything to do with my knee not being able to withstand the force of running into him and trying to kick the ball around him? I wonder if my shoulder were not so toughened and firmed up and could have softened when I went up against that guy if maybe my knee would now be in better shape? I wonder if I find now some way to soften that shoulder that when I walk maybe my rib-basket will be more spring-like and able to more lightly spring up and down over my very compromised knee?

And so he went to work/play, with that firmer shoulder and with his whole self. He noticed the ways his shoulders were involved with his whole self—that it wasn't just a game of improving one shoulder or one knee and his whole body was better. He discovered the important relationships within his own body, how his or anyone's knee would not bend without a low back that could easily move too. He studied the ways human knees move with the whole of any human body, even how other mammals' knees move. He watched babies learn to bear weight on their joints, grow in relationship with gravity—one of the greatest forces any of us ever confront and rarely ever consider once we've learned to stand and walk. He played with slowly moving on the ground, and listened to each tiny little movement.

The movements were clever, strange, interesting to him and to his brain, his nervous system, which ultimately coordinates where to move our muscles/connective tissue to put our bones in places and in such ways that support us in our relationship with gravity.

But ultimately it wasn't even so much the cleverness of the movements and their combinations—though that was important to interest his nervous system into paying attention—but the way in which he listened, he tuned in, he sensed his body moving . . . that's what made all the difference.

SENSING ONESELF IS THE MAGIC

Ultimately, it was the way a child moves and listens, the way babies can be so fascinated with their own hands and feet and moving from one place to another, sensing themselves moving through space. 'Noticing differences is the language of the nervous system,' one of the rally cries of this somatic work, 'and when we sense ourselves and notice differences, everything gets much more interesting! When we learn the language of one's own body, boom!'

So he sensed himself on the ground. Sensed his body moving this way and that. All the tiniest, slowest little movements, just like a baby does at first.

And before he knew it he was standing and walking.

How??! With three completely compromised knee ligaments!

He wasn't surprised to learn that others had been studying a bit of what he was experiencing, including the fascinating 19th century work that became known as the Weber-Fechner Law, this work of psychophysics having to do with human sensitivity to different stimuli like light and weight and other things. These researchers found that human beings could be so incredibly sensitive to changes in light—say even noticing the very slight difference between lighting a room with 100 light bulbs and then dimming only 2 of the light bulbs and seeing if humans could notice such a small change. Ernst Heinrich Weber and Gustav Theodor Fechner found that such a small change could be sensed by just about every human being! Could such amazing human sensitivity be true of movement, Moshe wondered?

Moshe found out that he could be <u>incredibly</u> sensitive to the ways he moved, when he moved slowly enough for himself to catch the nuances of every move he made. And he got better at it, that his sensitivity improved the more attentive he was to it. And he found his knee improving, he found he could walk with grace and ease, in some new way of walking—a way that seemed radically different for him perhaps, though any of us watching might not notice a whole lot of difference. At least until we trained our own sensitivity to notice more carefully and curiously the differences in the ways he walked.

Could it be this simple, Moshe wondered? Could sensitivity, noticing differences, be the key to life, to movement, to learning?

Moshe began developing 1000's of different movement lessons that helped one's brain and nervous system and whole self to organize around and to clarify relationships with all the joints of one's own body. He eventually called these Awareness Through Movement® lessons. And when someone wasn't able to do these lessons on one's own due to some significant issue, Moshe used his own hands to very gently move someone's body in the ways that he would normally invite someone to do on their own in Awareness Through Movement®. Later, he called these hands-on, one-on-one sessions Functional Integration®.

SENSATION AS A GATEWAY TO THE 'MIRACULOUS'

One of his most famous clients was a young girl born with a significant portion of her brain missing. He promised that she—this baby with so many vital deficits and difficulties—would dance at her wedding and graduate college. And sure enough she did!

How? By inviting her brain to learn through movement, and that learning is what creates the nervous system after birth in the first place.

Moshe's hunches about the nervous system are just beginning to be validated today through scientific studies in neuroplasticity, the notion that our brains can be changed instantly through learning, through curiosity, through movement, even through a clever story. Just like the stories of the what scholars assume was the first biblical writer, whom I call Sweet Lady J, who told her campfire stories 3000 years ago, stories that eventually would become much of Genesis in the Bible and then the foundation of three significant religious traditions: Judaism, Christianity, and Islam.

With people who had experienced the most significant traumas of life, of birth, of near-death, of World War 2, of injuries, of all manner of big and small traumas, of mental illness, of cerebral palsy, of all manner of diseases, Feldenkrais discovered that change is possible, when we move slowly, with awareness, sometimes even in gentle-clever ways.

It's really kind of amazing to me that one of Feldenkrais' biggest influences for discovering neuroplasticity through movement was Jewish wisdom, through the ways that stories change on a dime.

Moshe Feldenkrais was from a long line of rabbis, and even claimed Pinchas of Kortez as a relative and namesake. Pinchas of Koretz (1728 - 1791) was one of the main students of Baal Shem Tov (c. 1700 - 1760). Baal Shem Tov was a man of great healing-ability and wisdom and playfulness who gave birth to Hasidic wisdom. Hasidic stories are founded on the imagination found first in Sweet Lady J's stories in the Bible.

Neuroplasticity, the ability to change our brains through some gentle-surprise goes back to Sweet Lady J. Whether that gentle-surprise comes through a story or a slow and clever series of movements that Feldenkrais invented, it all goes back to her. As does nonviolence.

Taken, with some expansions, from the book, **Sweet Lady J: Mother, Muse & Root of Nearly Everything...The 3000-year-old Campfire Stories of Biblical Genesis Giving Birth to Judaism, Christianity, Islam, Nonviolence & Neuroplasticity**, *translations & invitations by Brian J. Shircliff (2017).*

self-shaping
niyamas

As we practice yoga more and more, we learn the importance of taking care of one's self in every way. There is no one right thing for all . . . each one of us will need to watch and listen and feel within one's own self exactly what it is each of us needs for life in all its fullness, its recognition of wholeness, of health.

No guru can tell you what you need . . . beyond the obvious: food, water, sleep, movement, rest. How much you need of each and what types is completely up to you, to how you know yourself and choose to love yourself.

Ultimately, as we begin to listen to the wisdom within our own selves, we come to know a great power . . . the Inner Teacher, the inner guru, the one within you that dispels ignorance and darkness.

The yoga tradition identifies three types of being, three types of energy with which we are all probably very familiar:

our own laziness and need for rest (tamas),

our own cultivation of truth, peace, goodness (sattva),

& our own inner-fire and passion and need to move (rajas).

The ancient yogins wrote much about these three different energies, these 'gunas' as they called them. *The Bhagavad Gita*, one of the classic texts of yoga study, has much to say about the gunas. As a matter of fact, it's these ancient yogins' way of saying that the oneness of the Universe wanted to share life and split into threes and continued to split and split and split—all still within this oneness, this whole of the Universe, THE ALL—and that every seemingly 'separate' creature or creation has these three energies within itself.

It would be easy to think that what we all really need to do is go after sattva and all will be well. Who doesn't want truth? goodness? peace?

But sattva doesn't motivate us to do the dishes . . . rajas does.

Sattva doesn't get us to finally surrender to dreams and the sleep we need . . . tamas does.

Our yoga journey might be to begin to discover when each of these energies and aspects of ourselves can best be cultivated. The better path, of course, as Patanjali points out in his sutras, is to rest in meditation, to avoid the pull of each of these three energies. And yet we 'house-holders,' we who live in the world and have things we need to do to live and thrive, must most days do way more than simply sit in meditation and have someone else take care of our food and clothing and shelter for us, as monks like Patanjali have such care provided. As *The Bhagavad Gita* wisely points out, we at times must be drawn toward action in our world—and we'd be wise to act and then let go of the result, to be unattached to the outcome of our decisive actions.

And that's where these three energies, these three gunas, can be helpful in our choosing to act.

Rajasic energy is probably not incredibly helpful when a small child is crying and needs to be comforted and calmed by us.

Tamasic energy is probably not the most helpful when a friend is pouring out their heart to us and we are unresponsive, practically asleep.

Life is a dance with all three of these gunas, these ways of being.

In your own slowing down and being mindful of how you feel and what you need in your own life right here, right now . . .

does anything begin to open up?

perhaps in your relationship to your very own self?

in your relationship with the world and all its creatures . . . THE ALL within which we all have our home and being?

The path to how we arrive is so strange.

I was a very active student in Vince Lasorso's White Willow Tai Chi School—probably went three to five times a week for about seven years, and loved every minute of it. Vince used to invite his teachers to town to offer workshops—long before holistic workshops were a cool thing. He invited the impressive Nganga Mfundishi Tolo-Naa to Cincinnati for a special Bagua workshop. At the time, Tolo-Naa was one of the world-experts in Bagua, walking the circle.

We all arrived at Grailville's big A-frame building in our own ways. We were giddy to be here, to be with one another, in this rural-retreat space—all of us chattering up a storm. This was a big deal.

Tolo-Naa walked into our giddy excitement, the room abuzz. He seemed none too pleased, though he did not say anything. After all, a sensible teacher—one tuned into sensation—meets their students where they are, and then invites them through a new door.

He simply and clearly invited us to stand tall with our arms at our sides, each of us to scatter ourselves around so that each could have a view through the window to the rolling field out beyond, to do all of this in the quiet.

And we stood. And we stood. And we stood.

Maybe 30 minutes went by. What in the world did this standing-still have to do with walking a circle?

I watched the field change before my eyes. Like a veil ripped off, as if experiencing, as if knowing it for the first time. The Knower and the Field, the deep wisdom of The Bhagavad Gita.

My feet felt like they were submerged under the floor, under the basement floor even. Roots.

Tolo-Naa stood with us. And then without any fanfare but a small giggle to himself, he said, "Good, now you're ready to begin."

relationship-shaping yamas

How aware are you of the people with whom you live and move and rest?

How aware are you of the people that you pass by every day—maybe even hundreds, thousands of people every day?

And all the online interactions with people in front of their own screens, sometimes even on the other side of the globe—maybe even an astronaut outside the globe and in outer-space?

Does your daily yoga practice,
the invitation to tune into your own self,
into ALL that is within you,
also invite you to be more mindful of all the people of your life . . .
THE ALL within you meeting THE ALL beyond your skin,
beyond ALL that is you?

Encountering THE ALL

reflections from VITAL-friends

We might like to think that yoga is a non-competitive engagement. Way back when and now.

Well, today we know yoga is competitive as everyone tries to get their corner on the $16 billion US market (*Forbes*, 15 March 2016) and teachers worry about people stealing their students, or undercutting class prices, or selling gear at lower prices or having some exclusive and new and much-needed prop available and on and on and on.

I often like to remind my fellow teachers that in our Cincinnati & Northern Kentucky area there are more than 3 million people. And if about 10% of the population does yoga (national average), then 2.7 million people in our very neighborhoods are not yet participating—so go find them! Show them why yoga might be helpful in their own lives! Be as wise as Krishnamacharaya and meet each student in a way that tailors the yoga-practice for what that person needs, that helps that particular human being grow in life, grow in awareness of THE ALL.

Competition in yoga has existed for centuries. The story I've heard—and can certainly see as entirely possible—is that Patanjali's monks would walk through town chanting 'here are the teachings of yoga! here are the teachings of yoga!' and all who were interested would then follow these chanting monks and meet under a tree and hear the sutras—the wise sayings—sung out, and probably repeated one at a time by the crowd . . . a sing-and-repeat way of teaching that Patanjali thought was the heart of yoga, of knowing THE ALL.

Well, eventually, someone HAD to decide there must be another way . . . and maybe someone reacted to the monk-like nature of life as being presented as the only way to find and know 'yoga' or the fact that sing-and-response sutras or wise-sayings teach one way and are helpful for a lot of people, and stories teach an entirely other way and are helpful, perhaps, for an entirely different group of people.

Study other wise teachers like Jesus or Gautama (the one people called the Buddha, one of the enlightened ones) and you'll quickly discover their love for both wise-sayings _and_ stories—all depending on what's most helpful in the moment. A wise teacher, after all, will want to meet each person in a way that is helpful for that particular person. A story works for some, but not every person. A wise saying works for some, but not every person. Silence works for some, but not every person at every moment of the day or night. A compassionate glance works for some, but not every person. A gentle touch works for some, but not every person. And for each one of us, what is helpful in this very moment might be completely different from what would have been helpful five minutes ago or what will be helpful five minutes from now.

So as monks shouted out 'these are the teachings of yoga! these are the teachings of yoga!' someone created another gathering, under another tree . . . and told the story of The Bhagavad Gita, the story of a man deciding if he should fight the people on the other side of the battle-field . . . family, teachers, friends who had stolen his side of the family's rights to rule. As it seems to happen every time, when this man was at his very lowest, this man's servant-assistant ends up being an incarnation of God (perhaps each one of us is?), and this servant-assistant invites the man to discover his path, the ground of his being in that moment, especially after a rather dramatic peek at THE ALL.

As was mentioned earlier, in the wonderfully helpful and detailed article "The Meaning of 'hatha' in Early Hathayoga," Sanskrit scholar and researcher Jason Birch points out that there is way more controversy in the centuries-old yoga world than just the assumed centuries-long oral and written competitions between Patanjali's monk-camp and the The Bhagavad Gita's followers' married-life, house-holder camp that I reference here. Yoga practitioners and 'gurus' constantly write and write-over each other and revise one another and say one another is wrong. Any philosopher or historian in any field would remind us that that's the way new and more helpful ideas get born, by chafing one another, by colliding with one another. Hopefully gently, nonviolently.

Disagreement can be helpful! Very helpful!

The canon of 'classic' yoga texts do not agree with one another on a whole lot.

Read them, study them, and you'll see.

For people of any ancient 'book' tradition, look carefully and you'll notice the same thing happening. I grew up Christian and began my own scholarship of the Bible—it's full of contradictions as well.

This trips up a lot of people who throw up their hands and either reject it all or invent their own patch-work of favorite passages from the yoga texts or from the Bible or whatever advice-tradition and then live by their favorite texts and reject entirely or at least ignore the other parts of their tradition that do not work.

When I find disagreement in a single tradition or in a single text, I no longer get frustrated by it—I get excited. Suddenly, I'm reminded that I need to find my own way, as the original writers / poets did by express-ing their exclusive view.

Surely, there are many, many ways to know 'yoga' . . . to get a glimpse of THE ALL, the infinite-nature of life. Sutra, story, reflection, devotion, service-work, relationship, making shapes with your body and sensing yourself, contemplation, silence, sex & love-making, dawdling along doing nothing while the clouds fly by overhead, and many, many, many more. Hopefully this book contributes to such a possibility of 'yoga' discovery.

Please enjoy some friends of VITALITY who share their experiences of yoga, their glimpses into encountering THE ALL.

And please do notice that all of these encounters are wonderful. And that not all of them agree with me (Brian Shircliff), the editor . . . some of the things that give them life do not serve me well, and some of the things that give me life might not serve them well either. After all, this is THE ALL we're talking about, the infinite possibilities that are and can be!

Each one of us must find one's own wise way. May these stories provide inspiration to discover your own!

Helen Buswinka's Encounters with THE ALL

GARDEN MUSINGS

...it doesn't take much. Just kneeling on Earth, working her soil while the bee on the flower next to me attends to her own task of gathering nectar. Is she as nourished by the fragrance of this sweet fluid as am I? Ants scatter as I lift a rock, carrying egg sacks as they go. I have disturbed their home. Is it beyond repair, I wonder? There is no otherness among us. Soil, me, the ants and bumble bee; each content in our own work.

...I tend the bed, giving each plant the space it needs to flourish. A few dill seedlings have sprouted among the flowers, not where I would have planted them. But who am I to say? Offering hospitality to the unexpected guests, I make space for them, too.

...recent rain has been especially life-giving to the plantain, generally considered to be a weed. What makes it a weed? Plantain was as sacred as eucharist to the ancient Saxons. Hindus associate plantain with the goddess Kali. And so, I dig out the plant with mixed feelings, thanking it for its work as a path to the Sacred.

...cupping a handful of compost, I side-dress the beans. Potato peels, carrots ends, and the remains of nourishing dinners, have been transformed into the black gold that is this compost. I now return the gift, nourishing Earth as she has nourished me. It's all of one piece.—December 2018

HOLY WORK

It is an unlikely place for Healing Touch, this crowded, bustling food pantry. Participants and volunteers come and go, carrying shopping bags or minding children, sometimes calling to each other, waiting with their tickets, receiving advice from the parish nurse. So much activity. So much noise. We three begin, handing out information, talking about Healing Touch. Our three pairs of chairs are squeezed into a space too small to work, but amazingly does.

Trust begins clumsily here, some not sure what Healing Touch is but curious, others distracted by their cares, and still others afraid their number will be called and they will lose their place in line for food. We reassure.

One shopper who has stepped forward begins to name her burdens, "My blood pressure, cancer, the rent, raising my grandchildren. Just the general stress of living." Holy ground, truly. One wants to remove one's shoes. I begin tenderly, hands on her shoulders, centering more deeply, both of us encased in the Light, and I can feel the energy flowing from my hands. For her highest good, I intend. Her shoulders fall in relaxation, hands open. One would like to let this grandmother be, relaxing into the only self care she may have, but her granddaughter tugs at her and another person awaits.

My Healing Touch partners are immersed in inviting, listening compassionately, laying on hands. We three move, overlapping space with one another in kaleidoscopic fashion. People come, one too overwhelmed to say much but wanting healing; another, one of our regulars, "It's my knees again, and just my whole body" and another "I just want to sit and close my eyes." Our tiny space has become sanctified with vulnerability, healing, and trust. The noisy activity of the food pantry, no longer a distraction, is transformed into ambient music for healing. —December 2018

Helen Buswinka *endeavors to live simply, savoring the beauty of each day. She can be found in the garden, immersed in a creative art, or in whatever sinks her deeper into Mystery. She is a student of Healing Touch at VITALITY and volunteers with VITALITY at Bond Hill Food Pantry.*

Penny Costilla's Encounters with THE ALL

Sitting in meditation I ask myself, Yoga?

Breathing. Breath. Stillness. Reaching all the layers inside the body physical, emotional, and spiritual. Part of life and living fully. Then for me, writing all I discover in my journal. Writing under the influence of meditation the thoughts go deeper and the insights broader.

Yoga opens the door to so much or as much as I allow.

Yoga gives permission for the search in whatever direction I decide.

Penny Costilla *spends her retirement strengthening her ties to Spirit through meditation and journaling. She has had the pleasure to volunteer at VITALITY since the beginning encouraging attendees to Inner Journey gatherings to understand and expand their use of journaling to enhance their personal growth and self-understanding.*

Mike Eck's Encounters with THE ALL

VITALITY Cincinnati and yoga helped open my eyes

To see anew
To see what I could not see
To see a vast open sea So

Come with me
Come and see
It's easy to be
A new me
When we all sea
what some of us don't see?

Some of us see the forest
Some of us see trees
Some of us see flowers
Some of us see bees
Some of us see dirt
Some of us see seeds

When we all sea the root
When we all sea the weeds
When we all sea the Vine
When we all sea the Fruit
We sea the Divine
We sea I AM

Mike and Denise Eck . . . *We build bridges between people and communities. We connect people with opportunities to learn, grow, prepare and share. We hope to light the path and show the Way.*

Kristen Iker's Encounters with THE ALL

Yoga is an evolutionary process for me. When I began taking yoga at VITALITY (my yoga journey began well before this but at a much slower progress), I had the idea in my head that I needed to meet a certain standard of technique. My years as a dancer had conditioned me to believe that there was one very precise way to master the art—through technique, which looked, or should look the same for everyone. I felt a pressure to make my lines, my angles and my breath fit this pre-conceived notion of a yogi mold.

After a few weeks at VITALITY, I started to learn that not only did I have a skewed perception about my yoga practice, but about the way my body is intended to move through space. I learned to stop looking at the angles and lines (it helped that there were no mirrors), and feel where my body was able to move with breath and where it was not.

Where I was not moving, my practice slowed in pace. Patience was tested, and I learned where I needed to breathe more. I found that even though I had, what I used to consider "limitations," the breath and awareness extended the posture beyond what I was physically able to do. I find it a little cheesy to say that my practice grew bigger than my physical body, but that's what happened. I came to realize that my physical body was the manifestation of my identity. Isn't that odd that I had never considered that before? And with each breath, and each sun salutation and each savasana, I was working through my very-much non-physical self, and that was where my practice progressed at a quicker pace.

I began practicing in a new space in the last couple of years. I have learned to find amusement on the days where my balance is off or my muscles are tight. I shrug or smirk at times, when years ago I may have shook my head and been frustrated. I refer to a mirror sometimes in my practice now. I use it in a totally different way than before. Instead of checking lines and angles I'm admiring the movement of my ribs and torso while I breathe, I'm admiring "how tall" I look in mountain pose.

I'm "noticing but not placing judgement" when the left side of the posture looks different than on the right. I'm admiring the surrender of a new posture I'm committing to the practice.

It was during my ballet career that I discovered yoga. I found it to be "a nice stretching class" with a terrific "nap time" at the end. But found it unproductive in my life of strict and full schedule. I stopped dancing in my teenage years, and during college rediscovered yoga as an enjoyable evening activity during final exams or when I wanted a break from roommates. I studied psychology and public health and during my graduate school career found a program in Cincinnati called VITALITY. It seemed like a great way of tying the two disciplines together at that time. A few years later, I'm learning more about myself and my potential through my practice. MY yoga is the reflection of my life in a breathable format. Each movement is with purpose, and each practice is a new page in my autobiography.

Kristen Iker is a developing artist who loves traveling and learning. She lives in an abundantly loving home with her husband and their pets. Kristen graduated from VITALITY's 2015 200-hour Yoga/ Healing Touch Internship (the 200-hour yoga teacher training program) and hasn't breathed the same since!

Crystal Judge's Encounters with THE ALL

LIVING IN GRATITUDE

Looking through the lens with gratitude as yoga in more recent years has lifted the veil from my vision. I am thankful that my life does not have the suffering that I carried for so many years. I am no longer holding the attitude that it's me against the world. I am no longer holding. Yoga has allowed me to let go physically, emotionally and spiritually. Finding comfort in uncertainty more often than not and feeling my whole body, my heart, my soul...EXPAND!

When I started my journey of yoga certification through VITALITY, I was very much on a path of self-discovery and it was ugly. The dirt and mess whirled around like a tornado and I was spinning with it. My journey has brought unexpected things into my life, and although I am still unsure of where I am intended to lead or follow or walk along, I am okay with that. Being okay with being, I am YOGA.

Crystal Judge *has a vision to live sustainably and to share knowledge learned through classes, workshops, healing modality techniques and empowerment. Find her family at* graciousfarm.com. *She is a graduate of VITALITY's 2013-2014 Yoga/Healing Touch Internship (the 200-hour yoga teacher training program) & 2015-2016 300-hour co-sponsored EmbodiYoga® with Becky Morrissey (Sangha Yoga) & Movement Intelligence® / Bones for Life® (VITALITY) Programs.*

Leann Kane's Encounters with THE ALL

SAVASANA

My final reflection.

My final "to-do" of yoga school.

My last asana to seal my practice into my heart, mind, and body.

I absolutely had no idea what to expect out of yoga school. It had been a loose goal of mine for awhile but I had never done anything to advance that goal. My wife is actually who contacted VITALITY and paid the deposit.

I had fallen out of love with my practice for some time. I was really into an intense vinyasa "power" flow in a corporate studio in town, the teacher I found was bigger bodied and short like me. I went religiously to her classes when one day, she was no longer around. The studio had been stripping away her creative freedom and had even restricted rituals like OM and Namaste salutes at the end of practice.

With that said, I wanted more. I wanted my practice to grow. I wanted to let myself be guided on a new path. I wanted to test myself. I wanted something different not just in my yoga practice but my whole life (which could be the practice). I found that at VITALITY. Six months ago, if you asked me if I wanted to do gentle yoga, I would politely decline. I couldn't imagine moving so slowly! After all, yoga magic only happens in a hot room holding asanas for a breath or two at most. Boy, was I wrong. Now after a long day of work I love nothing more than to get on my mat and take some time to be gentle and present with myself.

Nothing about me or my life is slow. I'd like to think it's a little bit intentional, but until VITALITY I had never tried to put those practices in place for myself. As a social worker I would teach or guide people towards doing this for themselves, as so has been said we often teach what we most need to learn. I am always rushing from one job to another, from one project or chore to another. While the rushing won't stop (for now) maybe now it will be easier for me to practice the slowness, the gentleness, the mindful intention VITALITY has so beautifully bestowed upon me.

I am so grateful to have gone through this journey with so many beautiful people. I am so grateful for what I have learned, which surprisingly is not necessarily all about how to teach, but rather why I teach.

My reasons for teaching are selfish. No way around it. I teach so that I can learn patience, gratitude, and flexibility. I teach so that I can be more mindful with myself and others around me.

I am still becoming comfortable with being the teacher, but I honestly think that may not happen. If I am doing this right, I hope to never become comfortable. I hope to only thrive in the present, learning as I go. I hope that through my classes someone else comes to find their path.

Just like savasana, while this paper in many ways signifies the end, it also welcomes a beginning. The lessons I have learned in seven months are invaluable and unforgettable.

With that I say,
Namaste.

Leann Kane *is a graduate of VITALITY'S 2018 Yoga/Healing Touch Internship, the 200-hour yoga teacher training program. Leann has dedicated her career as a social worker and life to bringing gentleness and understanding to those who need it most. Through her work as a yoga instructor she brings healing and joy to all aspects of the human experience.*

Nikki Leonard's Encounters with THE ALL

Yoga to me is community.

It's knowing that you are safe not because of an inherent right or any financial cushion but because of the people you surround yourself with.

We humans put trust in one another for many different reasons but the most common denominator is love.

This same love is the root of family, friendships, and communities that protect us.

Thanks and Namaste

Nikki Leonard *is a lover of all things travel, nature, and relationships. The things she values most are the connections she has built with her family, friends, and teachers along the way. Experiences, such as taking in the new sights and sounds this world has to offer, keep her going and cultivate a sense of overwhelming gratitude for this human form. She is a graduate of VITALITY's 2018 Yoga/Healing Touch Internship, the 200-hour yoga teacher training program.*

Tina Nelson's Encounters with THE ALL

What happened for me during the seven months with this group?

Going to my first VITALITY meeting right on New Year's Day was a fluke. Kathie Turner asked me to come after we had met for coffee and I had said that I was looking into getting a yoga certification. All major turns in my life have been met with I like this…I like this…I think I want to do this. That was exactly how I felt about yoga. The VITALITY experience was dropped into my pathway. No doubt the God of Universe opened the door for me. There is something about the energy of love, it draws possibilities and people to your pathway.

I am very grateful for the training that I received at VITALITY. The international online Feldenkrais Summit hosted by Cincinnati's own Cynthia Allen of Future Life Now enhanced my yoga experience and connection. I found myself resonating with teachings of David Kaetz and his explanations of the power of sound/energy whether it was in the form of a ringing bell or people singing—it was extremely powerful.

I found myself even more tuned into how I was experiencing the energy of a room and allowed myself to be playful or simply changing the position of my body when energy was overpowering to be more comfortable. I learned that the slightest movements could add clarity and to bring attention to my breathing for calmness.

I've enjoyed my yoga classmates and being on the journey together. Everyone added to the experience of the training. I am grateful for the opportunity to have shared this experience with such a great group of people. Endings are always bittersweet.

Through moving, breathing and resting, what have I discovered about myself, my life, this world? I am a kinesthetic learner. I have tremendous range for meeting new people and finding ways to connect. I am very sensitive to energy.

Yoga is a connector. People who do yoga love it or if they have not tried it...they are very curious to try yoga.

When did I get a glimpse of yoga (THE ALL), when did I find myself awakening to what is possible in my life or the life of the world? There are so many...

SoulCollage® with Fab Duell. I still look at the cards with awe. Some of my heaviest times were reflected with my shadow card; how those pictures appeared in my envelope to help describe my situation was uncanny. It gave me gratitude for my freedom and to look at my future with possibilities, with excitement!

The day that we did the downward dog observations and I said, "My downward dog always feels different each time I do it." Leann piped up and said, "That's because you are a new creation everytime you are on your mat!" It was like, "Wow!!" I kept getting confirmations about being renewed in spirit even the sermon the next day at church was, "You are a new creation."

I was very touched when Logan gave me a scoby to make kombucha. She made me laugh all the time.

Especially when I told her about my mental health clinic yoga teaching cancelation. Starting over can happen anytime of the day.

I found the gardening most challenging but was a very strong connection to meditation and reflection. The power of weeding, pruning, and harvesting are so reflected in the activities of our day-to-day life to be healthy, balanced, and renewed.

Tina Nelson *is a graduate of VITALITY's 2018 Yoga/Healing Touch Internship, the 200-hour yoga teacher training program. She found that you learn many things in teacher training to which you will never be introduced in a regular yoga class. It is a turbo jet start* to your transformation. First, it is the relationships/community you build with fellow yogins in your training class. They provide the support for building the foundation for your growth. What it taught her along the way...yoga connects people to people and it is about serving communities and leadership. Whether it is something we all strive to do together, building a garden in a neighborhood, hosting a yoga class out of a garage, donating items to the hungry, or simply showing up to class sharing positive energy...yoga has an impact on building healthier communities.

Aprilann Pandora's Encounters with THE ALL

I graduated from VITALITY's very first Yoga/Healing Touch Internship in 2012. While teaching yoga & meditation as a career at Cincinnati Recreation Centers, I became inspired to begin Eden Urban Gardens, LLC.

We have a little over a quarter of an acre in the city limits where we grow herbs, vegetables, and fruits using organic practices free of synthetic fertilizers and pesticides—heading into our 4th year of production now.

I still do a regular yoga and meditation practice and find that this has helped much with my clarity and guidance for life and work. Becoming a yoga teacher helped me to gain insight & open the door to a career change. It has been a challenging journey to start a business with only a vision, three hand tools, and my own enthusiasm.

We now are fortunate to have more resources to assist in our production. The idea of starting an urban farming business came to me in a dream; our business name came to me during meditation as I was seeking guidance for a name.

I am forever grateful to the opportunity to intern through VITALITY's Yoga/Healing Touch Internship—yoga teacher training otherwise would have been inaccessible for me due to cost. The best part of my yoga internship was being able to focus on bettering my practice, learning how to teach others, taking Healing Touch, and learning self-care. I found this incredibly helpful not only for teaching yoga classes but also in dealing with customers and business.

It is amazing to see how one seed idea can take root and grow.

Aprilann Pandora *is Urban Farmer & Managing Member of Eden Urban Gardens, LLC. She graduated from VITALITY's very first*

2011-2012 Yoga/Healing Touch Internship, the 200-hour yoga teacher training program. She sees herself as 'Enriching Lives Through Produce.' Interested in placing an order with Eden Urban Gardens? Find her on Facebook or call/text (513) 485-2679.

Logan Probst's Encounters with THE ALL

Breathe.
Inhale.
Exhale.
Slow down.

In the past seven months, I have learned to be a little slower, a little gentler, a little softer.

I've learned that it's ok to just be, in the moment, whatever that is.

I've learned that my pace is just the right pace for me and that we each have our own speed, our own flow. I've learned to grow, but not by stretching, but by expanding.

I've learned how to let things go — things that no longer serve me, things that no longer have purpose in my life, things that are no longer valuable

— and in that, I've created space.

Space within myself.

Space for all that I want and need.

Space for beauty, space for peace, space for compassion.

I've learned that nothing is more, or less, than it seems — it's exactly what it is in that moment. I've learned that we are all teachers, but more importantly, that we are forever students — always learning, wondering, exploring.

Following the retreat at VITALITY Cincinnati, I noticed a shift. A significant shift, but not one that happened over night. I realized that I slowly began to change, to unwind, to reconnect with myself and the universe around me. Since March, I've become more grounded, more at ease, and more aware of me and my being—my presence, my breath, my movement. I've developed a stronger sense of self, an awareness previously inexperienced, a spark that has grown into a much brighter light.

And for that, I will forever be grateful. The seed has been planted, roots have formed, and growth is certainly taking place. Namaste.

Logan Probst *hopes to share relief from both physical and emotional pain through the teachings of yoga. As a graduate of VITALITY's 2018 Yoga/Healing Touch Internship, the 200-hour yoga teacher training program, Logan is devoted to making the practice accessible to all by leading in nontraditional spaces.*

CJ Pierce's Encounters with THE ALL

Why is there always a dichotomy?
The yin-yang

Black and White
Polarities:
North & South
East & West
Right & Wrong
Good & Bad
Love & Hate
Heaven & Hell

These are never separate and one does not survive without the other.

What is this dance of Dichotomy that holds us together and also tears us apart?

Where are our moderates?
The Ones capable of seeing and knowing the blending spaces.

Where are our Universal moderates?
The Ones that fit and hold the dark into light and the light into the dark.
The workers that keep the whole together for the greater, without fanfare or privilege.
They are the keys that open hearts to the sacred, treasured, personal spaces to advance the synergy toward honor and respect.

How is it that the darkness cycles into the light and light cycles into the darkness?
Both the darkness and the light create elements of blinding distortions.
Blinded by the light into the deepest of darkness.

I am light
I am darkness

This dichotomy cannot be separated

What is in the dance of resistance within dichotomy that teaches us about one's boundaries?

The breath in, the breath out.
A pause at both ends that maintains a cycle.
Neither imploding, nor exploding.
A mere trust of safety within this divine synergy.
A mere trust, I am going to be alright.
A mere trust, My needs will be met.
A mere trust, I need not to fear.

As my body knows the beat of my heart with the rhythm of my breath as a surrender of acceptance.
It is yoga, It is all yoga.
The work has begun.
My job:
listen,
let go and
let it be.

Perhaps here, in Love,
In Yoga, A moderate will arise.
Within this complexity
I, my soul,
my heart,
my being,
my ID evaporates.
I am One
Of the One
Of the whole.

CJ Pierce *is a Professional Volunteer, ad-hoc, for non-profits address-ing social and civic causes. This passion of hers is fueled by her* *fundamental Yogic beliefs. A belief that ALL belong, a justice that ALL receive what is needed to promote and rise each one to one's highest self. As a graduate of VITALITY's 2017 Yoga/Healing Touch Internship (the 200-hour yoga teacher training program) & VITALITY's inaugural 2018 300-hour Advanced Yoga Certification course, she continues to attend, promote, and is a life fan of the ongoing education and work VITALITY provides.*

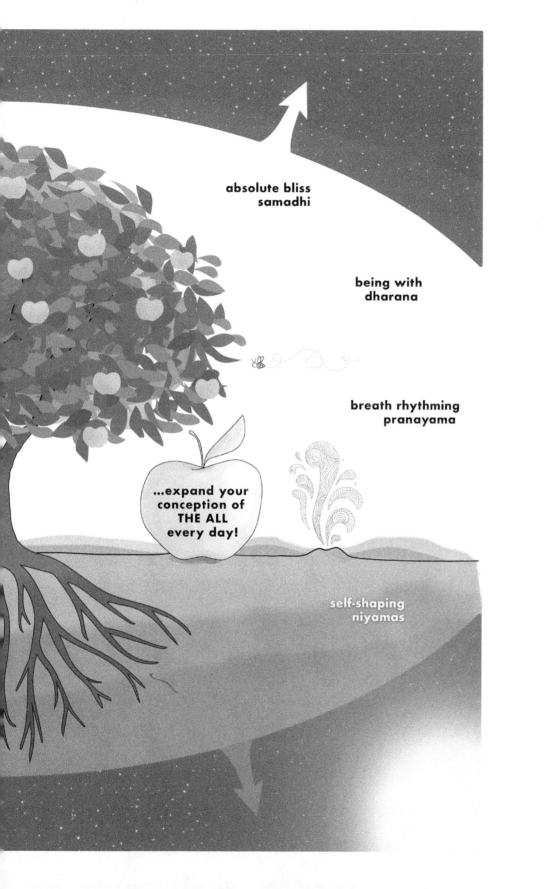

Encountering THE ALL

more reflections from VITAL-friends

Perhaps you're discovering that someone in this text says one thing with which you completely agree. Great! And then a few pages later someone else says something with which you completely agree, and that insight in one way or another contradicts the insight from the first person with whom you agreed. Haha, great!

When considering THE ALL, there are no 'sides' from which to choose. How can THE ALL—the infinite—have sides or divisions or even organized sections?

Even the attempts by this author/editor (Brian Shircliff) to so nicely section things off into bite-size chunks to consider might take away from the ability to consider or conceive of THE ALL.

And yet, no one of us can know the full scope of THE ALL.

We have to start somewhere, right?

And as Emily Dickinson so wisely reminds us in her poem "Tell all the truth but tell it slant" . . . we can only take in, glimpse, experience so much of the 'truth'—so much of THE ALL without losing completely our ability to notice any of it.

Check out her poem . . . quite nice.

These pieces, these little sayings and quotes and stories and philosophies and invitations in this or any book, they all are simply helps, little windows through which to experience the larger world. None of them is the whole 'truth' in itself. Anyone who claims to have the 'truth' and demands that I agree with them I usually run from! :)

Yet we all have glimpses. People with whom we agree. People with whom we disagree.

In my life, I've probably been helped the most by the people with whom I originally disagree.

They invite me to consider that I don't know the whole ALL yet. Of course, at least in this lifetime, I probably never will know it ALL. Though still my experience of THE ALL can grow, right?

And yet the-active-and-then-lazy-pursuit, the invitation to sit here and then move and then sit here again and do nothing and marvel at the wonder of it ALL . . . movement and rest, movement and rest . . . well . . . that seems to be a reliable path to wisdom . . . to notice what I'm experiencing, to be with it—this experience—with all the sensations that I am able to notice in moving and resting and even some I'm not yet able to notice, to discover in my own self what it's ALL about, and to let that discovery be, to hold it all gently, lightly. Whatever conception of THE ALL I have today might be vastly different compared to tomorrow. Hopefully it is. You don't experience the world or yourself in the same way as you did when you were 5? or 10? or 15? or whatever age ago, right?

So consider sitting back and enjoying a few more VITAL-friends sharing their encounters with THE ALL . . . hopefully through their stories you might glimpse your own life, your own experience—either because you've had a similar experience, or because something someone says reminds you of something entirely different in some strange and wonderful way.

THE ALL is vast. And so are your depths, friend.

Amanda Sanders' Encounters with THE ALL

I began the 200-hour yoga teacher training program March 2018. I can hardly believe that training is over. I have had so much fun learning with Brian and my classmates. Everyone has something unique to offer.

The community that is created there is gentle and easy-going. A new home is the vibe.

I have learned to be creative with my practice and push to expand. Traditional yoga is beautiful but for an ever-growing and awakening world, tradition is the beginning. We adjust to the changing of our mind, body, and environment.

Knowing your body and understanding that everyone is different in flexibility and body structure will guide you to the right practice.

The spiritual side of yoga is important. Exercising the strength within is an ever expanding practice. Breath, compassion, community, all are a part of a full yoga practice. Most important, love for yourself.

In our training program we are required to complete 100 hours of community gardening. This is so great, to connect one to the earth by touching it. Most don't realize how fun it is to garden until you are out in it. My kids said, "I didn't think this was gonna be fun but it is."

There is so much out there to get involved in to help the community. My eyes have been opened to the joy gardening brings.

I am so thankful I am involved with VITALITY and for the people I have met. Much love for the future. I will share what I have learned.

Amanda Sanders is a retired Cosmologist and loves helping others. She wanted to be a yoga instructor and graduated from VITALITY's 2018 Yoga/Healing Touch Internship, the 200-hour yoga teacher training program. The program was exactly what she was looking for, kind people, with like minds of creativity. Amanda is a Reiki master and with encouragement infused it into her yoga practice. Visit Scorpiusreiki.com for Reiki and Officiant needs.

Liz Smith's Encounters with THE ALL

The practice of yoga introduced me to a new way of thinking about leading my life.

I believe the experience of living is a practice. An experience that doesn't arrive, but is continuously expanding and changing with each breath and each moment.

Yoga helps me negotiate change, the only real constant. It has taught me to slow down and observe my thoughts, actions, and the actions of those around me.

This practice, along with meditation, has created a much needed space between events that happen, and my reaction to them. Every time the space in between event and reaction grows larger, there is more opportunity for choice, thoughtfulness, compassion, breath, and ultimately, freedom from suffering. A freedom that comes from within.

Lots of love,
Liz

Liz Smith *is an artist, teacher, and life-long student. She calls both Kentucky and Alaska home, depending on the time of year. Liz is a proud graduate of VITALITY's 2013-2014 Yoga/Healing Touch Internship, the 200-hour yoga teacher training program.*

Tonia Smith's Encounters with THE ALL

My introduction to yoga began in the late 1990's with a VHS tape, done quietly in my bedroom. Even then, in my 20's, with noisy city streets just outside my window, and a small dog and cat who insisted on being a part of my practice, I quickly began to see the benefits of yoga in my life. Unknowing of its history, unfamiliar with the Sanskrit names for asanas, and unaware that yoga would make a huge impact on my life nearly twenty years later, I only knew that I felt better and stronger.

On my first day of yoga teacher training at VITALITY Cincinnati in February 2018, I arrived with a new yoga mat, enthusiasm, and a bit of concern that I would not be as flexible as the other students. As it turned out . . . my new yoga mat was quite comfortable, the other students were equally as enthused, and I was, in fact, not as flexible as most of the other students. To my surprise (and relief), I was not asked to place my leg behind my head, but to listen to and honor my body. Wow!

The ensuing seven months were a yogic revelation, filled with movement, meditation, reading, discussion, journaling, laughing, gardening, and eating (a lot!). Together, we created SoulCollages® at Spirited Hand Studio, listened to singing bowls and had a chili cook-off at the Monastery Studio, got our hands dirty gardening at Eden Urban Gardens, and learned of energy healing from Dr. William Bengston. During these adventures, as well as in quiet moments together on our mats, my fellow yoga students became my yoga friends . . . they are now family.

The most valuable lesson that I learned as student of yoga at VITALITY Cincinnati is that yoga is practiced both on and off the mat.

I am ready to share what I have learned with the world!

Namaste.

Tonia Smith is a 2018 Yoga/Healing Touch Internship & 300-hour Advanced Yoga Certification graduate and now volunteers with VITALITY. Tonia's mission is to make the practice of yoga and mindfulness accessible to all.

Jean Marie Stross' Encounters with THE ALL

While my husband was attending a conference, I was enjoying a walk by the ocean at North Myrtle Beach. It was in early November when the sun was setting in the late afternoon. It was then that I experienced an unlikely freedom as told in this poem. I made a quilted wall hanging of this poem for a unit in my doctoral studies in Spirituality.

SILVER DRENCHED! An Anniversary Poem

Visiting the ocean at dusk, the moon struck the waves
glistening
dancing
making silver jewels before my eyes.

In the distance down the beach,
condo towers and hotels were lit up,
lined up, poking the sky, silhouetted like ripe, plump
phalluses against the setting sun,
offering an artist's palate
colors of oranges, reds, pinks.

For a few minutes, in my eye's span,
I held both energies,
feminine, masculine or rather they held me.

Balance, harmony, "at-one-ment" —
move, live, have your very being in me.

As a sentinel, I watched the sun sliding
behind the rim of the horizon
sucking with it the colors and hues.
Only the lights of the buildings remained now
in the distance.

Before me, the waves rolled in

rounded
curling
enfolding labial movement,
forming and
reforming at my foam-soaked feet.

The moon continued to make silver on the water.
Silver was
glowing
glistening
shimmering
dancing at my toes.

I was adorned with silver jewels. Being silver drenched, I felt so affirmed in my own silver-ness—my greying hair, my changing vagina, and a stir in the deep dark cavern of vaginal mystery of who I am. As I near the first anniversary of my hysterectomy, I welcomed this renewal of my feminine energy for my well-worn masculine dominated life.

Balance, harmony, "at-one-ment" —
move, live, have your very being in me.

This silver-drenching continued as I heard "Shall we Dance?" and so I did . . . a greying haired, richly jeweled princess on the beach.

Jean Marie Stross *is involved in Spiritual Direction ministry as a spiritual director/reflector. She listens to her own journey and listens with others for movement of the Spirit—the invitations, the blessings, and the challenges. Jean Marie has been a participant, supporter, and fan of VITALITY as it keeps the vital signs on the journey alive.*

Val Vogel's Encounters with THE ALL

In this weary world of distractions and unrest, there is an oasis of peace and purity only a breath away.

This is yoga to me.

It puts me in a space of being relaxed but alert and I feel purified, radiant and in a perfect state of wellbeing after I practice.

It brings reference to my body and makes me conscious of what I put in this vessel that has now been sanctified by yoking it to the universe and its cosmic pulse.

I teach yoga where I work and am amazed at the miracle of unfolding divinity I see in my students after we have practiced.

Moreover, in the inner courtroom of my mind there is an eye I cannot escape that witnesses to my highest potential and I'm once again hungry for the next time I enter this joyous union of breath and body. Namaste.

Val Vogel *enjoys teaching ashtanga-inspired yoga specializing in gentle (hatha) yoga, chair yoga and meditation at the Recovery Center of Hamilton County and also at Plan of Southwest Ohio. She started practicing yoga in 1995 and has been hooked ever since. Val Vogel graduated from the 2016 VITALITY Yoga/Healing Touch Internship, the 200-hour yoga teacher training program.*

Patricia Williams' Encounters with THE ALL

Yoga is about connectedness—the state of being joined or linked. As humans, we are designed to be connected. Many times in my life, I have felt alone, and that's when yoga has helped transform the situation.

At VITALITY Cincinnati, community is nurtured and embraced. I graduated from the 200-hour yoga certification program and it was a wonderful experience. I met great people, learned so much about myself and found my voice! Since then, I have continued my studies, learning more pranayama and graduating with training in EmbodiYoga® with Lisa Clark and Becky Morrissey.

My experience on my mat and in the yoga community has helped tremendously with the anxiety that has been a part of my life. I have learned the gift of self-compassion and self-acceptance. When I forget these gifts, yoga is there to bring me right back to my truth. Yoga is about how I live my life, doing my best, being connected to my humanity, divinity, nature and one another.

I feel so grateful to all of my teachers. Namaste.

Patricia Williams *believes her purpose revolves around a life of service. Through her work as a massage therapist and reflexologist, she helps others heal, feel safe, respected and nurtured. Pat is a graduate from VITALITY's 2016 Yoga/Healing Touch Internship (the 200-hour yoga teacher training program) & Movement Intelligence® / Bones for Life® basic certification. She has been a long-time supporter of VITALITY.*

Linsay Wilson's Encounters with THE ALL

My lower back has bothered me since my 20's:
During my early 20's,
I had a hard fall on an icy concrete surface and hurt my tailbone.
I had two car accidents, in one of which I slid across 5 lanes of traffic and up on the curve, luckily I was able to walk away.
During the child birth process, I had repercussions from a spinal tap.

Other things happened as I grew older,
I fell off a handicapped school bus lift and someone in a wheel chair fell on top of me. In addition to landing on my hips my ankle twisted. It was several years before I got full use of my foot. And my lower back especially on one side hurt more.

But from my 20's on, there was a constant annoying pain that I assume was part of life, part of getting older. But it wasn't until I was nearly 70 that I discovered Bones for Life and Feldenkrais. The pain left completely. Stayed gone.

In my 50's and 60's I discovered that yoga helped bring some relief especially while I was doing it. When I was getting ready to move, I asked my yoga teacher what to look for in a new teacher and what made her different from some many other yoga teachers. She said she went to Feldenkrais classes herself and was adding a bit of that to her classes. So when I moved to Cincinnati I found Future Life Now & Cynthia Allen and through that found VITALITY. I am so grateful. It has changed my life and what I expect and what I am willing to do. There is no more pain. It is gone completely. My posture is also better.

I wish that more people in their 20's, 30's, and 40's would give it a try. We would have a more peaceful, productive, and happier world. Gratefully those of us a bit older are discovering the benefits of this extraordinary work.

Linsay Wilson *is a graduate of the first co-sponsored training in Movement Intelligence® / Bones for Life® offered by Future Life Now & VITALITY Cincinnati. She and her fellow graduates teach at VITALITY, all over the city and world!*

Carol T. Yeazell's Encounters with THE ALL

Yoga is more than downward dog and sun salutations. It's even more than mountain pose and exalted warrior.

Yoga is the grand entrance to a life that is more thoughtful, calm and productive.

Mindful breathing through yoga poses becomes mindful breathing in life.

The mind clearing that is necessary to practice poses becomes a part of daily relationships and experiences.

In times of personal difficulty or crisis, the lessons learned through a yoga practice are keys to living with and through personal loss, fear and sadness.

Carol T. Yeazell *advocates the health-promoting benefits of a whole-food plant based lifestyle. She offers Healing Touch to friends, grandchildren, and nursing home residents. She is a founding member of VITALITY, as well as a Board member.*

relationship-shaping yamas

The yamas are concerned with what we do with our power, how we live with and honor all beings, all creatures, all life:

- nonviolence (ahimsa) . . . avoiding violence and having a sense of yourself and ways you might be bothering and stirring up violence (even microaggravators); trying to be reasonable in your needs and theirs; and especially using cleverness and equanimity and courage to transform conflicted-relationships in ways that wake you both up and give you both a chance to know THE ALL and respond in kind...

- courage to be your authentic self and allow others to be their authentic selves (satya)

- living simply so others can live as well (asteya . . . the opposite of stealing)

- finding the middle, equanimous, equal-minded path in all things . . . relationally, energetically, sexually (bramacharya . . . the celibate monk Patanjali understood bramacharya much differently from the house-holder, family-oriented Krishnamacharya, and gratefully for most of us!)

- realizing that I have all that I need right here and now so there's no need to hold onto anything tightly (aprarigraha).

Ultimately, though, all of these yamas come down to inviting us to find ourselves in equal relationship with all humans, with all creatures, with all life . . . to remember each one of us humans wears a crown (the top of each of our heads), to move away from those strange desires we humans have to attempt to hold power over people, to trust more deeply the equal-relationship that is within us ALL.

And when we find ourselves resisting equality and just when we are about to attempt to hold power over someone, we can pause and catch ourselves and love ourselves in that very moment and then choose a different way, a way toward equal relationship.

Equal relationship has to do with giving and receiving . . . the 'divine marriage' within and without, we might say, where there is a glimpse of the no-separation, the whole. Equal-minded relationship . . . where all possibilities exist and dance together without stepping on each other's toes. All possibilities. The Infinite. THE ALL.

Perhaps you might be curious to consider how much you try—consciously or unconsciously—to try to hold power over people, the earth, your own dreams and visions for life?

How much do you let other people hold power over you? The insistence of the yamas—even and especially of nonviolence, ahimsa—is that we are NOT to be doormats onto which one another can wipe our filth. Sure, yes, we are invited to be hospitable—to provide space for people to grow—and yet that doesn't mean we let people use us. We invite people and our very own self to awaken to the way the universe is—to the realization that we are ALL life, each one of us, and yet I alone am not the ALL of life.

A NEW WAY FORWARD

There is a deeper dream seeming to invite us to a new way . . . glimpses of that dream all the way back to Patanjali's time, Gautama's time, the writer of *The Bhagavad Gita*'s time. Maybe long, long before.

Might you give yourself permission to be present to your dreams and visions for life unfolding around you and from within you . . . without trying to control or even steer them?

Might you trust what Nature—THE ALL—might be offering you, to be 'equanimous,' to be even-keeled, to find the gift in every situation? To do something besides demand your cravings be yours, to do something besides demand your dislikes and hates be cast away?

Might you trust that the deeper pulse of life within you and within the whole earth is inviting you to know a life that is amazing? that _is_ bliss?

Might you give yourself permission to discover a new way forward in relationship, a co-stewarding of what is possible?

Ah, but what about those 'doormat' moments when they creep up . . . what to do when people try hold power over us? Equanimity—being even-keeled and non-reactive—doesn't mean we let ourselves be door-mats to oppressors or to friends who subtly try to hold power over us . . .

there must be another way, right? but what is it? how can we even conceive of it?

could there be a third way that doesn't involve running from our prob-lems, or the usual two ways...

lashing out in violent ways toward oppressors in word or deed or grimace...
letting oppressors have their ways with us without our doing anything to defend ourselves . . .

there must be another way, right?

ANOTHER WAY...AN INNER JOURNEY!

Here's a short story, a conversation that might happen within you, an invitation to exploring nonviolence, ahimsa . . . clever strategy for awak-ening people who hold power over us that we might all know our common humanity, our equality as equal beings in this One World, in THE ALL.

First, to prepare for the conversation, you might take a minute or two to list out some of the qualities in others that you cannot stand, qualities that really, really bother you . . .

it's okay . . . no one will judge you . . . so make your very honest list for yourself and discover what happens for you as you be with these qualities and this conversation, a conversation that's nearly as old as the hills through the wisdom of the world—or at least 2000 years old . . .

He asked me, "So, after having some time to think about it all, have you noticed any moments when you have said or done to someone else the very thing you hate in others . . . you know, something on your list?"

"Well, I have to admit there were a few moments where I caught myself doing that. But there are so many others where that didn't work, that mimesis theory that you were telling me about, that we become what we hate, that we react to what bothers us in others and then 'mime' or copy what bothers us because it's already within us, that we already are what we hate. I mean, I don't do **all** of those things on my list of qualities I can't stand in others!" He just smiles at you as you read through some of them. Compassion seemed to radiate from him, maybe a peace you wish you knew better, a peace you wish you could find within yourself more often.

Even so, you might find yourself getting defensive: "And besides, what about all those people who hold me down, who have bullied me some-how, who have exerted power over me? What about them? I mean, I can offer them love upon love upon love, but sometimes I just feel like a doormat, like my attempts at love for them do not change anything!"

"Ah, that's very good. How very good of you to bring that up. Well, it seems to me that there are some choices when people try to hold power over us . . . we could lash out at them in some way, physically or verbally or emotionally . . . but does that solve the situation? Nah, doesn't it usually seem to make things worse? And besides, doesn't that then mean that you are playing their game? That you are holding power over them, dominat-ing them in some way? What are some other responses, huh? We could run away from them, avoid them, try not to think about them, right? But does that really solve it? Maybe for the time being, but every time you see that person, don't your bristles stiffen and you find yourself on edge? And doesn't that anxiety then ripple over into your other relationships? Or even every time the person comes to mind, you feel the rage simmering within you? Fight or flight—those reactions don't seem to do it do they? Maybe there's another way, maybe other ways, to handle the situation, a third or fourth or fifth way, perhaps. Let's say that you got into a some kind of accident with someone and they feel you are at fault, negligent, and they said they were going to sue you for everything you've got, you know the standard American line. What could you do?"

"I don't know. I guess hire a big-time, expensive lawyer!"

"Sure. Maybe you'd do that anyway. But why does someone do that? Why does someone 'sue you for everything you've got'?"

"Well, they probably want all my money to soothe their pain. But I think there's more to it than that. It seems like they are trying to get even, maybe even get one over on you, control you somehow."

"Yes. Say you are in the courtroom and that person's lawyer has made their case and it's your side's turn to speak. And you stand up and place your wallet on the table in front of you, your car keys, everything of value you have on you. You take off your expensive clothes you wore for the court proceeding, your shirt, you slip off your shoes. You begin reaching for your belt before someone asks what in the world you are doing. And you say, 'He said he wants everything I have, so I'm giving it to him.' And he chimes in, 'I don't want those,' he points to what's on the table, what's left on you. 'But these are very nice pants, and these socks are worth a couple bucks. You can have them both. Clean pair of underwear too, pretty new,' you say as you slip off each item of clothing, each possession. And what do you imagine he says?

"'Stop! I don't want those—'"

"And you respond 'But you said you wanted everything. And here it is,' as you stand there completely naked in the courtroom. Sure, you're probably in contempt of court, but what have you exposed before the whole world?"

"Your naked self!"

"Yes, and what else besides this man's attempt to hold power over you. What's he going to see? Well, pretty quickly, he's going to see that you are a human being just like he is, you're made of the same stuff as him. And when we see that, how quickly we have the opportunity to realize that there is indeed no reason to hold power over anyone. We're all human, we're all made of the same stuff, we're all children of this same world. The sunlight and the rain fall on each one of us, whether we are good or bad in each other's eyes."

*Taken, with some expansions, from **A New Setting of Ignatius' Spiritual Exercises: Hearing, Seeing, Feeling, Old Stories in New Ways** by Brian J. Shircliff & the Companions of VITALITY Cincinnati (2015).*

There is a cleverness to nonviolence, not only a wriggling free of the chains of the oppressor but also an invitation to change the situation, to allow the situation to change the both of you. Nonviolence is an invitation for both parties—the 'oppressed' and the 'oppressor'—to be engaged by the wily, cleverness of nonviolence, of ahimsa.

How so? That the clever words or actions stop the moment in its tracks. That in that split-second there's a possibility for each party—the 'oppressed' and the 'oppressor'—to choose a new way of relating with one another. A new way not mediated by any particular morality, not directed by any particular law or doctrine. Nonviolence's cleverness is a new way towards relationship, the giving and receiving that is two parties, two people responding with one another, working it out together with an aim toward their equality, their equal status as human beings.

After all, relationship has to do with sharing power, a realization of the oneness of creation. THE ALL.

Nonviolence, one of the Patanjali's yamas, was used by Gandhi to welcome the freeing of his own Indian country-people of British rule. The nonviolence Gandhi practiced invited India and the British Empire to work out a new relationship with one another. And they did. And soon the British Empire left India!

Gandhi played with nonviolence through his satyagraha, his experiments with truth, which he based upon the nonviolent jujitsu Jesus invites in the Gospel of Matthew 5: 38-41 alluded to in that conversation above. Sadly, with rare exception, most biblical commentators through the past 20 centuries have missed the clever nature of Jesus' nonviolent philosophy and action. Some would say that the writer of the Gospel of Matthew who inherited these lines from another source might not have understood the clever wisdom himself!

As complicated of a person Gandhi was during his life—like all of us, gifts within himself we love and 'gifts' we wish we didn't have to deal with—Gandhi found it, Gandhi uncovered this nonviolence and found it useful in throwing off the chains of oppression and hierarchical-power . . . as did people like Leo Tolstoy and Francis & Clare of Assisi and perhaps a few others in the deeper past, people who have sensed the power of nonviolence in the breeze and brought it forward in new ways in their own present circumstances of being oppressed.

Like most Christians—even after all those Sunday sermons and even through his own seminary studies—Dr. Martin Luther King, Jr. did not discover Jesus' nonviolent approach in the Gospel of Matthew 5: 38-41 until he read Gandhi's writings! Gandhi lit a fire and a vision and a dream within MLK that gave a new birth to the Civil Rights Movement in the mid-twentieth century United States. Check out the roots of the renewed movement in Montgomery with the incredibly organized bus boycotts, the local and national soul-searching begun again by Rosa Parks' noncooperation. MLK tells the story so brilliantly in *Stride Toward Freedom: The Montgomery Story* (1958). It is a story of love.

This same nonviolent philosophy re-sparked by Gandhi and MLK began the Arab Spring a few years ago in toppling dictators and welcoming some change in the Mediterranean world, change that many hope will bear more equal-minded fruit some day.

May such clever nonviolence—such radical love that turns the power structure upside down, indeed flattens it!—may such clever nonviolence resound in every heart, in every relationship, in all 'corners' of the world and universe.

Nonviolence recognizes that there's wisdom in not going head-on into anything but finding instead a clever way around, with a 'goal' toward being with everyone and everything in a new way. THE ALL.

May we be so wise to explore and wonder about such a way as nonviolence and equal-minded relationship with all creatures, all desires, all life—a way that Patanjali notes is key to the ultimate experience of bliss!

What relationships we can have . . . when we tune into that deeper dream being born within you and me, within THE ALL!

The path to how we arrive is so strange.

The impressive Nganga Mfundishi Tolo-Naa came to town often in my early holistic development. I'm grateful.

One of the foremost martial artists in the country, if not the world, Tolo-Naa was a helpful and gentle uncle to me . . . though we were warned by his more experienced students, maybe jokingly, not to awaken him while he napped in the next room unless we wanted to experience great pain!

When he was sharing his insights into tai chi and qigong with us one night, he said something that affected me deeply, something that took me years to understand. "You know that you can use this tai chi and qigong for others, right? In helping them in their own healing. You know this, yes?"

Um, what?

I certainly got a helpful buzz in my own tai chi and qigong practice, later with bagua too. I had watched all kinds of my own illnesses and aches and pains disappear through my own personal practice. It was one reason I had kept coming back for years.

But harnessing that power for others?

Bullshit. That's what I initially thought about what he had said. That's what I thought about a lot of things he said.

And many of those things, those gems of wisdom Tolo-Naa offered I have since found to be true in my own experience, in my own way. Indeed, they are the foundations of all I continue to learn in Healing Touch and reiki and Feldenkrais Method® and The Bengston Energy Healing Method® and more.

Maybe you too? Maybe there's something here—some invitation or idea—you'd like to push away, something that offends you. Good. How good of you to notice how you feel, right?

And who knows what you'll discover as you listen to your own experience over the days and weeks and years. Who knows . . .

self-shaping niyamas

Some say that the most important asana is savasana, which often gets translated as corpse-shape (or, in my opinion, more problematic: corpse-pose) in the English-speaking world of yoga . . . but maybe a better understanding is complete-relaxation-yoga-shape, or let-it-all-go yoga-movement. After all, no yoga-shape is ever still, even complete rest.

Sure, the 'death' image can be quite helpful . . . the ever-present 'rising to new life' we find in just about every religious-imagination that gets picked up here too in savasana, in the corpse-shape . . . as long as you give yourself permission to feel into it, to let go of as much as you can in this shape as one would in death. The name of the game here, after all, is <u>letting</u>!

Do you give yourself permission to be lazy for awhile every day, to let your body find the earth, the ground, to let it unwind on its own? Or if the ground is not an easy option for you, maybe your bed.

Perhaps when we give ourselves such permission to be lazy (tamas = laziness, darkness), we then find our way and know exactly what is our work, what it is toward which we are invited to offer our time and energy (rajas = passionate inner-fire), to discover our way of proceeding that is uniquely ours (sattva = truth) through which everything seems to flow around and within us.

Giving ourselves time in the darkness—savasana or even sleep!—can help us to cultivate a deep reflection that is, perhaps, mysterious—where and when helpful ideas well up within oneself. The Inner Teacher speaks.

Patanjali clarifies that bliss cannot be ours for long unless we live a well-reflected, a well-chosen life through these five particular precepts:

• seeking authenticity inside and out—in whatever ways seem right for us, again different for each person—letting our inner truth shine (saucha)

• seeking and enjoying the calm and equanimity within us and having no desires for more (santosha)

• enjoying fiery inner cleansing a little at a time, in our own intelligent ways (tapas)

• enjoying self-study and self-observation (svadhyaya) a little every day, the playful reflection that can direct one's life in wise and authentic ways

• noticing the infinite in the finite, the divine in all creation, the ALL in everything you sense, everything you see and hear and touch and taste and smell, and responding accordingly, reverently, humbly, knowing you are and we all are swimming together in the infinite ALL (ishvarapranidhana).

Imagine what your life just might become! Imagine the life of our world if you—if all of us—have the courage to live such a life of gentle reflection!

May we be so bold!

Marion Woodman

joining Jung, from stage to stage
. . . the power of dream and story

She loved the clever energy of adolescents . . . their passion, their ability to so easily take on roles and then slough them off, their gift at times to have such inspiring and genuine compassion for people.

She recognized such gift in adolescence—to teach high school English and drama for 20+ years. A very long time!

I try to imagine Marion's reveries, her preparing for class or the upcoming play, her own staring into space at this season in her life. The characters and poetry that floated through her daydreams and nightdreams. The dialogue. The words. The sounds. The silences.

She was fond of Shakespeare, the one who gave us such a deep view into the complicated inner life of human beings. Shakespeare seemed to know it all within himself to be able to write with such clarity . . . all these feelings, the sensations involved with each one . . . greed and grief, love and lust, anger and awe, darkness and light.

What got into Marion that she would one day decide to go to India all by herself? To seek her soul, as she said.

She nearly died there.

What got into Marion that she would one day decide to resign from her much-loved teaching position and leave behind the students and colleagues who had so much love for her? To seek her soul, she said.

She left teaching high school to become a Jungian analyst.

She found a new life here for herself, discovered what she later termed her 'pregnant virgin' self.

Yes, you read that right.

What would make someone leave her life, her husband behind temporarily, to seek out year-upon-year of not-easy, introspective study as a student of Carl Gustav Jung, the 'father of modern psychology'?

It's the dream, of course. The dream.

The one that calls you, the one that is being dreamed through each one of us in our own wild ways.

Marion followed it. She looked deeply into the bizarre images, wondered about them. Even if they were erotic and crazy and violent and embarrassing.

She listened deeply to the tenor of her dreams—even if they seemed full of noise.

She allowed herself to feel whatever she felt in the dream and in her remembering each one of them.

METAPHOR...LIFE'S DANCE WITHIN

Such was the wise advice of Jung, even with all his own complications and contradictions. He knew something worth knowing, and Marion let him teach her, even after his death.

Marion knew that life is metaphor, that all of our authentic desires for life and all of our fleeting cravings and dislikes/hates have something to say to us.

Craving sugar . . . then where in your life are you craving sweetness?

Falling into gossip . . . what part of your story do you long to tell or to live yet?

Stuck on alcohol or drugs . . . then where in your life are you longing for new visions, new dreams?

Overworking yourself . . . then where in your life would you really like to work / play?

Hating someone or entirely annoyed by someone's actions . . . then what is within your own self that might be annoying you and taking you out of your equanimity? what needs love within you?

For Marion, addiction and stuckness and habit are invitations to awareness, invitations to notice some desire within us has entangled itself around maybe what it is we really want, the deeper pulses of our lives.

What many might not know is that Jung, Marion's imperfect grandfather-like-teacher, was an avid reader of the yoga texts, the classic texts on yoga.

Jung decided that people should not seek 'yoga'—that it would drive the seeker insane.

Perhaps like the old saying, often quoted in Zen circles: "Better not to begin. Once begun, best to finish."

And Marion did. She did begin. Through her daily practice of writing her dreams in a journal, of dawdling with them every day, quietly turning them over within the fresh soil of her own soul, her imagination. Through a life of listening to people talk about their dreams, their hopes for life. Through her vast writing and world-wide lecturing.

Do yourself a great favor and read her writing—*The Pregnant Virgin: A Process of Psychological Transformation* (1985) is a great place to start.

Or her book with Elinor Dickson, *Dancing in the Flames: The Dark Goddess in the Transformation of Consciousness* (1997).

Or Marion's personal journey through bone cancer toward health, *Bone: Dying into Life* (2000).

Marion died in 2018, many long, full years after her bone cancer experience.

Perhaps Marion and Jung are right—there is wisdom in listening deeply, drinking deeply at the well of our nightdreams, bringing them forward in our daydreams. Wondering about them, turning them over as we stare out a window or at a wall and sip some tea. For hours if you'd like.

To be curious about what stirs within us . . . without any need to do anything about it at first. To simply be curious.

Of course Patanjali would remind us that dreams are illusion. The not-real.

And of course everything is illusion when we forget that everything we experience is but a wrinkle in THE ALL, the vast ever-expanding REALITY that includes us all.

HAVE YOU MARRIED YOURSELF LATELY?

Jung called such a realization of THE ALL 'the divine marriage' . . . the realizing that the so-called splits or aspects of ourselves . . . 'masculine' (Sanskrit: pingala) and 'feminine' (Sanskrit: ida) are not separate at all, that they are always swimming together in THE ALL, that they depend upon one another for life, in the wholeness of life.

As we all in the 21st century world begin to wake up to the reality that the binary-game—masculine & feminine, darkness & light, bad & good—is no longer all that helpful or wise, I offer that THE ALL includes third and fourth and fifth + possibilities that are 'not masculine' and 'not feminine' but something else. . . a third-and-more way that indeed saves us all. It's the realization within oneself that life is far from binary, that life is not black and white, but indeed gray too and a million shades and colors in between these three.

This, of course, is what we are all waking up to in the 21st century—that gender, that not much of anything is binary. That it never has been. That we limit ourselves if we do go the binary route.

SHAPE-SHIFTING INTO LIFE, INTO 'THE ALL'...

The shamans of so many peoples today and in the deep past know this—the third-gender being the border-crosser, the one who can cross over the usual ways and meet us, take us through the veil to THE ALL, whether for a glimpse or a long-stay. The third-gender is the shape-shifter, the one who can know all possibilities. On this side of the dream, on any 'side' of it.

Marion must have enjoyed noticing her conception of the THE ALL expanding her whole life. Certainly, Shakespeare and teaching and poetry and drama were her initiators to the deeper pulse of life, to wanting to drink more deeply from the well-spring of what was being dreamed within herself. And then she knew she had to follow these dreams . . . not so much as an acting out of every image within every dream of hers . . . instead perhaps a growing confidence and trust in the queer ways of life, that THE ALL beckons even outside the social expectations that family and friends demand of us.

Marion knew the niyama of svadhyaya—she knew the importance of self-study. Little did she know, perhaps, that such honest and playful reflection is yoga, at least as far as Patanjali is concerned in his niyamas. Such is the movement from the budding of adolescence eventually giving way, with much self-study, toward becoming adult and then crone, the wise old hag, the genius who visits us with wisdom, within one's own very being in so many ways, sometimes within our own dreams. The best teacher is within one's own self, right? And surely we need friends to remind us of that, friends like Marion.

When we dream, we get an unusual window into THE ALL, the realization of infinite possibilities.

May we be bold and brave enough to 'stay with it, to be with it' as Marion invites so often in her writing, to wonder . . .

the ever-deepening mating-ness of life . . . the divine marriage within us . . . of all these energies . . . 'masculine' (pingala = sun) and 'feminine' (ida = moon) and 'something more' (perhaps the stars! these infinite third+ genders) all dancing within one another in the gigantic whole space that is you . . . THE ALL.

Such is the path toward wisdom, even if 'hatha' does not mean 'sun' and 'moon.' Perhaps we need to be nudged (hatha) to notice the sun and the moon and the vast horizon of sky with its limitless possibilities to experience the divine marriage, THE ALL, within one's own self, within the world.

So put on some tea, friends, feel it in a cup in your hands and stare out the window awhile . . . let the deeper dream be dreamed through you, in your daydreams, and your night...

shape making
asana

Patanjali was known as the snake-man . . . a shape-shifter. Perhaps that says something about his ability to contort his body in all kinds of slithering ways. Perhaps it had to do with his ability to take on with equanimity any idea or any challenge and 'go with it' or move with it.

And yet . . . while his sutras celebrate asana, there are no specific shapes recommended. There are certainly no pictures!

Perhaps this is the ancient wisdom of asana—that there are no prescribed shapes, no particular ways that you need move. Instead, it's a game of noticing oneself in a shape, of noticing your wanting or needing to move . . . all of it sensation-led.

As a matter of fact, the only prescription Patanjali offers about asana is to make it easy, to find the easier way, to do only what's easy.

This actually sounds quite a bit like Moshe Feldenkrais' advice in his Awareness Through Movement® classes!

Patanjali even adds an image to clarify . . . to move so easily as a snake slithers and moves so beautifully and gracefully through the water.

Perhaps all of the yoga-asana books and videos have become an incredible hindrance to what Patanjali was up to in his shape-shifting ways, his vision for asana and how asana is a way to experience THE ALL, the bliss of samadhi, the realization that there is no separation from THE ALL, the infinite nature that is LIFE.

And yet, perhaps we don't even need to shift shapes to know THE ALL . . .
.

ONE SHAPE!

If you only knew one shape—one particular 'asana' or shape in which your body likes to rest (on your back, on your front, on your side, in seated, in standing...on the floor, on a mat, on a bed, in a chair...in some way right for you)—and you used that shape every day as your practice, would it be possible to know 'yoga' . . . THE ALL?

Say you chose to be on your back, maybe with your knees gently bent with a bolster or a blanket rolled-up beneath your knees. Maybe you're comfortable without any props.

You could just as easily choose to be in a chair in some relaxed way.

Whatever shape you choose for yourself . . . maybe on your first day, you really focus your awareness on one leg.

It could be any one place within yourself. If you don't have a leg, start with a different place within yourself.

Wherever you've chosen within yourself, you can bring awareness to the place where you feel bones touching the ground and where you don't. Maybe see if you can sense the shape of that place—the joints, the layers of musculature, your skin.

Maybe you see if you can sense just how much that particular place moves as you breathe . . . maybe with your natural breath, maybe with a few more full breaths.

Take some time with this sensing yourself!

Perhaps discover at first if you can do this—if you can sense yourself, this starting place—without touching this place you're noticing, perhaps too without even looking at this place with your eyes opened.

You might find that such a knowing yourself changes as you invite yourself to be aware of yourself in such a knowing way.

Really having trouble? Maybe sit in some easy way and touch this place that you are inviting yourself to know. Lightly touch yourself as if smoothing out your clothes over this place that is you. Or gently rest your hand there. Can't easily reach this place? Then imagine your hand or the hand of someone you love is lightly touching this place, just enough that you can better sense yourself. Luxuriate in the sensation such gentle self-touch brings, real or imagined.

Do all of this without the need to try to change anything. Simply become aware, and watch how this awareness actually creates change.

See if you can let go of judging the touch in any way. No need to say, I like this! No need to say, it's not bad, but it could be better! Revel in such equanimity, such calmness, such evenness, such level-headedness.

Maybe as you let go of touching yourself gently, sense if this place feels differently than other places within yourself. Did something come alive within that place by directing your awareness there? Does some 'residue' of that touching still linger there—even long after your hands have left this place? What is that, do you think?

Such awareness is falling in love with you, with yourself. You yourself are a window into knowing the infinite, THE ALL.

AND THEN TOMORROW...

The next day, bring yourself into the same / similar shape and invite yourself to know a new place within yourself . . . say if you chose one particular place on your leg the previous day, this new day you choose your arm, some particular place on one arm. Or your head, or anywhere else within your body.

This is yoga, this kind of knowing . . . this, I guess, is what the ancient yogins knew . . . long before the asanas had names, long before the asanas had prescribed shapes with particular alignment cues and all those words and all the magazine articles, the pages upon pages and words upon words and photos upon photos of some prescribed shape, some asana.

Relish in what you know through sensation.

Relish in what the ancient, first-generation yogins knew there on the cusp of the Indus River, as they lazed their lives along. ('Yogin' is the all-gender version of 'yogi,' which is the Sanskrit masculine version.)

EARLIEST ASANA BEFORE ASANA WAS A 'THING'

Your body has a shape to it no matter what shape you put it in.

You are constantly making shapes. That's what Krishnamacharya's teacher essentially told him in his cave-training. That there were 8.4 million types of creatures on the planet, and if we notice that each one of these creatures is a little different, then imagine the nearly-infinite possibilities. More and more and more difference between each creature when we put a fine point on it—so to be precise, there are way more than 8.4 million asanas possible. If each creature is counted—there are nearly 8 billion humans on the planet, right? And each human can take on how many nearly-infinite shapes? We're all shape-shifting creatures—even and especially with every breath that alters your shape and mine with each inhale, each exhale.

We are so vastly different from one another—and you as a creature are so vastly different each second, each breath. You are different from second to second to second.

And yet, beautifully, we all exist in life, in THE ALL. In every shape we take.

ASANA & THE ALL

As you rest in some restful shape, some asana that feels right for you, discover what comes to you . . .

maybe your thoughts begin monkeying around with you—so be it AND BE WITH IT,

maybe bliss comes to you—so be it AND BE WITH IT,

maybe you find yourself bored—so be it AND BE WITH IT,

maybe some inkling of your deepest desires for life comes to you—so be it AND BE WITH IT.

And whoa—definitely no need for judgment here about any of this!

Give yourself some space to become aware, to notice, to be with yourself and whatever Arises. No need to try to rush and fix anything.

Can you love yourself in the light, in the goodness of who you are? You are light!

Can you love yourself in any brokenness you might encounter within yourself? Dare you love the tangled mess that is you?

Can you give yourself permission to notice that the dirt and crap in which you find yourself—now or in the past—is simply rich soil just waiting for you to sit here, to rest in asana, and root down and grow! grow! grow! . . . ?

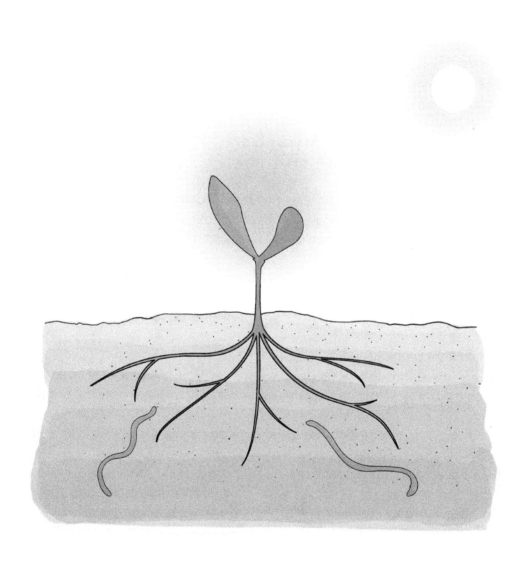

breath rhythming
pranayama

Find some easy seat for yourself.

Where do you first notice your breath in your body . . . without trying to change anything?

What do you smell or taste in your breath? What temperature? Does it change as you begin to notice?

Does your belly move when you breathe? your lower ribs? your upper ribs? your collar bones? do your eyes follow anywhere as you sense your breathing? even if your eyes are closed? what else?

Be here awhile, as long as you are interested in your breath.

What happens for you as you slow down and observe your breath like this?

As you move through your day, whenever you remember it, consider remembering and practicing this observation of your natural breath.

And at night, we'd all be wise to let it all go as we surrender to dreams.

There's plenty of writing out there about purposefully shaping your breath and doing all manner of things with your nostrils and belly and tongue and all that—and all of that might be helpful for some people. It was helpful for me at times too.

But the greatest power, perhaps, in pranayama, is not shaping your breath but realizing your breath is shaping you. In every way. That this 'breath' has a life of its own. That we are all swimming in this breath together. That we breathe the same air. That breath is life, a life-force all its own, prana, as we say in yoga.

Indeed, imagine the forces—the expansion and the drawing inward—that happen on our planet with all these creatures breathing. Perhaps it's as if we are all being 'breathed.'

Breath is powerful, as we well know. If your body doesn't breathe for you, you shrivel up and die. Fortunately, something very primal—a deep intelligence within you—reminds you when to breath.

When your life feels like it is spinning out of control, and your breath probably is too, consider simply coming back to your breath, coming home to your breath —

feel it, listen for it, some days depending on the weather or a steaming room, you can even see it, taste it, smell it . . .
so quickly such a remembering has a way of grounding us,
of slowing the spinning within and without,
of helping us remember we are alive in this moment,
and that is enough.

Pranayama practice—first noticing your breathing and how it changes, a noticing that nudges your breath in some way—is perhaps the most important practice of yoga.

A TOUCHING INVITATION

Today or another day, consider gently and lightly wrapping your fingers around different places of your body—as if gently, lightly holding yourself, letting your thumbs be with your other fingers—and breathe . . . what do you notice? stay in one place for awhile . . . stare out the window or close your eyes . . . breathe easily, naturally and feel . . . maybe every now and then breathe a bit more deeply, more fully . . . what do you sense? what do you feel?

The ancient yogins understood that the human body had these very subtle energy-streams (Sanskrit = nadis) rolling on through it—72,000 (or many more, depending on the yogic text) of these energy-streams, in fact. The ancient yogins taught that, when we breathe, we feed these energy-streams—that prana, life-force, flows through these streams and gives every body life in a very subtle way.

The medical / scientific world knows a lot about human beings and can dissect the heck out of every little 'part' and 'system' —

but they haven't yet figured out where this life comes from and goes to, how the 'whole' of you works, is alive, comes into being.

A lot of people get all worked up about energy—get worried that we are now in the land of woo-woo or whatever. I did too for a long time.

And yet it's so easy to feel sometimes too, right? Like when someone is very near you and you feel the heat of their body. Heat is energy, of course.

I've begun wondering if the subtle-energy of the ancient yogins and the subtle-energy that my tai chi teachers used to tell me about through acupuncture and acupressure and tuina and all those tai chi and qigong forms and all that —

what if this subtle-energy is actually the nervous system of the human body—indeed of any body? We know that it is electric current that flows through us, through what we call the nervous system, that something that flows over the liquidy synapses between neurons, the grand communicator of the human body, of any body.

What if these ancient yogins and ancient tai chi masters were onto what we simply call the nervous system? What if they were onto sensing so subtly the dance of electricity that takes place through us, between every neuron? What if they became so sensitive to themselves that they could feel the electrical impulses running through them and termed them meridians and nadis and chakras and subtle energetic body and all that?

Sometimes you do too, right, you feel it? Like when you get a bright idea and suddenly the 'light bulb goes on' within you, right? Neurons reached out for one another and electricity flowed over the new synapse between these neurons and—'oh wow'! You feel it!

If you're reading this while standing up under the tremendous force of gravity (have you even noticed it?), we often say in Feldenkrais Method® that 80 - 90% of your nervous system is on high alert sending electrical impulses through the ever-complex musculature—the flexors and extensors, to put muscles in two special movement categories—to keep you upright under the tremendous force of gravity. And the remaining 10 - 20% of your nervous system is keeping your heart beating, your breath flowing, and all the amazing things that happen within you under the radar of your usual awareness.

Maybe that's why we get such a buzz from movement, whether in standing or sitting or whatever that involves moving through gravity! Maybe it's the movement of electricity through you! Maybe that's what the ancient yogins and tai chi masters surmised.

A-HA! WHAT IS THAT?

Of course, we'll never know. We'll never know what the ancient yogins experienced exactly, we'll never know what the famous tai chi masters experienced, we'll never know if what they all experienced—even if they were the same thing!—was really the electrical impulse of the nervous system, of the very life-force flowing over the liquid-gap between neurons and the 'a-ha!' we feel when we get an idea and the light bulb pops on within us because neurons have found a new way to reach out to one another.

Professor of Physiological Science at the University of California, Los Angeles (UCLA) Valerie Hunt thought the human energy field and chakras and meridians was a bunch of hogwash until the scientific instrumentation in her research labs began picking up weird things (light frequencies) just beyond people's bodies—and it seemed to have something to do with what emotions they were feeling. She called in famous healer Rosalyn Bruyere to test her and what she saw around people to see if the color Rosalyn was seeing matched the color-frequency of her scientific instruments. And—a-ha!—sure enough it did. Valerie Hunt's book *Infinite Mind: Science of the Human Vibrations of Consciousness* (1989) is fascinating.

With all we know scientifically at this point in the 21st century, maybe there indeed is more, more, more that we don't yet know, yes?

And how incredible that the ancient yogins of the Indus River Valley 3000 - 5000 years ago had an inkling about something they were sensing, something that they were feeling through observing their own experiences with moving and breathing and resting!

And maybe the game is not so much to <u>believe</u> them as it is to have our own experiences and test things out.

As Moshe Feldenkrais discovered, what the medical and scientific world knew about the nervous system in his day in the 1940s and 1950s was very, very little. He was sometimes boo-ed off the stage when he spoke about the human and animal ability to grow through movement, that the human brain could be changed quickly by movement if the movement was slow and gentle as it is so often for a baby and the baby's development, that this movement was 'learning'—and that such learning never needed to stop at any age. Moshe Feldenkrais even surmised that human beings don't have to lose neurons as they age—as medicine and science in the 1940s and 1950s were SURE that humans lose neurons as they age. And all of Feldenkrais' guesses, all of those hypotheses that Feldenkrais had in the 1940s and 1950s that seemed so far-fetched to medical and scientific researchers then are being proven correct in the 21st century through scientific research.

Move and breathe and rest and grow your neurons—especially if you sense yourself in as many moments as you can!

Medical doctor and researcher Norman Doidge's groundbreaking work on what doctors throughout North America are doing with their patients through movement and through a whole host of interesting strategies is fascinating—an easy way for medical-types and people like you and me to discover the power of neuroplasticity, that the human person can be changed quickly. Doidge's book is *The Brain's Way of Healing: Remarkable Discoveries and Recoveries from the Frontiers of Neuroplasticity*. Published by Viking Press in 2015 by a *New York Times* bestselling author, it's far from woo-woo or anything of that sort.

BREATH...AND THE A-HA!

Discover for yourself, what you can sense for yourself. When you simply notice your breath a few minutes, when you find rest with your breath even for a short while, you might begin to notice that you feel refreshed, as if something found some balance within you. True too by getting up and moving, even for a moment!

Rest has a way of doing that! Moving slowly and playfully—as we are invited with asana, even just by breathing—does too! Observing your breath—pranayama—can have the same effect.

The ancient yogins knew that moving and resting and breathing effected something very subtly within humans—their own feeling was that moving and resting and breathing had a way of balancing the flow of all of these 72,000 energy-streams and especially the main channel—the shushumna nadi, the column of light around which your spine is said to form in the yogic imagination.

When we move and breathe and rest, when we take care of ourselves and are gentle with ourselves, we are kinder, yes? We are more authentic, ready to respond to every situation, yes? The moral-invitation and self-care of the yamas and niyamas seem much more possible, yes?

Welcome a new world! Give yourself time to breathe and move and rest in ways that feel right for you and you renew yourself and the world and know more deeply THE ALL!

sensation appreciation pratyhara

Of course, what you take within yourself becomes you.

Imagine it.

What you eat eventually gets rolled over and crushed within you in this amazing way without you even aware of it happening and transformed into energy that feeds your cells and even becomes your cells. Super tiny bite-sized 'units' of energy.

Incredible.

What is it that is said? That after just a few years, a human being has a very new body? That many of the cells that are 'you' get replaced in some rather remarkable way that is life.

What you listen to and feel and see and touch and sense (or don't sense) creates you too, right? What you take in shapes all of you, your responses to life, your way of moving and breathing and resting in the world.

Imagine it.

Sometimes quieting one way of sensing the world awakens other ways of sensing.

Perhaps today, consider taking a break from something for a few hours. Maybe a morning or an afternoon. Just a short time.

It's of course up to you whatever this 'break-from' might be.

It could be food, a favorite drink.
Music.
Your phone.

Being inside.
Being outside.
Talking.
The news.

It could even be taking a break from your usual yoga-practice to opt for something else.

See what happens for you. It's not like this needs to be a permanent practice, that the way you choose to spend these few hours needs to become what you do with the rest of your life.

Discover what happens for you when you give yourself a different experience, even for a short time.

Just how much might you appreciate your senses when you fast for awhile from them, from their usual ways of sensing?

And what comes alive within you as a response?

Ruthy Alon

speak the language of the organism
with Movement Intelligence®

I'm always amazed that very often in history—at least with the fields in which I'm interested and curious—that a man begins the work and a woman carries it forward in new and often richer ways, and often in ways that make more sense to beginners like me.

Hear me out . . . that's not to say that women and non-binaries can't invent anything great without a man beginning it! For sure! After all, Sweet Lady J and her wildly clever campfire stories gave birth to the modern world . . . Judaism, Christianity, Islam, neuroplasticity, and non-violence! If we'd all today be as wise and clever and playful as Sweet Lady J was 3000 years ago—much wiser than the men who crafted religious traditions from her playful imagination!

Regarding this phenomenon of 'man beginning, woman generously improving' I have noticed something interesting . . . Marion Woodman certainly carried forward in abundant, new, and more accessible ways Carl Jung's work with dreams and story as rich avenues to improve human life, to get to the roots of who we are so that we all might live. In Jungian circles in which I sometimes participate, Aniela Jaffé and Carl's wife Emma Jung are sometimes said to have understood Carl Jung's ideas better than he did!

Some would say—myself included—that Bonnie Bainbridge Cohen has done a great service to yoga and martial arts and the whole developing field of somatics through her playful, experiential Body-Mind Centering®. She saw how complex are the things of yoga and martial arts and my own beloved tai chi and wanted to create a more accessible gateway to experiencing these things for beginners and long-time practitioners alike, by first experiencing one's own amazing human body, to rest in—say, your thyroid gland—for the rest of the afternoon through slow and gentle moving and breathing and resting that might look nothing like the yoga-asana or tai chi or qigong forms that we are used to. With such unusual experiences that Bonnie invites, imagine re-engaging your 'traditional' asana practice or your tai chi or qigong forms—they would certainly feel differently as you come to know more of yourself in these rich ways Bonnie offers. I'm grateful to Becky Morrissey for keeping Bonnie's work alive in Cincinnati.

RUTHY'S GENIUS

Ruthy Alon has found a way to bring forward Moshe Feldenkrais' ideas in rich new ways as well.

Perhaps my own story is helpful here.

My mom was taking Movement Intelligence® / Bones for Life® classes with Cynthia Allen (Future Life Now) about fifteen years ago. She wanted to explore if this gentle movement might help her with preventing or at least slowing our family's hereditary osteoporosis.

My mom enjoyed the classes and said she felt better, though Cynthia was clear that the research was still being done as to whether or not Bones for Life® could indeed improve bone density on its own.

So at the dinner table my mom proudly told us about the classes and what they did. I nearly choked I thought it was all so stupid. I remember my dad having to tell me to be more respectful of my mom and her forms of exercise. At that time, I was in my 'handstands-will-save-the-world' phase.

Fast-forward about ten years and we had VITALITY up and running and our dear friend Penny Costilla who shares journaling with us every month passed along a postcard advertising an upcoming 'Tea & Learn about Bones for Life with Cynthia Allen.'

"If you're going to be so into movement and stuff, you might want to explore what else is out there with Movement Intelligence and Feldenkrais Method," Penny told me.

God, not that weird stuff, I told myself.

I went to the event just to be polite. And I went with some painful joints I had been trying to work with for years through yoga and tai chi and massage and chiropractic and acupuncture and Healing Touch and a whole host of things.

In five minutes of whatever it was Cynthia led us through—these weird, gentle movements that seemed to have little to do with those painful joints—I was pain-free. Amazing! How could this be, I wondered.

So I signed up for the Movement Intelligence® training and became a Bones for Life® teacher, and that led me to the bigger umbrella of somatic work from which Movement Intelligence® emerged: Feldenkrais Method®.

Whenever I return to the asanas of a yoga class, something in me seems more informed about my body and the ways I can move with ease and ways that seemed to cause the pain through what we have called 'traditional yoga-asana' and 'vinyasa-yoga'. . . which, I noted through Krishnamacharya's life story earlier, might not be all that traditional at all. At least if a tradition is to exist more than a few generations.

Sanskrit scholar and yoga practitioner N.E. Sjoman has a wonderful book about Krishnamacharya and his combining the yoga-asana that he had learned in his life with British gymnastics and perhaps other things to create 'modern yoga' . . . the ashtanga-vinyasa style and sequence so many of us across the world have found endearing. Check out Sjoman's fun little book: *The Yoga Tradition of the Mysore Palace* (1999).

Might we yoga teachers be so creative and clever and open-minded as Krishnamacharya, 'the father of modern yoga'?

Might we yoga teachers and practitioners find 'yoga' in any activity that marries sensation and mindful awareness in moving and breathing and resting—

even if the shape is not a 'traditional' asana?

Krishnamacharya didn't use traditional asanas all the time either!

SOMETIMES WE MUST STEP OUTSIDE A FIELD TO KNOW A FIELD, TO GLIMPSE 'THE ALL' THAT'S THERE

Ruthy Alon's work—Movement Intelligence®—has been quite helpful in my journey as a yoga-practitioner . . . as a mover and breather and rester.

Perhaps we might find 'yoga'—THE ALL—anywhere, yes?

With her playful movements and style and ways of inviting oneself to listen to oneself, Ruthy invited me to think of myself as a creature . . . as an organism that learns—'consciously' or not.

Through her work, I was able to begin wondering about yoga-asana in whole new ways.

Check out her work online—there are many free videos available to pique your interest to want to find a class or a training near you. Ruthy is quite generous about sharing her work to invite people into the greatest secret hidden in plain sight: that we are creatures who can learn and grow and change—and fast!

OBSERVE CREATURES—EVEN HUMAN ONES!

When I watch my little nephew move, I see his creatureliness quite clearly. And perhaps my own too. And the dog or cat who happily crosses my path, same thing.

Creatures play. They move in ways that feel good, that are interesting to them. If they find something that doesn't feel or taste good, they howl, they move away from it. And they are smart in that way. And they learn through this play, this seeking out what it is they want to do. And they do it without thinking much about it . . . at least until societal-forces (parents! teachers!) start clamping down and trying to restrict behavior—all the behaviors that little kids have the luxury of enjoying . . . screaming with joy, barking, touching themselves or others in ways or at times that seem socially awkward but are just playful curiosity, etc.

While we have many things to teach children and we have many ways of avoiding danger to teach children, the things we adults sometimes do to 'civilize' children often can be so harmful! We adults might be discovering that we are paying a price for it, unless we recapture the wise-play of children in our own adult lives.

Perhaps we'd be wiser to invite experiences for children—and adults!—to learn on their own, in their own wise ways.

Ruthy Alon and others have taken this understanding of creaturely movement into some amazing places and ways of being. Ruthy created Movement Intelligence®—Bones for Life®—to work with her own issues, her own osteopenia and rounded upper back at age 65. She knew through her studies with Moshe Feldenkrais that the human brain was easily changed through moving with awareness . . . and she wanted to study how she could possibly change her bones, invite them to find strength again as she aged. All the studies on osteopenia—on the slow loss of bone density—pointed to walking as the best remedy. Sure, genetics and nutrition and supplements and a host of other things might help—though the studies of her day pointed to walking as the best medicine for improving bone health, without negative side-effects. So Ruthy became curious . . . who might know something about walking that she could study and learn?

Ruthy became fascinated by the women of Africa (and throughout the world) who carry water and all kinds of pretty heavy material on their heads with such grace and ease—and often without a lot of muscular effort. Ruthy—like all of us, I imagine—hope that there might be a day when people don't have to walk long distances to get fresh water . . . though Ruthy was fascinated by these women's tall moving with ease with a jug on their head and sometimes a baby (or two!) strapped to their backs, often on uneven pavement, sometimes even in bare feet. What was it these women knew in their bodies that allowed such graceful movement?

Ruthy knew that simply putting a lot of weight on her head and walking around wasn't the trick—that such a thing would be harmful to her and nearly all of her students and our necks and our whole selves. Most of us didn't grow up doing this! So Ruthy created some gentle processes that invite us to have a small taste of what these water carrier's know about tall, elegant walking without adding unnecessary muscular effort. Each Movement Intelligence® process informs something in human walking that could be helpful for walking well and more efficiently under the greatest force of our lives—gravity. After all, it's walking efficiently in relationship with gravity that increases bone health. Much like Moshe Feldenkrais' great work, Ruthy's processes create subtle and yet substantial changes in one's body. Two of my teachers—Cynthia Allen and Carol Montgomery—have published a study about this in *Journal of Functional Neurology, Rehabilitation, and Ergonomics* (Summer 2017).

Bones for Life® is what brought me to this first understanding of neuroplasticity, that our brains—our whole selves!—can change in a split second with some helpful and easy stimulus. And, as I write this in 2019, now Ruthy is 89 years young and strong-as-bone (as her ancient Hebrew-speaking relatives would say), has the most elegant upper back and movement, continues to travel the world to teach, and is as sharp as ever! So many of us have found freedom with her work, with Movement Intelligence®.

SO WHAT'S THE WALK-IMPROVING DEAL WITH RUTHY?

With Ruthy's playful processes, we are invited to move a little bit slowly, on the ground or from a chair or in standing. As we do in Feldenkrais Method®, we move slowly and only do what is easy. We're invited to tune into a very small, specific range of movement . . . to notice the way your foot moves, your shoulder moves . . . each place within yourself so dependent on the other. Indeed, no one place can move without the whole moving. Incredible, really.

There are interesting—and quite surprising—sequences to Movement Intelligence®.

Want to improve the way your right shoulder moves or feels? In Ruthy's Movement Intelligence® we might take your shoulder gently out of play and instead invite everything around your right shoulder to move. And being the intelligent creature that I am and that you are—any creature who breathes and moves—some deep, primal intelligence within us human beings learns something. Ah, maybe my right shoulder doesn't have to work as hard when at some deep level it realizes that it has the support of the rest of my body.

This of course could be true of every joint in my body and yours. This is the taproot of neuroplasticity that Ruthy's teacher, Moshe Feldenkrais, figured out.

Lifelong habits can even change, when we pay attention and when we are given new possibilities from which to choose, from which one's brain can choose.

I am always amazed by Ruthy's playful—and highly effective—creativity!

Indeed, when we look at Feldenkrais Method® & Movement Intelligence®, we find the wily, nonviolent playful imagination that can be found in Sweet Lady J's imagination, the deepest and often forgotten foundations of the biblical imagination from which practical nonviolence (ahimsa) springs.

One of my Feldenkrais teachers very intelligently noted that Ruthy Alon is the quintessential role-model of which Moshe Feldenkrais had hoped. Feldenkrais' greatest wish was that he would be people's last teacher— for what he was most interested in was people learning how to learn again and then teaching themselves whatever it was they wanted to learn in their own intelligent, personal way. Moshe told Ruthy and his first students that he had hoped that people would learn from their own playful-curiosity and 'write with their own handwriting'—and not try to copy his handwriting.

Some 'traditional' Feldenkrais people get all wrankled with Ruthy's teaching—that it's not Feldenkrais' teaching. And of course it is not. Though with both of these wise and playful teachers, the proof is in the pudding, in the flexible and strong goodness I feel within myself when I play with both of their ideas. Many people indeed say this!

It was a great gift for me to study with Ruthy for about five days in person a few years back. I walked into the workshop in New York City all twisted and turned from a late plane ride, the subway, a mile walk with luggage. After just the first 15 minutes of the workshop, my body felt so good.

Ruthy is so quick to be able to find helpful change and ease for each person—even after only watching you walk for like five seconds! That's how sharp her perception is—the greatest gift of her 'toolkit' from which she can pull out a move or create one on the spot to stimulate the 'organism' that is the human person to learn something—within their own moving-with-awareness—and grow.

We human beings are incredibly powerful creatures—when we continue to allow ourselves to be surprised through growth.

A NEW WAY FORWARD...A GURU-LESS AGE

In some ways, Ruthy and Moshe and Marion and Krishnamacharya are the wiser ones who follow no 'gurus' . . . these four people—human ones—who have transcended the old need within humanity to give power away to some authority, to instead trust the authority within one's own self.

Sure, these four wise ones might have a great deal to teach us, as they all had teachers too. These four wise ones have gifts that are incredible, and like the rest of us they have gaps in their own learning that we as their students might wish they'd learn more quickly! Welcome to human beings we love and who love us! We are all tangled, beautiful messes!

Having studied these four people quite a bit myself and read a great deal and pondered and used their ideas, I can say for sure my life is richer. I have had more glimpses of THE ALL—and more often, more sustained.

And most importantly, they have helped me to know THE ALL in my own bones, in my own breath, in every cell within me and 'beyond' me.

THE WISDOM OF ASYMMETRY

Ruthy is fond of telling a story about her early studies with Moshe Feldenkrais in her twenties. She happened to be that week in terrible pain—I think it was in her back or hip. All of her colleagues kept trying to help her by making the painful area more symmetrical to the non-painful side.

She said she only felt worse!

When she was resting on the ground trying to figure it out, she decided to take one of Feldenkrais' concepts into play, to go with the pattern that her body was presenting. If one leg wanted to move or rest this way, then let it. If the other leg wanted to move or rest in an entirely different way from the other leg, then let it. As a matter of fact, she even exaggerated in a very small way these differences.

Immediately, she was pain-free!

Trying to make yourself conform in some symmetrical way only makes you worse, yes? Maybe we'd be wise like Ruthy to appreciate the asymmetry within ourselves, to be curious and nonjudgemental about it. Maybe even to love it.

It's asymmetry that allows you to walk, to move, to take the first step. And her body of work—Movement Intelligence®—invites a more harmonious asymmetry within every organism, through learning, through playful curiosity.

And when I consider this, the realization that I am an asymmetrical creature, the root meaning of the Sanskrit word 'hatha' has a whole new meaning for me . . . to nudge, to have an effect upon, to strike . . . in a sense, to take me just ever-so-slightly off balance so that something within me—my whole self!—responds in kind, all of me cascades toward a new way forward, and all with gentle ease.

Perhaps the greatest change for us might be in letting go of our need for symmetry and better appreciating the asymmetry—even barely-noticeably deepening the asymmetry as Ruthy did.

Such an appreciation of asymmetry might create the hatha that I've been inviting through this book . . . the small, gentle change that we need to awaken ever more deeply to THE ALL.

*Small portions of this taken, with significant expansions, from **Sweet Lady J: Mother, Muse & Root of Nearly Everything... The 3000-year-old Campfire Stories of Biblical Genesis Giving Birth to Judaism, Christianity, Islam, Nonviolence & Neuroplasticity**, translations & invitations by Brian J. Shircliff (2017).*

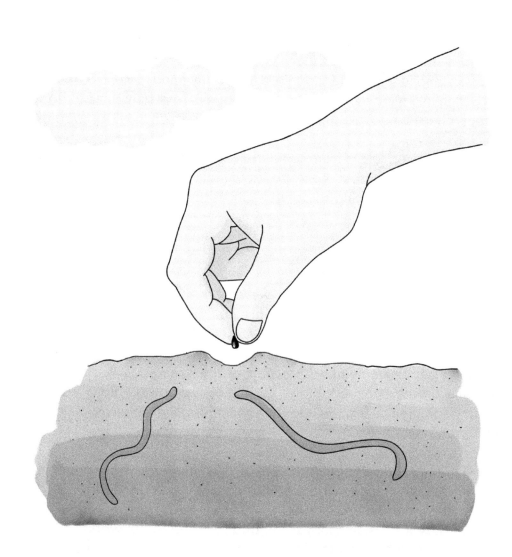

being with
dharana

When I left teaching religion at a Catholic high school to practice yoga &
meditation more deeply and teach yoga full-time with VITALITY, I received
many puzzled looks. Some suggested I'd lost my mind; others that the devil
had gotten into me because the devil, of course, had something to do with
yoga. (Where do people get these ideas about which they are so sure??)

I actually received letters from some friends who were gravely concerned
about the state of my soul, because, from their perspective, the very idea
of meditation has nothing to do with Christianity. (Or Judaism or Islam,
for that matter.)

Incredible, yes?

I very much wondered how they were with themselves in the quieter
moments. What was it they really feared in meditation? Could they ever
'be with' themselves?

How little people remember the roots of their religious traditions, and
how little do they notice that the very thing that all religious traditions
have in common is indeed meditation—though it goes by a 'million'
different names in each tradition!

Sure, it might be wise to be careful about assuming that what one person
experiences is similar to what another person experiences, from person
to person or tradition to tradition. We indeed have different bodies,
different nervous systems that sense and respond to the world, different
upbringings that have shaped how we sense and what we must assume
and how we respond, often in very different ways.

To my myopic Christian friends who worried about the state of my soul
because I was meditating or participating in yoga . . .

+ What did they think Jesus was doing in the desert for 'forty days and forty nights,' ancient-speak for 'a very long time'?

+ What did they think biblical Samuel was up to on the hillside with all the misfits of society, all of them naked and high on the breeze, up on The Heights, in the land of the honeycombs?

+ Naked?! In the Bible?! High on the breeze?! Look carefully and nearly all the important experiences of the Bible indeed happen in nakedness, when someone chooses to be naked. The very heart of the prophetic tradition involves nakedness . . . a blood-thirsty and jealous King Saul chases his harp-boy David on The Heights where Samuel and the misfits hang out. When David and then King Saul get there, they fall into the trance with all the prophets gathered there with Samuel. David and then Saul take off their clothes like all the others and fall on the ground and are in that ecstatic-healing-vision—that's what 'prophet' actually means in Biblical Hebrew—and all that jealousy and rage disappear in the once-raging King Saul!

+ What about all those prophets that came after Samuel—including the shepherd and tree-pruner biblical Amos (his part-time jobs that in the ancient world would be of the lowest classes, perhaps like garbage-sorters today)—who stared into space and heard the new rap, the new lyric-poem, that might free us all? Or even the upper-class power-brokers of the ancient world, priests like Isaiah or Jeremiah, to whom a small space of quiet in the midst of daily, city life brought on such visions and such raps? Or even the surprising ones like what we have called 'Second-Isaiah' (the composer of the raps in Isaiah 40 - 55 of the Bible), most definitely a woman's voice?

+ What do you think John the Baptizer was up to in nearly drowning people in the river? Think that big first breath as he drew them up from that drowning ritual was important? And they were naked too, right?

+ And what about the gospel that Jesus shares—"YOU are the light of the world, the spice of life, the best stuff of life!"—which is so radically different and at odds with the so-called 'gospel' shared about him, about a seemingly innocent man who was state-executed and dead on some tree limbs that were deader than he was and that God raised this man back up to life in all its fullness?

During college, when scripture professor Art Dewey was inviting me more deeply into Jesus' sayings and parables and sparking me to wonder about this ancient man's experience, maybe even those strange possibilities that might have happened in Jesus' being drawn to the solitude of the desert, I started wondering on my own what was the allure to a story about this bloody guy on the dead tree. The bulk of Jesus' life and teaching are so at odds with the domination-system that executed him—let alone the theology we've used to try to dress up and make sense of the execution.

Why such violent blood-fondness in the Christianity of my youth, of my upbringing? Why had I for years been so fascinated by the bloody story of Jesus' death, the bloody artwork and hard-to-avoid dead man on a dead tree that is so often the centerpiece of Christian churches, maybe even the bloody-nature of my own life—even at the same time not giving much of a care for all those who were in line for execution in my own state for crimes they did or did not do, just as Jesus, this ancient man was so accused and executed?

What was it?

Eventually, I had to say to myself . . . 'Maybe you see yourself up there on that dead tree, hanging by the thread of your life. Somebody's sick sacrifice. A victim. Powerless. Just like that Jesus was. Well, it doesn't have to be that way, friend,'—I said to myself—'get yourself down from that tree. You are the light! You are the light! You are the center of the universe—THE ALL. And that's what the dead guy on the tree—that's what Jesus told you, told all of us, before he was executed. You are the light of the world! And the reason people killed him was because there weren't enough people around who were on that wise wavelength to agree with him about each one of us being the light of the world. But now there are—so join the bigger family waking up more and more each day!'

My life changed a great deal when I saw the fuller scope of this Jesus and his whole story and his whole philosophy of life through his clever sayings and hilarious parables—yeah, you read that right—and let go of clutching so tightly and surely the last few days of his story about blood and death and unjust execution and all that.

Sure, it's important to know this part of this man's story. But it alone is not THE ALL of him or of his life.

So what of ALL this . . . what might I say to my myopic friends worried about the state of my meditating soul, if sitting there on a hillside or in the desert or even in the midst of daily city life, all of these biblical men and women ecstatic-visionary-healers ('prophets') who ushered in the very foundations of what today we call Judaism or Christianity or Islam, were they all wrong? Was Jesus wrong to say that "<u>YOU</u> are the light of the world!" . . . a realization just about anyone who meditates from any 'tradition' comes to quickly? Were these biblical greats' souls at risk of this very dangerous 'being-with' that is meditation, call it by whatever name suits your fancy . . . prayer . . . resting in God . . . contemplation . . . intimacy with God as Christian mystics like my own birth-saint Teresa of Avila lean into?

To anyone who still worries about meditation being wrong, please sit with all that awhile.

SO . . . WHAT IS THIS 'BEING-WITH'?

Patanjali might say that this dharana limb, this step into 'yoga,' involves a LOT more concentrated effort than I'm inviting here or elsewhere.

But I think such concentration only produces more tension within oneself. And causes more trouble.

At least at first.

Of all the modalities I've tried and with which I've played and been certified, the only one that TRIES to change things is yoga.

In fact, the gentle-human who revealed the inadequacies of yoga—Gautama—his enlightenment didn't come about until he stopped trying to change himself and accepted himself as he was. <u>Always as he was</u>. Kind of like Jesus was said to do with all the people around him—even those who accused him of crimes and executed him. In the stories that we have, he seemed to accept it all, even the injustice of it. And he offered love.

There are many stories about Gautama offering such love—even to accusers!

For both of them—Jesus and Gautama—the 'game' of life is simply to be with whatever comes up within oneself or to be with whomever crosses your path or shows up at your dinner-table. And not to try to change them—be with them!

Imagine it . . . what would it do in your life if you stopped trying to change everything—yourself, everyone else, the world—and simply stayed with it, were with it. Would love be possible? Even with all your flaws? Even with everyone else's flaws?

Would such a love as this nurture growth? Who knows, right? Much like good soil and water and sunlight nurtures a seed, coaxes it to open and root down and grow up . . .

to accept things as they are . . . and let Nature take over . . .

that's a much different kind of concentration, a much different kind of action.

Maybe yoga doesn't even have to be this way of trying to change things. Maybe the gentler nudge of observation and acceptance is all that is needed.

DHARANA = CONCENTRATION? EH?

It very well could be that we do not translate Patanjali's ideas all that well from Sanskrit to English. I intend to learn Sanskrit myself to find out!

The more I try to concentrate, the less concentrated I am. The more I let my attention, all of my senses take in the ALL around me and within me, patiently, quietly, curiously, the more concentrated my attention becomes and suddenly—'oh wow'!

Perhaps the real invitation here is to 'be-with' something . . .

maybe you do listen to your breath,
to the wind coming into your body and leaving it . . .

maybe you feel the breeze on your skin,
how it comes and goes,

maybe you rest on a seat or on your back or front or side
and sense how everything within you settles
as the minutes unfold—how it keeps happening! —
as you unfold and unfurl,
no matter how wild your thoughts at first get,

maybe you 'be-with' a lover, a beloved,
and quietly hold that beautiful human
and quietly sense one another
a sensing that might begin love-making
or be its beautiful result,

maybe you hold a cup of tea and sit in your favorite chair,
stare out the window for awhile . . .

Some might say that they 'are-with' something like their music-with-buds-in or their work or their reading or whatever . . . and yes, for sure, there is a beauty with that. We might be wise to 'be-with' whatever it is we are doing in the present moment. And perhaps that's what is invited for those of us who are not monks who have lives and people to whom we are responsible in the world.

But I think 'dharana' is an invitation to **receiving** . . . with welcoming something arriving, from where we do not completely know, at a pace and in a time that we cannot predict, with our buds out . . . a welcoming something that cannot be controlled . . . a something that just arrives, a something that we allow, that we welcome within.

IT IS INDEED IN THE WIND

Something like the wind. For all the biblical greats, the wind is the true initiator into life, into THE ALL.

The wind is the true initiator for all of us. At that first breath outside the womb.

Try as you might to run from the wind, you can't. The wind cannot be controlled. Lock yourself in a house, and even then it will find you. In its own time. It will seep into cracks and crevices, under doors. It will seep into you and keep you alive, without you even knowing its wild and clever work.

Can't feel it, this wind? Then you can hear it. You can even watch it move the leaves or the fibers of the draft-dodger you bought to keep it out.

Such is the wind. Such is Yahweh. Such is THE ALL.

Check out the Hebrew roots of the word the ancients used to name THE ALL—Yahweh—and you'll know something of the ancients' wily ways . . . of what Sweet Lady J was up to. And the writer of Samuel too.

Say Yahweh out loud.

Even sounds like the breeze, like someone breathing, ya?

UNJUST JAILING LEADS TO WISDOM

One of my meditative teachers through history—Pedro Arrupe—called what arrived to him 'the guest of my soul.' Arrupe was a Catholic Jesuit priest from the Basque region of Spain who steeped himself in Japanese and Zen culture to better know the people he was invited to serve, before and during and after the atomic bombs were dropped on Japan at the end of World War 2.

He came to that insight—'the guest of my soul'—as he was in prison, thought to be a spy when he was a missionary in Japan, not long before those atomic bombs were dropped on his city.

As he tells the story, he was cared for in such beautiful ways by what arrived to him there in prison. In the quiet. Even in the noise.

Equanimity can show up when we 'are-with' ourselves. Arrupe even came to love his jailers, talked with them in friendship when they delivered his food. They even came to him with questions, with their problems. And Arrupe listened to each one of them, offered advice for them to 'be-with' in new ways in their own lives. This is what happens when we allow 'the guest of my soul' even a small entrance within oneself. Such a gentle 'guest' invited Arrupe to one day play table-tennis with his once-jailers after the war. Such a gentle 'guest' invited him to love his oppressors as friends.

And I think that's just it. Isn't it?

Can you welcome it, this 'guest'?—by whatever name you choose to call it. THE ALL.

Can you offer this gentle 'guest' hospitality within you?

Perhaps the question of 'dharana' is
what draws your attention?
what life draws your attention?
can you be with it, allow yourself to be with it?
and then wait for the buzz of life . . .
the deep hum that is the earth
in the earth, your own heart
and all life on and in it . . .

deepening rest
dhyana

I once watched my mom holding my little nephew and suddenly knew something of the meditative life that I had not know before.

My nephew had been his wild and inquisitive little five-month-old self that morning. Beautiful.

My sister and my brother-in-law were in the other room getting ready for the day.

So giving them a little break, my parents and I all took turns being with the little one, sometimes entertaining him, sometimes letting him entertain himself. He was always entertaining us.

My mom was holding him and walking around our place and showing him artwork and pictures on the wall. He loves that. And then all of a sudden, this little bundle of rambunctiousness put his head on my mom's shoulder and something in him let go almost completely and he fell asleep. Out of nowhere.

Something in him took the shape of what he was resting with. And he rested very deeply.

Movement and rest. Movement and rest. The path of learning, of becoming.

And the wise ones will discover that, within any human being, there is never a 'stillness'—that life teems within us. Impulses to breathe, to beat out the heartbeat of life, to keep you upright or moving or resting are always going—even in the deepest rest, the deepest sleep. In fact, any time some limb of you is trying to be in an upright relationship with gravity, we often remind one another in somatic learning circles (discovered first by Pavlov's student Ivan Sechenov) that 80 - 90% of your nervous system is on high-alert to send the impulses through you that talk to muscles to put your bones in places to keep that limb upright and weight-bearing in gravity. And of course, such an enterprise of uprightness is not about that one limb but of your whole self. For your arm to reach upward, everything else under it has to be sure, to know the ground beneath you, or else you topple.

That's what my little nephew was taking time to discover at five-months-young, even in taking shape in my mom's loving arms. He was still figuring it out—indeed we all are every minute if we open ourselves to learning in new contexts. Even walking on a new surface involves a learning within us with each uncertain step—all these new calibrations happening within us with each step, some deep intelligence within us figuring it all out.

We humans have to learn to sit upright or to stand without toppling, to crawl and roll and walk in so many different contexts. We're the only mammal that arrives into the world that does not walk within minutes.

Such complex beings we are.

And such potential!

NATURE'S GIFTS

Without trying to change anything . . . see if you can sense yourself, what Nature offers you in this moment. You might sense soreness or delight or even a blankness within your whole self or even in some places of yourself. See if you can be unattached to and non-clinging with whatever Nature has given you this moment—and watch whatever it is change, morph, wave-like.

In order to find such deep rest, we need to be with ourselves. As we are. And then as we are a moment later. Without any need to change anything.

Sure, you might want to move a leg, an arm, whatever. Do so!

The deep rest of meditation . . . that hazy place between sleep and waking life . . . that 'in-between' opportunity where we pause and so often it feels like a million ideas come to you . . . what to do then?

For me, it's a lot like being with the crying and fussy baby—the more you try to do to calm the baby, the more the baby squirms and gets uncomfortable, even more stimuli. The more you can allow the babies—human or your thoughts—to take the shapes they want to be in . . . the happier the babies!

So be with yourself, perhaps, as all those thoughts come. Maybe just sit there, notice your breath, maybe just through your nose. Which nostril does your breath find more easily. Of course you could try to change it, try to make it equal, but that will disturb the baby. Instead, just rest here. Let the baby find the way, the way to settle into your arms. The less you do, the more you both might be.

Of course, you must do what you know to be right for you!

It's so easy to think that you need a huge change for your life to change—when in fact all it takes sometimes is a little nudge. A beginning.

The temptation is to think that you're powerful—that by doing something special or by breathing in some special way you can change your pain or your day or course of life whatever. And you can. For sure. And you are powerful. Though you don't need to breathe in a special way to realize the power or the change. It changes without you changing it! Just naturally, in your own rhythm of the moment, of this second, whatever that something deep within you invites. After all, you are Nature. You are THE ALL. Just not all of it by 'yourself.'

NATURE'S WISE WAYS WITHIN

Ah, not getting what you want in life? Try changing your nature. Not so much through willpower as by arriving in some easy way everyday for a little bit of time. Stare out the window. Make a cup of tea. Sit. Feel the life within you. It doesn't take much. Maybe 20 minutes a day, for a week. Watch how you change without you doing much of anything . . . .

Does your mind 'monkey around'?
Do your thoughts sometimes go every-which-way?

Good!
That means you're alive!

Be with yourself here.

And not only 'be' . . . .

Can you fall in love with yourself here,
at the complexity that is you —
the tangled mess, the beautiful mess —
at the beauty of breathing
of moving
of resting
of letting yourself take shape
as the wisdom within you
allows it
no matter your seams or knots or inconsistencies?

Can you fall in love with yourself here,
wherever you rest your head,
your whole self?

absolute bliss
samadhi

Consider sitting in a coffeeshop or a park or a place where people mill about and watch each person and each creation there a moment. You know, gently, without judgement.

Can you feel the connection you have with each person, each creation you experience?

Can you feel the connection with every plant? with the air? with everything that involves life-force?

Can you sense the love, the life between you and every creation you witness?

Perhaps not a 'love' that is overtly sexual . . . at least not as we sadly imagine sex to be.

Consider a new 'love-making' . . . a 'love-being' that might be possible with each creation, human or not-human.

Perhaps this is a being-with, a gentle, flexible, moving-with, accommodating, offering hospitality.

Like my mom with my nephew, the ways they held one another, let themselves be shaped by one another. Relationship.

Without even reaching out—imagine it—how would you touch to communicate such love with whatever or whomever is before you? What tone of your voice might emerge from you? How would you be that appreciates and respects the authenticity of each particular creation and THE ALL in which we all exist and move and have our being? In what ways would you respect THE ALL within this person as the same ALL that is within you?

Can you feel the love within yourself, can you feel THE ALL within your-self—even with all the tangled mess that you are as a growing and learning human being—and can you feel THE ALL in the space between you and the person or creation that you let yourself lightly notice?

Can you feel the love, THE ALL, within that person or creation? Even with the tangled mess that they might be . . . the seams and inconsistencies, the knots, the so-called 'imperfections' that allow the person to be 'per-fect' and authentic in their own unique way? Can you appreciate the whole of this person or creation, that this person or creation is growing too? Can you appreciate this person even if you think this person might have offended you at some point in your life, even if they wear a hat or a shirt that offends you?

Can you appreciate THE ALL of all life?

Although you're simply imagining it...
in what gentle way
would you move your hands through their hair,
or over their surface or skin?
in what ways would you allow your hands to hold,
in ways that meet and melt and respond,
in ways that do not inflict your power
over the person or creation,
in ways that sense and respond
to a 'knowing' this person . . .
such recognition of your equal-status in life, for life, with life,
with such gentle-love,
in which we all live,
this bliss . . . ?

And now we are ready to <u>begin</u> . . .

Are you prepared to accept your divinity—that you participate in the divine unfolding, of life giving birth to life giving birth to life, the Infinite? That we all do, all creatures, all life? That truly, when the veil of daily life is seen for what it is, that there can be no separation between you and the Infinite reality, right?

Dare you trust this wisdom, this goodness within you?

Dare you trust this goodness, even with the tangled mess and the brilliance coexisting within you? dare you love ALL that is you? ALL that is anyone?

The path to arriving is far from linear, no? Patanjali knew that. His eight limbs are not 'steps'—not a methodical way to arrive. Nor is the unfolding story in *The Bhagavad Gita* a specific 'method.' They both invite. So does *The Dhammapada*. And so can you.

Dare you invite others into a glimpse of who we truly are as humans, as creatures? Dare you invite a glimpse into the Infinite reality—THE ALL—in which we participate . . .

on their own terms,

in their own time,

through invitation,

through love?

Indeed, it might be the only thing that works – this love

. . . an invitation to a new way forward for our world!

And why a new way forward?

The history of yoga is quite interesting.

I find it pretty incredible that we 'move'

from Patanjali's Sutras and *The Bhagavad Gita* with ZERO descriptions of asanas

to the centuries upon centuries later . . . *Hatha Yoga Pradipika* with its about fifteen descriptions of asanas

to today with BKS Iyengar's *Light on Yoga* and its MANY pictures of asana and Swami Sivananda's students and their books and descriptions of not only MANY asanas but very complex asanas at that. Pattabhi Jois' primary series and later series all have their posters of the order of their asanas too, plus his book *Yoga Mala*.

What happened in the 20th century that we needed asana so much? What is it within us yoga-people that we have evolved the need for asana in our 21st century world so much? Especially when the roots of yoga seems to be more meditative, more interested in stillness.

And why such complex asanas in the 20th and 21st centuries too?

Patanjali's only advice about asana is to make it easy, to make it snake-like, right? And the only way to make any movement easier is to sense oneself, right? to sense the varying degrees of ease we are invited by Patanjali to welcome, right?

For me, asana—any movement in fact—stirs up the sediment within me. Perhaps that's its helpful purpose!

I rest for a time in meditation, and I begin to sense and notice most days just how settled most of myself is and then I feel the need to move, to take on a different shape . . . and if I move slowly, with the ever-so-slightest move . . . it's like everything within me changes, like sand being spilled out within me or the creek within me getting all muddied up. All that once-settled sediment within me gets stirred up! It's fun! And once I've moved to my heart's content I find another good perch upon which to rest and meditate, all that stirred-up sediment settles again.

Movement and rest . . . asana and meditation . . . movement and rest.

So why all the 20th & 21st century fascination with asana, with moving all the sediment within us, all that sediment we've inherited from previous generations of life on this planet?

Maybe this fascination with asana these days is to heal the madnesses of the world, the madnesses within us that we've come to know all too well.

What madnesses? The 'only real devils in the world are the ones in our own hearts' that Gandhi talked about . . . what today I would call gender-inequality, the multi-century effects of slavery and racism, the multi-generational effects of warfare and violence, even the multi-generational effects of nature's violence, whether climate-change-induced violence or just nature's queer ways.

What madnesses? All the sad ways we try to hold power over one another to try to get a grip on life and all the forces that get thrown at us in daily life.

Maybe something within us knows that movement is critical—especially as more and more of the world relies so little on movement for survival, for getting daily needs met as previous generations did.

Maybe something wise within us knows that asana is key to healing the past and finding ways to become equanimous and more equal-sighted in the future of our relationships.

So imagine it . . . each one of us moves and that sediment within us gets kicked up. And then we rest for a bit and the sediment settles again, in some new arrangement. Maybe an idea comes to us in our resting after we've kicked up the sediment within us by moving, by asana . . . or maybe we come to know some of our own violence and we somehow grow with that realization, catch how our words or thoughts stirred up violence in a relationship earlier. Maybe we then can catch ourselves later, stop ourselves before we create more violent-waves on the planet.

Such is growth. Such is growth for all who desire to grow on this amazing planet.

Movement and rest . . . asana and meditation . . . movement and rest.

After we stir up the collective past and one's own personal past slowly and peacefully through movement, we are wise to sit with it—with this kicked up sediment, centuries of pain—and watch it change. How important it is then to rest and let it all re-settle again—maybe with some new idea of how I might grow as a human being, how I might be the light, how I might trust more deeply my own authenticity and authentic voice as a human being, as a creature who KNOWS, as a creature who seeks to hold no power over anyone or anything!

How important it is to have that rest, though, after stirring up all that is within us! How many yoga classes I've been to and how many yoga classes yoga-teacher-trainers report back that they've visited where there has been no rest, no meditation, no savasana—or that these things were optional.

Eek.

Imagine what happens in the world when that class leaves with all that sediment stirred up within them and no time for it to re-settle, no time to learn from its new arrangements. I don't want to be on the road when they leave class! I don't want to be their partner or child or parent!

Movement and rest . . . asana and meditation . . . movement and rest.

As I pause between moving and resting, all kinds of things come to mind for just how much I could improve my relationships, what a schmuck I've been too many times to family and friends and lovers, all the ways

I could have responded differently to the circumstances . . . and with all this the collective sum of dis-ease and violence we've inherited, it seems, in our DNA, the various madnesses that swirl through our news cycles, no matter which 'side(s)' of the political aisle we're on.

How to find equanimity in such madness?

How to forgive and know love, remember the love in which we live and move and be . . . THE ALL?

Yoga is an opportunity to heal such madnesses . . .
to let Nature do its thing within us . . .
to let the breeze have its way with us
and transform us . . .
how? we don't even need to know.
Give ourselves a hint,
a nudge,
and everything seems to move,
to cascade—in a helpful direction.

Movement and rest . . . asana and meditation . . . movement and rest.

It doesn't take much to count as movement, it doesn't take much to stir up what's within us so that it all can later settle down again. Perhaps this is a new way forward . . . what is invited here next . . .

An Invitation to Begin (Again)...
7(00) Shapes, a Think & a Nap

BRIEF INTRODUCTION

One time I had a very 'traditional' group of yogins who wanted me to use more Sanskrit and more Latin anatomical names and only teach 'traditional' asanas, yoga-shapes.

So I usually obliged them.

But one day I decided without any fanfare to lead an entire 90 minute class with movements that went by no Sanskrit names in yoga—some things I invented, other things that are 'riffs' on things we kind of might do in yoga.

At the end of the class . . . "That was the best class you've ever taught us!"

So I responded, "Oh, thanks." After they began telling me all the things they liked about the class, I gently chimed in, "How many of those things we did have Sanskrit names? How many of them are 'yoga'?"

They got quiet. Just as I was learning through Krishnamacharya's wise teaching-life, this class figured out that this 'yoga' was much bigger than they realized.

What follows here is much of that same spirit—very different from what we'd usually term a 'yoga' class. And yet, I hope you'll be able to enjoy this dollop of whatever it is that follows as an invitation to yoga, to THE ALL.

WHAT TO DO

It should go without saying . . . only do what's right for your body.

You can enjoy the experiences that follow anywhere you are most comfortable . . . the floor, a chair, the center of a bed (so you are safely there and don't roll off!) . . . wherever you are most comfortable and supported and safe.

No gear needed unless you would like things to help support you in rest . . . a mat, blankets, pillows, bolsters.

BEGINNING . . . ON YOUR OWN

Take a moment to just sit there, however it's most comfortable to sit.

Can you notice the shape of your body, the 'edges' of your body, at the surface of your body, your skin?

Notice every limb.

Notice every inch of your torso . . . front, back, sides.

Notice your neck and head.

Can you even tune into the creases of your joints, where the skin has little lines that allow you to move more easily?

Take time to discover just how much sensation you can notice on the surface of yourself, your skin . . .

of course, you've been moving since the very beginning of the exploration, you've changed shape slightly with each inhale, each exhale . . .

maybe move one limb just slightly . . .

and then go back and sense yourself . . .

do you notice the cascade effect of how moving one limb moves them all, even just slightly?

do you notice that your breathing changes slightly depending on what shape your body takes . . . that some places within yourself now move with your breath more easily because you moved one limb . . . and some places are slightly restricted, they don't move quite as easily because that one limb moved? all this change with the smallest of movement!

and maybe there are places within you that you have difficulty sensing? maybe a cleansing breath or two will provide just enough movement through your whole self that you can more easily sense yourself . . . . the surface of your body, your 'edges,' your skin . . . .

LIGHT, LIGHT TAPPING

Once you have a sense of your whole self and the constantly moving self that is you . . .

use your fingers and hands to **very, very lightly** tap your whole body . . . just enough to play the drum that is you. As babies would playfully tap their own bodies for fun. Light. Easy.

If you do not have hands available for this exploration, you could imagine that your hands or someone else's hands are lightly tapping your body.

There will be places where it's easy to tap, there might be places that you do not want to tap. All good! Enjoy as much of it as you'd like. <u>All</u> of it very lightly, gently! And only do what's easy—no need to try to get your back, any of it, if it's not easy. Perhaps imagine someone you love and trust is tapping those places that aren't easy to reach.

What do you notice as you lightly touch your body in this way?

How many times does your body change shape as you tap here, tap there? Perhaps discover if you can tune into how your back changes shape as you touch one leg and then the other. Or even watch as your belly moves this way and that as you touch one leg and then the other. Incredible, yes?

And then when you've had enough, let it all go and pause and sense the surface of your skin. Is your body easier to sense now? Do you have a better sense of where the edges of your body are now, from head to toe?

SMOOTHING IT OUT—ON YOUR OWN

And now with your hands, smooth out every inch of yourself with the palms of your hands—lightly, easily, happily, pleasurably.

It doesn't matter where you begin. And as always, only smooth out the places that are easy. Can't reach some place easily? Then imagine someone else is smoothing out these places for you.

Take your time and move oh so slowly—like a full minute or more for one arm. Or luxuriate in even more time for yourself.

Notice how your body changes shape with every move of your hand? Say if you reach—easily! not that far!—for some place on your leg, that your back changes shape? That the curves of your back and neck change so slightly . . . do you notice that? Can you sense yourself in that way?

Discover if you can sense with your palms and fingers every crease of every joint. Perhaps questions arise within you about the ways your body moves and why things are the ways they are. Judgements might arise too. Maybe you can let all those ideas go for a time . . . and simply be with yourself, with your whole self.

Luxuriate in soft, gentle sensation.

Once you've had enough, rest completely. Maybe that's reclined with props and pillows and all; maybe that's in a chair. Stay here awhile and sense yourself again.

Are you more able to sense every place that is you?

Maybe there are even places on or within your whole self that you had never touched, never explored . . . maybe not since you were a baby!

Rest here. Luxuriate in the goodness of you, of the beautiful creature that is you. And when you're ready, move on to either this next section or the one after (A Think & a Nap).

SMOOTHING IT OUT—WITH A TRUSTED LOVER

If you'd like, consider asking a lover to do what you just did for yourself . . . for your lover to lightly and easily touch all that is you, very slowly and lovingly deliberately.

Try to rest in a place and in a way that's easy for both of you.

Of course you can do this clothed or nude, as you're comfortable with your beloved.

See if you both can luxuriate in the slow appreciation of this whole body that is you. And consider doing this in silence, resting together in the quiet.

As lovers, there are places you're probably accustomed to finding, places that you might always kiss or be drawn to noticing. That's lovely. Here, though, in this invitation, consider offering your full attention to the whole of this person . . . and linger nowhere any longer than any place. This is your lover, so love all of this person lovingly.

Take your time. Communicate a gentle, nonjudgemental love with your hands. And invite yourself to receive this love, this gentle touch.

When you're ready, switch roles.

And after you've both had a full chance to offer your hands and to receive your lover's hands, then consider resting next to each other without touching one another—on the ground, in your bed, in a chair, whatever is easiest—and sense all the sensations happening within your own body.

Perhaps too, without even touching one another, you can sense your lover nearby . . . the heat radiating from your lover's body, the rhythm of your lover's heart (possibly even finding a rhythm with your heart, a mutuality), the feeling of your lover's breath, even if your lover's breath is not directed toward you.

Luxuriate in it all.

This too is yoga . . . an invitation to THE ALL.

A THINK & A NAP

After you've sensed your whole self again, by yourself, rest awhile . . . bask in the sensations, perhaps without any judgement . . . and notice, as always, that sensation offers you choices—both in how you rest here and in how you live your life . . . and then as you're ready . . . consider wondering about all that you crave in your life, and all that you desire in your life.

What you crave and what you desire is what you crave and what you desire . . . no need to let shame or embarrassment get in the way of it.

It's your life.

Ignatius Loyola—the man who today is revered for welcoming a new way forward with the contempaltives-in-action Jesuits, some of the best educators the world over—was a man who once was known simply as Iñigo. He knew lots of cravings . . . fine food and drink, sex, violence, being recognized as studly among his friends and people of his town.

It wasn't until he found himself wounded and nearly dying in battle at the age of 26 that he began to discern his cravings from his deepest desires for life. And he did so for about a year from his hospital bed—all without any modern, push-button entertainment to distract him.

As you consider your cravings—the chocolate you know is in the refrigerator, the pizza you could order, the drinks you could be having with your friends, the sex you want now and with whom, the car, the vacation, the house, the ritzy clothing and jewelry, all of it!—notice your feeling for each thing, each opportunity.

Be with yourself here. No need for judgement. Just observe, just sense what it is that you feel for each of these things, these opportunities.

Of course, no need for embarrassment or shame about any of them, or anything else you crave or desire. They are on your radar for a reason—perhaps they are waking you up to life in some way, Ignatius would remind.

After you've felt each one, after you've had the opportunity to know each one a bit more deeply, begin to be with them all.

Some of these cravings might be quickly passing already. The pull you felt toward them might now feel kind of blah.

Fine. Just notice.

And some of these cravings might have gained some steam—their pull is even more profound than before.

Fine. Just notice.

And then, begin wondering if any of these cravings are calling you more deeply into life . . . maybe one or two of them call out to you, beckon you to another side of the river, of the tree, of life . . . does this feel differently, this tug, this attraction, than the chocolate bar or whatever it was for you that was craved a bit ago but now you've almost forgotten? (If not, go eat the chocolate bar!!! Just kidding…kinda.)

As you sift through all these cravings and desires you have . . . maybe there's one or two that you have a sense of being your deepest desire(s) for life.

Fine. Just notice. Feel. Sense. Just as you did your body in the earlier invitations. Let it all play out in your imagination . . . sense your deepest desire(s) as much as you can.

Let these deepest desires play out as if they were a movie . . . something in the future . . .

notice the people you see, the expressions on their faces, the ways they move and rest and even breathe . . .

the sounds around you, and voices and tones of voices . . .

the feeling of the air on your skin, the temperature of the air . . . just right for you

the smell or taste of things . . . even of the air . . .

the feeling of something of your body (your feet?) on the ground . . .

let it all play out, these deepest desires for life.

Ignatius—far removed from his days as Iñigo and all the cravings of his younger years—arrives at something profound about our deepest desires, the ones that call our name seemingly from some other world, that keep us up at night, that sometimes have us in tears we feel them so much.

Ignatius claims that our deepest desires are where we meet God, THE ALL.

Is this life calling your name, this movie playing out in your imagination . . . and dare you be with it, be with yourself every day?

To be, or not to be . . . ?

questions, controversies, & quandaries
about 'yoga' as a practice / play
for teachers & play-ers

Much of this section was written during a short, recent visit in Sedona, said to be one of the healing centers of the world . . . Sedona, with its massive and wild red and brown rocks and vortexes where the wind whips around and dances gleefully, the community of people who stay and who come and go and welcome some new way there together for our world.

I planted myself in a little coffee shop that overlooked the rocks and much of what follows here came through in a morning before a grand hike. I do hope there is something helpful here for you to consider that brings you to new ground where you know . . .

from the roots of who you are that you are enough,
that all you need is within you,
that you are THE ALL . . .
though not all of it in 'yourself,'
in the dancing, permeable container of molecules that is 'you.'

Some of my teachers used to tell me that Cincinnati will be very soon the next healing center of the world, like Sedona. I used to laugh when I heard that. What a ridiculous thought!

But now I'm beginning to remember that Greater Cincinnati, say a 50 mile radius around Downtown Cincinnati and including Northern Kentucky and Southeastern Indiana, perched here on the winding Ohio River, that Greater Cincinnati invented the modern world . . . airplanes, cash registers that presaged computers, lager beer, rock'n'roll, professonnal baseball, Reformed Judaism, Marriage Equality, soap that can be packaged and shipped and sold, massive grocery stores that are one-stop-shops for just about everything.

Even though it's guessed by historians that most Cincinnati locals cared little about the issue of slavery in the pre-Civil War and Civil War days of the mid-nineteenth century, Cincinnati was the first northern stop on the Underground Railroad, that compassionate channel of freeing southern slaves to the north.

There is a hunger here in Cincinnati, a longing for more life, a land of mystics seeking THE MORE, THE ALL.

Come, see . . . here in word and invitation, or here in person.

So what follows here is a gathering of things I've been thinking about for some years, questions about yoga and how it relates with other holistic disciplines that have a mutual interest in THE ALL, questions within yoga that seem to never get talked about very loudly or that seem to need some resolution . . . perhaps through another question. As I've pointed out quite often, the study of 'yoga' is a multi-century tangled mess of teachings that contradict and fly one away and then another. Just like any and every person I know. Just like me.

The tangled mess of yoga, of course, is true of any holistic discipline and any religion. Any tradition is a working out over centuries what the most helpful way is, even as times and contexts change.

I offer these questions and quandaries not so much as answers as ways to soften the edges of yoga and these seemingly different holistic disciplines . . . that you might find the way that is best for you.

Only you know . . .

To be, or not to be . . . ?

be

right?

To breathe, or not to breathe . . . ?

breathe . . .

though what kind of breath is the million dollar question!

I began my holistic studies with tai chi and qigong, and with the wise Vince Lasorso we were encouraged to let our breath do whatever it liked nearly all of the time. Every now and then, he invited us to breathe more fully, deeply, especially on an exhale, to experience something quite interesting in our groundedness. I remember too the general wisdom—in class and in print—of breathing in such a way that would not disturb a feather under one's nose.

For the most part, among all the various breath-ideas in tai chi, there seemed to be a curious wisdom about letting oneself breathe how one needed, of letting Nature do what Nature does, without much 'conscious' interference.

When I later followed my mom into yoga and began my yoga journey with ashtanga-vinyasa yoga, we were invited to breathe in a very orderly way. Ashtanga-vinyasa yoga encourages a loud inhale and and even louder exhale through one's nose (if possible)—a breath designed to build heat as one's breath is a bit forced through the body. Such a breath in the yoga tradition has been called ujjayi breath, 'victorious breath' as in victory over the monkeying around of one's thoughts. Pattabhi Jois encouraged such a style of breath to burn through impurities, especially with the use of the bandhas (more on that below).

If such a breath-style floats your boat, then go for it of course.

I found it burned me up too much inside, and actually increased the tension within my body—especially and interestingly/strangely around my eyes. And through my Feldenkrais Method® studies, I've come to discover that using a whole lot of effort to breathe in movement seems to reduce greatly the help of the movement itself in drawing some attention within myself, to helping me sense myself. So for many of us simply using one's natural rhythm of breathing—interestingly, as I was encouraged with tai chi and qigong and later with vipassana meditation and Feldenkrais Method®— might be most helpful, and certainly relaxes more all those areas within that are needed for breathing. And well, that seems to be my whole body!

An exception, though, could be when I'm having difficulty sensing something in a movement. When I take a slightly larger breath, I'm sometimes more able to sense a particular place within myself. Why? Because a single breath ripples through one's whole being, every single muscle is affected by, well, every movement, and breathing is movement.

THE WISDOM OF THE WIND WITHIN

One other way of considering this too is to listen in on what Gautama has to say about breathing, what kind of breathing helped him to know the absolute bliss of enlightenment. Who is Gautama? the one people came to eventually call the Buddha, the enlightened one of 2500 years ago.

Gautama sought enlightenment in all of the yoga teachings of his day. And his search was no small thing. After all of these yoga studies and hatha / 'forced' or 'directed' breathing-styles, he still found himself miserable and suffering . . . his inner world was still unsettled and unhelped by all of the yoga that he was taught.

So he sat himself down under a tree and crossed his legs meditation-style and told himself and the Universe that he would not get up from this spot until he'd found the answer . . . until he was enlightened.

Who knows how long it took . . . !

But what he discovered—as taught by S.N. Goenka in the vipassana tradition, the technique of what Gautama discovered, not the 'religion' or 'religiosity' or excessive ritual built around him and his discovery—was that simply observing WHAT IS and not trying to change anything is the key to enlightenment. No ritual needed, no special chants or prayers or priests, no special breathing. No props, no perfect weather or temperature. No bows to gurus or gods or goddesses, no religious devotion of any kind. Not even any yoga-shapes besides sukkhasana, the 'sweet' yoga-shape of simple crossed ankles. Even that was probably not necessary.

Gautama's discoveries of course caused much controversy in the yoga world—and generations later Gautama's teaching wrankled many Vedic and yoga scholars and priests who were teaching such specialized breath and movement techniques.

What Gautama discovered worked for him, and he found it worked for others. Nothing special needed but time and attention to WHAT IS. Only and always WHAT IS.

Perhaps WHAT IS is THE ALL, and all we need to know. Not the past. Not the future. Not all of those places one's mind, one's body, one's whole self darts off to.

So I've been bringing the wisdom of such breath—what S.N. Goenka teaches of simple natural breath awareness in vipassana (dhamma.org) and what Moshe Feldenkrais teaches in his Method—to the yoga I practice and teach. I very rarely even say much about breathing in a class.

This is sure to wrankle a lot of my yoga-friends.

I know. I get it. I too used to say the 'magic' of yoga was in one's breath.

All I have to say now, after about 30 years at meditation and movement, is maybe not . . . maybe controlling or limiting or expanding one's breath is not necessarily where the magic is, at least most of the time.

Perhaps your sensation will lead you to know what is best for you.

Your sensation is WAY wiser than any guru or any teacher. The guru or teacher does not live within your skin, does not know your sensations. You do. So listen! To yourself!

And know that 'how to breathe' is a question that has an answer that might change for you each time you ask.

So be it.

Pay attention to sensation and have no attachment to the way you think you should feel or would like to feel and you'll know some 'magic' alright, some significant clarity.

To engage your bandhas, or not . . . ?

Bandhas are 'energy locks' within a person that have been part of the yoga-teaching tradition for millennia. Some yoga-instructors simply say, "engage your bandhas." In classes these days that seem to have drifted from using Sanskrit, the directions or verbal cues for engaging bandhas are often 'pull up your pelvic floor' or 'internally squeeze your sex organs' or more specifically 'engage your perineum (space between sex organs and anus)' for one of the bandhas and then 'pull in your belly' or 'engage your abs' or 'pull your navel to your spine' for another of the bandhas.

Pattabhi Jois encouraged the use of three bandhas in his ashtanga-vinyasa practice. My teachers used to say that a good yogin would engage their bandhas all day long, on mat and off, and only let them go when in savasana (resting on one's back in full relaxation) and when sleeping.

I followed such advice and two years later found that I was incontinent, that I had over-toned my pelvic floor. Not to mention that my low back hurt and I couldn't figure out why.

I was doing yoga, for crying out loud! I should be feeling good!

But I wasn't.

In my first classes, I was shocked to discover that Movement Intelligence® and then too Feldenkrais Method® encouraged—at least most of the time—a letting go of this idea of purposeful core/pelvic engagement and letting the deeper wisdom of oneself take over . . . that something within oneself knows when to engage these places within oneself and when to let them go.

For example, when you stand up from a chair, do you usually need to tell yourself what to engage and what not to?

With each step that you take when you walk, are you telling your pelvic floor or your abdomen what to do?

Most of the time—if not all of the time—of course not. Something within you is wise to know how to bear your weight under the biggest force we all encounter every day: gravity. And this inner knowing is learned by each one of us in infancy. Your pelvic floor and your abdomen know when to engage and when to release when you move, as they 'talk' with your whole self.

Might a physical therapist or doctor suggest that purposeful inner engagement is necessary for a particular condition? Of course! And it goes without saying that you'd better listen to them for the particular condition that you have!

But for most of us, this whole engaging bandha-business can be quite problematic.

When I started letting my pelvic floor and abdomen do what they wanted as I moved and breathed, when I let go of engaging bandhas on mat or off, after awhile I was no longer spilling urine all over myself on the way to the bathroom. I later learned that gymnasts and athletes often overtone these places within themselves too. And to them and all I'd recommend taking a few Feldenkrais Method® Awareness Through Movement® classes or having a few Feldenkrais Method® Functional Integration® sessions with an experienced practitioner to speed along some freedom in these over-toned areas, to give your body a new education in how these places can work more efficiently in all the ways that you'd like to move and perform.

To drishti, or not . . . ?

The Sanskrit word 'drishti' has to do with where one puts their sight during yoga-practice. We often call it one's 'gaze' in yoga-practice.

I grew up in yoga learning that there were prescribed places to put my eyes and sight during every yoga-asana, within every yoga-shape.

For awhile, that was kind of fun. After awhile though, lo and behold, my eyes felt like they were bulging and far from relaxed or useful after yoga-practice. As with engaging bandhas, putting my drishti in the same places every day, in all those shapes, sometimes practicing twice or even three times a day, had overtoned the small, so important muscles of my eyes—and probably my whole self.

In Feldenkrais Method®, the wisdom most of the time is to let your eyes go where they'd like to during each slow-movement and rest. Sure, sometimes there are specific instructions for what to do with one's eyes. For the most part, though, we let them go where we'd like. And sometimes I catch myself with my eyes—whether open or closed—fixed on some place and the movement with which I'm playing is suddenly very, very difficult. It's like having my eyes on some static spot gets me stuck there. While most of myself wants to move one way, my eyes are stuck in one spot and prevent much (all?) of me from moving optimally, easily. Feldenkrais would call this 'trying to do the thing and its opposite.'

He figured out that one's senses are very powerful—especially one's eyes. Your eyes direct your whole self to look here and there. Where your eyes go, every muscle of your being is involved with going there. Direct your eyes in the same way to the same spot every day—say in every shape you allow your body, on your mat or off—and you have a very limited scope of life!

Take for example Utthita Parsvakonasana, Extended Side Angle Shape. If you don't know this yoga-shape, you could look it up online to see what it looks like, if you're curious. The prevailing wisdom of this yoga-shape as I was taught in ashtanga-vinyasa yoga is, once you are in the shape, to extend your eyes up to the hand raised in the air and keep your eyes there as you breathe your five or more breaths.

That's all fine and good until someone's neck starts hurting, or someone topples over due to losing their balance.

YOU HAVE A DEEP WISDOM WITHIN YOU!

Maybe it's wiser to let your eyes go where they'd like to go. Sometimes that might mean up toward that raised hand, other times it might be letting your eyes and head/neck turn toward the ground, or even the horizon-line, or some other place that is easy, gentle, or curious to you.

If yoga is indeed about sensation, about sensing oneself, about being with these sensations, about becoming curious about them without any attachment or assumption about how things should be and responding accordingly, if at all, then how indeed can you do all that—all of the deep tuning into sensation—and at the same time follow someone else's directions about where your hand and eyes and the rest of yourself are supposed to go?

Maybe there's an inner wisdom that knows better for you—not some outside teacher or guru.

And maybe we'd be wise to play with even easier shapes than Extended Side Angle Shape! As much as I love this shape, standing shapes are very complex puzzles, as Bonnie Bainbridge Cohen has noted! Even just standing up tall on your feet is a huge demand on your nervous system . . . as it is often said in Feldenkrais Method®, about 80 - 90% of your nervous system is engaged in simply keeping you upright in gravity when simply standing there.

All the more reason medical doctor and researcher Norman Doidge celebrates the study that confirmed that walking—essentially moving your body over a surface in a very inner-coordinated way in relationship with gravity that never stops—is the best self-care, the best medicine. Check it out yourself:

The Brain's Way of Healing: Remarkable Discoveries and Recoveries from the Frontiers of Neuroplasticity. Norman Doidge, M.D. New York: Viking, 2015, p. 85.

Walking has been one way yoga—encountering THE ALL—has thrived in my own life . . . the free-flowing movement on relatively uneven sur-faces, the ever-changing air, the flowers that need visiting for a quick sniff, the trees, the wildlife (human included), the hawks, the breeze, the bees buzzing . . . THE ALL. Lovely.

To mudra, mantra, centering prayer, OM, or not . . . ?

Mudras are particular hand positions and placements used in moving and breathing and resting, yoga-practice.

Mantras are repeated words—Sanskrit or English or any language—that are repeated over and over, in a sense, to anchor one's attention on something during yoga-practice. Soothing sounds or words with special meaning are usually chosen. Centering Prayer essentially uses a mantra as part of its practice.

OM is said to be the 'universal vibration' often used in yoga-practice to bring good vibes within and outside oneself, to bring oneself to be in harmony with the Universe.

If any of these work for you, by all means use them. I have and I do.

Just know that Gautama seemed to notice through his discovery—at least as taught by S.N. Goenka (dhamma.org)—that they might get in the way of your noticing WHAT IS, of THE ALL within you, within ALL that is you.

All that's needed to know THE ALL is to notice WHAT IS, and to be at peace with whatever that particular sensation is—not to crave for some other sensation, not to try to push away what you are indeed sensing either by craving for something else instead.

Sensation is constantly changing, right? Sit awhile and notice.

Even the most unbearable pain is not a constant. There are waves to it. Sometimes even waves of pleasure in the midst of pain. I noticed that when I was eighteen and experiencing a kidney stone moving through my body . . . the most awful pain I had ever experienced and then strangely some ripple of pleasure, and then pain, and then pleasure, and then nothing, and then pain . . . on and on and on, the only constant to any of it was that it changed. And often.

Nothing is permanent . . . Gautama's most important realization.

To play music during yoga-practice, or not . . . ?

I love music.

Let me be clear about that. Very.

The first yoga teacher training I embarked upon was under the tutelage of Amber Jean Espelage (Yoga Ah! - Cincinnati) and Larry Schultz (It's Yoga - San Francisco). Larry was the hired 'guru' for the Grateful Dead when they were out on tour in the mid-1990s. According to yoga-Dead legend, Bob Weir even named Larry's style of yoga 'The Rocket' because it sped along one's yoga-learning.

So there was a LOT of music being played in yoga classes offered by Amber and Larry. Often ambient, often long guitar solos, not a lot of words. Often fading to quiet in savasana - quite nice.

I got a lot out of those classes, for sure. And yes, the music helped with the choreography, with moving the class along in its own winding way that can be the dance of The Rocket. And yes, every now and then the most perfect lyric would arise and save the day of my life—some few words that I needed to hear just then, at that moment, that place in my life.

Later on though, as I was teaching more meditation in high schools and with other groups, I found the quiet helpful, especially with a lead-in of my voice inviting some gentle awareness and then a <u>long</u> space of quiet and then a few words to invite us back together in the full sensate sharing-experiencing with voices and facial awareness eye-contact and more. As I'm fond of saying and used to be very fond of donuts, leading meditation is a bit like a donut . . . a small mouthful of words . . . a long, long quiet in the middle of the donut . . . an even smaller mouthful of words to close.

The long quiet in the middle of the donut is a full symphony in itself for those who have ears to listen or those who have sensations to feel.

THE SYMPHONY OF SOUND...WITHOUT MUSIC!

Take some time to listen in, to feel the quiet around you . . . the noises well beyond where you are, maybe outside the room . . . the noises within the room around you, maybe of the breeze, maybe of other creatures nearby or whizzing by . . . the incredible noises within you, the creature that is you . . . the breath that comes and goes within you and beyond . . . the sounds of food bring digested . . . the sounds of liquids constantly moving within you . . . the sounds or feelings, if you're able to listen deeply, of your own heart beating . . . the incredible inner and not-so-obvious movements of the very alive creature you are.

Play a symphony or any music in the yoga class and you might just miss the symphony happening within and around you.

In my explorations of tai chi or qigong or Movement Intelligence® and Feldenkrais Method®, usually no music is played. The teacher-leader will wisely offer little pauses for quiet in between instructions and invitations so that people can listen in on what they are feeling within themselves, in their own ways.

Something pretty incredible begins to happen as we move and rest and move and rest and listen and drink deeply from this well.

Listen in on it as you move and breathe and rest . . . in any ways that seem right for you.

What happens for you when your senses are not bombarded with a lot of stimuli . . . when some of those places within you can quiet . . . .

Just what do you think the play-list was for the ancient yogins of the Indus River Valley? 3000 - 5000 years ago?

If you're going to have music . . . to have 'recorded music' or 'live music' . . . ?

I've always felt that a yoga class where someone is playing some instrument live—a single drum or a single guitar or a violin or flute or whatever—can be very interesting. Musician and mover communicate with one another, sense one another, invite one another on some journey together. It's a love-making.

At least it can be.

If both can sense one another. If the music does not overwhelm and dominate.

In any relationship, the 'divine marriage' is not possible, in my humble opinion, if one partner is 'roled' into the dominant and the other into the submissive receiver and those roles stay static without any sensing of one another, without any sensing oneself and what one needs or would like in every moment of life in that 'relationship'—in that relating with one another.

For such wholeness to be realized in any relationship there can be a tumbling, an offering, an inviting, a giving, a receiving . . . and that can only happen when all creatures can sense one another and respond to one another and know.

Recorded music doesn't have such an opportunity. It doesn't know the vibe being created by the movers. It just squawks on.

Even my favorite songs don't know what I'm feeling in this moment—so, so different from live music.

Even if the artists in a live concert don't know what I am feeling in particular, they do know something of what's 'in the breeze,' what's happening in the larger life of the room or of the world that day, that moment.

And sure, of course, recorded music can be helpful—I play recorded music quite often. But it responded to 'the moment' of however long ago when it was recorded.

Play the same song live now—even by the same artists on the same instruments (as if any of the artists or the instruments is the 'same' from second to second to second)—and it will be different because the song played now responds to the moment, to whatever is within that person today, to whatever that artist senses and responds to—within themself or with other players or whatever is in the breeze that second, whatever the feeling of the moment.

I'm ready to play with more live music with moving - resting - breathing opportunities, by whatever name we call such opportunities.

Some call it 'ecstatic dance.'

And ecstasy is certainly possible when we sense, when we feel, when we choose to respond . . . .

And all of that without any need for drugs.

It's the heart of the biblical tradition that no one wants to talk about— what the prophets—literally 'ecstatic-visionary-healers' in Hebrew (nabi)—were doing with one another up on the hillside outside of town, where the bees buzz, where the wind blows, where nakedness is welcome because you want that sexy breeze that is God—THE ALL—to be in contact with all of you, without any barriers, where all are welcome to move and breathe and rest and respond to and with one another.

Let's find out again, yes?

It's probably quite close to what the ancient yogins knew in the Indus River Valley 3000 - 5000 years ago.

And so can you.

And so can we.

To use alcohol / drugs, or not . . . ?

We all need to find our own way.

Of course.

The buzz I get from a single cup of coffee or rich yerba mate, from a single gulp of good wine, from sitting outside and feeling IT, all of it, the breeze and ALL, or at least as much as I can . . .

it's all a drug, right?

I prefer to get high on the wind.

What works for you? Today, tomorrow, that you might have many days of it, of this high, with only helpful consequences?

To eat meat, or not . . . ?

It's up to you, my friend.

I don't eat meat, but not for any moral reason. Not even for any health reason other than eating meat seems to make me sick, physically ill.

I suspect that most people in the world need to eat meat. I doubt though that any human needs to eat meat at every meal, or even every day.

Figure it out for yourself, friend. What food or drink makes you feel healthiest day in and day out?

The original ayurveda, of course—long before there were doshas / types and all that—was to notice what works for you personally.

And so can you!

To anatomy-talk in yoga classes, or not . . . ?

I think it's very important for yoga-teachers and movement-geeks to study anatomy, to look at books and cadavers and plastic skeletons and the many incredible on-line resources available today where you can peel away layers of human models to wonder how a human walks or moves or breathes or whatever.

What a gift to be able to wonder about the great within!

Of course, the 'within' of a book or model or cadaver is VASTLY different from the very-alive creature that is you!

And of course the 'within' of you and the 'within' of me will be similar in many ways, and yet very, very different too.

Sure, we probably each have something that will be called a 'heart' and a 'liver' and a 'brain' and all that.

Though each of these similar organs are most certainly different shapes and colors and sizes and sometimes even places within each one of us.

There are no two 'same' human beings.

Even identical twins are vastly different if you have the eyes to see, ears to hear, self to feel. And your noticing these subtle differences among all people is the key, right? The language of the nervous system, after all, is sensing differences, appreciating differences.

Looking at anatomy books or even gently and lightly touching into a human being who trusts you—a beloved partner, perhaps—might invite you to wonder about what is within you and me as each one of us moves and breathes and rests.

Most importantly, though, remember that you are a 'whole self'—just as your beloved friend is too.

'PARTING' IS SUCH SORROW
TO THE SWEETNESS OF 'THE ALL'

There are no 'parts' to each one of us.

The naming of this as 'heart' and this as 'pulmonary artery' and this as 'sinoatrial node' that is the inner pacemaker and this as 'nerve' that gets impulsed by something up in the very primal area of the brain is all pretty arbitrary. Where does 'heart' begin and end if it does not work without all of these particular 'things' or places within you and me—not to mention the need you and I have for the air and food to be 'digested' and converted into useable energy by other places within you to keep alive every place within you?

The names aren't the game, are they? Naming some place within you might confer some certain power over it—but sensing something is way different and perhaps more important than naming it, right?

Just how helpful are yoga classes where teachers talk about "here, feel your IT band—that means iliotibial band—feel that and how there's a stretch there"?

Especially if the student doesn't feel the 'stretch' there but somewhere else?

Especially if the student doesn't even know where the IT band is?

Especially if you start thinking of yourself in Latin terms that mean not a whole lot to a student who knows nothing of anatomy?

Especially if the experience of yoga is to invite you to know the whole of you—not yourself as a bunch of parts—let alone in Latin!

"Come on now, get into that piriformis!"

Or..."this is all about finding length in your psoas—so..."

Ugh.
Ouch.

The threat of teacher-student power-plays and guru-ship is close when we call places within us by terms that mean nothing to a student and serve to only claim power over the student—as in 'look, I know what things are called in medical textbooks and therefore you had better listen to me because I know more than you.'

Even with his vast medical / scientific studies, Moshe Feldenkrais was wise to call things in his classes by what a middle schooler would. Hips, knees, head, fingers.

Feldenkrais hoped that people would follow their own curiosity, be self-learners after just a little experiential reminder about how learning happens within human beings, perhaps within all creatures. Of course learning is a little different for each person—learning is a personal enterprise. Each person in Feldenkrais' class would have a different experience and a different 'result.' Maybe one person's self-learning would take that particular person into deeply studying anatomy books and such like Feldenkrais did himself. Maybe self-learning would draw out poetry from someone else in the same class. Maybe another a dance. Maybe another person—like Ruthy Alon did—is inspired to create a whole new body of work/play. Maybe another person becomes a much happier parent who calmed themselves through turning sensation into a guide, through moving and breathing and resting with sensation as the guide and letting other 'noise' quiet itself by tuning into something else for awhile, and can now return to their family having remembered their wholeness and the wholeness of ALL.

Wise, yes?

To 'guru,' or not to 'guru' ... ?

The roles of teachers and gurus are quite different, in my opinion.

Usually with gurus, we pledge some kind of allegiance to them and to their teaching. We trust that we will grow through them, through being connected to them and their teaching. All too often, too many of us do so without seriously questioning them or their teaching.

With a teacher, we are free to learn what we'd like, to take what's most helpful and let go of the rest.

Even then, we teachers with our students can create unnecessary and unhealthy power-dynamics with students that take away from both student and teacher discovering all we can of THE ALL.

In my opinion, anytime one tries to hold power over another or projects their own power onto another person, relationship is impossible. Same is true if we give our power away to a guru.

To give your power away to anyone—no matter how wise—so that that person can decide what you need to do misses the point . . . the invitation to find it oneself, to trust that the Universe, THE ALL, is reliable, that it / you / THE ALL can be trusted.

This could be true of anyone in any role, right?

WHERE YOU SIT MATTERS, TEACHER!

When I walk into someone's yoga class, I can get a very good sense of their politic—classroom, sexual, relational—by where they are in the room, by the tone of their voice, by their position and the position of their students.

Check it out. How do you feel in the room?

Triangles, squares, rectangles, circles . . . each classroom arrangement tells a story—especially in where we as the leader of the class or conversation chooses to sit in the room. Even worse, of course, is to stand over people who sit below us when we have no particular need to do so other than to inflict our power-issues on others 'below' us.

Platforms and the level of the leader with the students tell a story too. I have been in a number of yoga gatherings where the teacher—talking to a small group of eight of us—wanted to sit on a platform, a riser, to show us that what was being taught was important, that what he was conferring upon us was 'truth,' literally down onto us.

If you really think you are better than people, then by all means situate yourself in some arrangement where you are higher than everybody and where the only person with whom anyone else listening can make eye contact is you, the 'leader.' But don't be surprised when the Universe casts you down from your perch for the tangled mess that you are—that we all are.

In high school teaching, some of us used to call it 'sage on the stage' syndrome—the need somewhere maybe within each one of us of trying to make oneself more powerful than another and to privilege one's message over all others in weight and length.

NEW WAYS FORWARD
CAN WELCOME NEW WAYS FORWARD!

Set the room up in a circle or semi-circle and people can see one another and the conversation begins to happen more readily—with words or facial expressions and body language and more. We communicate in so many ways when we can face one another. Set the room up so that the only face someone can see is the teacher / leader and, well, you get the sense...'sage on the stage'...'guru.'

This of course depends on what the lesson involves! But if it's a conversation we're trying to have—an active back and forth with one another to know more together, to uncover together some larger vision of possibility . . . !

Try having a conversation among equals where everyone sits in rows and cannot see one another. Is it even possible?

Even an auditorium with a big rectangular setting and a stage set high off the ground where most people sit below the speaker—for very practical purposes in a large crowd—can be set up in such a way that is more conducive to eye contact and reaction and conversation. Maybe a few people are on the stage with the speaker where the speaker talks to and with those on the stage and those in the auditorium-seats . . . such an arrangement in a very locked-down, not-so-easy-to-change room like an auditorium can even improve the presentation when some mutuality is invited.

When the speaker is the only one talking in the room or even in a podcast—even if stringing out pearls of great wisdom—the opportunity for learning is lessened. Conversation—verbal or nonverbal—is communication, yes?

Communication . . . the word itself says a lot.

We need one another to learn, right? I have benefitted from all of my teachers—even the ones who were one-way-choo-choo-trains who just kept right on without letting any of us into the conversation.

Though the ones who invited me to have an <u>experience</u> of myself and the THE ALL—with as little of their commentary as possible—probably helped me the most.

Or when the teacher acts as a 'facilitator' who invites us to share through conversation and story-telling and story-listening something of our experiences—as each person is ready to share on their own terms and in their own time, . . . we can get a larger sense than just our own and than just the teacher's.

HOW TO INVITE 'THE ALL' . . . ?

We need one another to sense THE ALL. We need people to point out things for us to wonder about and test out.

Maybe the way I see and hear and feel is very limited—that I have limited myself in too many ways.

Maybe someone else's words will invite me to sense in new ways within my own self.

Maybe not, too.

THE ALL is vast—immeasurable.

The ALL includes you, me, the air, the breeze, the rock, the water, the bee, all creatures, the spaces between and among all of these and more, all possibilities . . . THE ALL.

My trying to fill the supposed 'space' between us with a lot of words or noise just might limit you from having a sense of THE ALL.

What can we say or do or offer that might help us all to know the fullness . . . THE ALL?

Sometimes —
often —
the best thing I can do is shut up.

To Sanskrit or OM or namaste, or not . . . ?

A lot of people get off on using big words and words from other languages to hold power over us—to show they know something more than I know . . . 'gurus' or teachers that hold power over us by trying to create an air of mystery.

I've done it before.

And when I have, I've missed an opportunity to meet the person with whom I'm talking.

When one holds power over the other, communication is impossible...

meeting the 'other' is impossible, relationship is impossible.

When I hold power over another, the 'other' and I cannot dance and relate—to give and receive and sense when to move in and when to give way and when to allow and when to receive and when to step in and step out. Such an awareness is the 'divine marriage' unfolding <u>with</u> one another. Permeability.

ON BRIDGES AND BORROWING

If we study language deeply, we discover that 'language' is ultimately sounds that are recognized with some mutual meaning unfolding between the 'sounder' and the 'hearer.' Language is where both 'sounder' and 'hearer' try to sound out meaning with one another. Communication.

In *Truth and Method* (1993), Hans-Georg Gadamer talks about communication and language as building a bridge between one another, working out meaning with one another.

I kind of like that.

'Language' is a story of borrowing, right? It's not like 'English' or 'Sanskrit' or any language emerged from the ground or the air or anywhere. It's the hard work of generations meeting one another and colliding with one another and finding some way to communicate with one another and then beginning the slippery-slope of assuming words have meaning, of guessing we're really understanding one another.

And recognizable words, of course, do not emerge in vacuums, in small pockets or silos that we call 'English' or 'Spanish' or 'Sanskrit' or whatever. Language is permeable. Words get borrowed and created and re-purposed across the divides of one another.

And we bring forward meaning with them. At least we hope so.

Sometimes dogs and cats and pre-verbal human-babies are more percep-
tive of the tone-meaning of adult-humans speaking words than adult-humans trying to parse out meaning through word-choice and all, right?
Have you noticed this too?

I think it's fine to use Sanskrit in classes—especially as we hearken
back to the roots of whatever we think 'yoga' was 3000 - 5000 years
ago in the Indus River Valley. I have obviously done that with this
book—and I hope I have done so in a way that invites each one of
us to have our own experience of what I'm playfully guessing the
most ancient yogins had in the Indus River Valley long before anything was written down as 'the way it should be if it's yoga'—when
ancient human-creatures were creating and playfully wondering and
figuring it all out just as we 21st-century human-creatures are trying
to do the same.

IGNORANCE AND 'THE ALL'

A friend of mine once told me that she lost interest in her religion
when its rituals moved from an ancient language to English instead.
"It lost its mystery," she said, a person who had been part of this religion her whole life but never had any interest in knowing the ancient
language that was being spoken. "It lost its mystery." What it lost in
my opinion was the power-dynamic of some sage-on-the-stage trying
to mediate a powerful experience for people instead of allowing the
participants to have that experience for themselves, on their own
terms. In a sense, by speaking only in that ancient language to the
congregation, the sage-on-the-stage preserved their own ministerial
air of mystery and special knowledge. Consciously or not, that minister set up a power-dynamic between self as minister/mediator and
their congregants.

Sure, the minister could have been more of a bridge between the deep-
past of the religious tradition and the congregant-friends. The minister
could have taught the congregants the ancient language so that they
too could bring forth on their own some of its great and important wis-

dom from the basements of the past. The minister could have talked in ways that connect the congregants with the tradition and that ancient language—a move that might inspire their own self-learning. Or the minister could talk and act as if the minister were the only one who knew and would be content to keep it that way—the air of 'mystery' and knowledge that would keep the minister separate from their congregants, the minister's followers.

Power-dynamics. We can create them in our 'relationships' with people in all too many ways—often perhaps to ensure that we have some value to the group, that we are needed and important and able to fulfill some special role that no one else can fulfill.

Or we can trust that all of our gifts are needed, that no one has 'special gifts'—that all things can be discovered and learned and brought forward in new ways—maybe even more helpful ways—and that no one needs to have a lock on anything.

Power-dynamics like this of course happen not just in religious congregations but in yoga classes and all areas of life.

Using words to hold power over one another as 'teacher' over 'student' makes relating with one another—communication—impossible.

Then should we never use Sanskrit in our classes? In my opinion, of course not.

I use Sanskrit (or Hebrew or Greek or whatever) when it seems appropriate and helpful—and I hope I do so in a spirit of inviting people to be curious about the past, about the wisdom of the past—in a spirit of inviting them to find out for themselves and to share in the circle, in classes, what they've discovered.

Such a strategy invites us all to learn, I hope —

and fashions the class to be about something way more than all the wisdom that I have accrued as 'teacher.'

TO OM OR NOT TO OM...

And for us to assume that the most ancient yogins – long before the first Vedic / yogic writings originated—OM'ed at the end of their practice or whatever is completely ridiculous. We don't have the recordings, friends. And whatever was written about them was probably multiple generations removed.

Maybe they did OM. Maybe they didn't. Maybe they made a different sound.

I love to OM.

For us to assume that OM is 'the universal sound'—no matter how much I like it or how good it feels in my belly and my chest and my head when I OM—is ridiculous. Why take on someone else's teaching without wondering about it yourself?

As much as I love to OM, some days it feels better to me to make a different sound. To play with it. To sense what feels best today, and then sense again tomorrow and be able to lean into what is good, what feels good, what is most helpful for me—and not to be attached to it or any particular feeling and to allow my students the same freedom. Walt Whitman was onto that, yeah? His 'barbaric yawp'—his whole invitation of *Leaves of Grass* is just that. I often think he knew more about 'yoga' than most yoga practitioners I've met.

If we do invite our students to OM—and I certainly do sometimes—we might be wise to let them have the experience of it—the vibe, the sound, within and throughout the room, the feeling, THE ALL—without trying to convince them that OM is 'the universal vibration' . . . wherever or whenever that overlay emerged.

One's own experience can lead to THE ALL. Someone imposing a power-dynamic to any situation usually gets in the way of knowing THE ALL.

Telling people the way it should be—even these too-many words I've assembled here—limit the experience, and even hide it—as some linguistic scholars guess that language actually <u>hides</u> meaning. My hope is that all my words here help to pull back my / our assumptions about yoga so we ALL can better know and experience more often THE ALL.

To chakra, or not to chakra . . . ?

I do something with my 'chakras' every morning as part of my personal practice / play.

That being said, I'm not sure they exist.

Again, let's not let someone else's experience prevent us from having our own experience. Let's not assume that someone saying there are 'chakras' or wheels of energy spinning like disks around the center-line—the shushumna nadi—are real . . . no matter how 'wise' the person is!

Have your own experience! Today! Tomorrow! Forever!

What happens within you as you touch places within yourself and breathe naturally and stare out the window and discover what bubbles up within you?

Try resting a hand on a joint—say an elbow—and see what happens. Or even just imagine doing so.

Try resting a hand on your belly just below your ribs in the center of yourself—what happens?

Try anywhere on your body that feels right and is easy to reach.

There is something there, everywhere, yeah? And strange and wonderful :)

Call it chakra or whatever. Or just enjoy the sensation.

Regarding the wisdom of meditation . . .
to side with Hinduism,
or to side with Buddhism, or what?

Too often we forget the origins of human experience that eventually got concretized in religious ritual—ritual being a prescribed thing and too often not an invitation to sense and choose what's best.

We'd be wise to have our own experience, yes?

Of course sometimes people like myself (non-Hindu & non-Buddhist) forget the great tension between Buddhism and yoga with its Hindu/ Vedic roots. Gautama, after all, is the real live human being who grew up living out the Vedic-inspired life that today we would call 'Hinduism' and who had tried all the yoga of his day in what we call northern India where he lived; yet he did not find enlightenment in any of the yoga of his day. He found that he continued to suffer, that even as relaxed as he was there was still something within himself holding him back from bliss, from enlightenment.

"Ah, but it's all changed so much, right? What we have in the 21st century is so much better—you know, with 200 & 300-hour yoga teacher trainings and all, right?"

Far from it, of course.

Gautama did not find enlightenment in the shapes/asanas of yoga,
nor in very deep and detailed meditation instruction,
nor in ritual,
nor devotion (bhakti yoga = religious devotion),
not even in selfless service alone (karma yoga),
not in raja yoga, the 'royal path' which is essentially all of these paths above . . .

Gautama found enlightenment
in something much simpler (and way more complex):

noticing sensation within his own body and finding some way of preventing himself from becoming attached to any sensation in particular —

to let go of his craving for lovely feelings
and to let go of his tendency to push away the not-so-lovely feelings —

to be with them all, with every sensation,
to let them all be.

And to do that—let everything be without needing to try to change anything—with people too. Even despised presidents of every generation!

And you can too. Find a place that is relatively comfortable for you—a chair, a cushion, whatever—so that you are supported by the earth enough that you CAN observe the coming and going of sensation. Nothing lasts for long now does it? Not even the concrete parking lot over there. Come back in 50 years and it will be cracked and penetrated by weeds—if it's even there! Your body too will change quite a bit in 50 years. Your body is changing from second to second.

Why let ourselves be attached to much of anything, huh? This is Gautama's grand realization—and it's in this that we too might find liberation, freedom, enlightenment, samadhi, bliss.

SEEK NO GURU EXCEPT YOUR OWN EXPERIENCE

Find out for yourself, why don't you? Put no trust in Gautama—neither as wise human being nor as Buddha / enlightened one. Sit and find out yourself.

Yes, your thoughts will go every which way and dart to places and memories and future dreams and why that blind over the window leaks just that little bit of light and how in the world you still smell like hot sauce when you ate that two days ago—how your thoughts will dart anywhere and everywhere you don't want them to go. Ah, this is good. Greet this madness with a kiss.

Yes! Kiss some place that is you. Especially when such 'madness' sets in.

It's a heck of a lot easier and friendlier greeting yourself with a kiss than getting mad at yourself for something that, well, just might be beyond your control. And who wants to control anything? I haven't found control very helpful with much of anything. When I lived at Abbey of Gethsemani for a summer a few decades back, the monks with whom I lived and worked would often tell the story of fellow meditator and spiritual writer Thomas Merton. He used to say the same about control and the hogs he tended at the monastery—try to force the hog to go and it'll dig in its heels. Be with the hog, let the hog know you're interested and present and the hog might just go through the gate on its own. And what a gift!

In my experience, breakthrough is on the other side of days when I sit and my thoughts go absolutely every which way. As long as I be with myself, greet myself in this madness, stay with myself, kiss myself. And if a breakthrough doesn't yet come, so what. I'm still alive and can try again tomorrow and tomorrow and tomorrow after that and discover for myself what shows up. Greet it all with a kiss and life is so much, well, so much.

After ALL, enlightenment is not earned or accrued. Enlightenment or bliss arrives . . . how we do not know. Much like the wind, the breeze.

Maybe there's wisdom in taking what's helpful now, appreciating its helpfulness now and letting go of what's not helpful now—AND committing to come back to what's not helpful now to see if some day it very well might be helpful!

To reject nothing outright, and instead put it aside for now with love—this might be the wisest thing we can do. After all, everything is within THE ALL, right?

To myofascial-release, or not . . . ?

Do you want to work with the tissue that seems painful and feels tied in knots or do you want to work with what organizes the tissue into knots or no knots? (the nervous system)

That's Moshe Feldenkrais' greatest insight. Check it out.

That's how he walked on a knee that had three compromised ligaments.

I used to teach myofascial-release styled yoga classes. I do not anymore.

Sure, like massage, they can feel good. And sometimes I need that 'feel good' experience. And indeed, 'feel good' is a sensation, and a helpful one to recognize when we are not too attached to it, when we don't expect 'feel good' to happen every time with our efforts — 'feel good' is not THE ALL.

Something special happens when we know the whole of ourselves. If I'm going to seek out massage now or ask a lover to massage me, I request it to be Esalen-style. (Esalen® is a retreat center in Big Sur, CA where much of the human potential movement gained traction in the 1970s. Some of Feldenkrais' best work and teaching indeed happened there. The massage-style associated with Esalen® has nothing — or at least very little — to do with Feldenkrais' Method in particular, though they do share the wisdom of knowing the 'whole' instead of just a bunch of parts.) And what a gift it is to knowing gently my whole self. And then so many of my troubles disappear!

To asana-only or meditate-only, or what?

Indeed there are whole schools of yoga — ancient, medieval and modern — that espouse only one shape (seated meditation with crossed ankles) as the requirement for any possibility of enlightenment and that the other shapes are merely distractions.

I have to say that I love to sit in meditation and I love to move in other shapes too. Don't get me wrong. But all this hopefully makes you wonder as it does me!

We'll all need to find our own way, perhaps with some helpful input from others and teachers past and present, input that we try on and wonder about, input that we decide upon if it's truly helpful for me in this moment of my life or not.

Though it's important to remember, as Gautama reminds, that enlightenment doesn't come from knowing what to do, it comes from doing, being with — 'practice.'

To offer or accept hands-on adjustments, or not . . . ?

I've had some of the best-trained hands of yoga adjust me and injure me.

Even with decades of training, many yoga teachers' hands are still not sensitive enough to be helpful to me. It's often taken me weeks to get back on track after someone adjusts me during a yoga class. Feldenkrais-trained or Healing Touch-trained hands are a very different story — especially since they aren't trying to correct or change anything . . . these disciplines seek to meet the person where the person is without any need to change . . . and almost always the person changes. Such is love.

I've had plenty of teachers — men and women — let their hands wander over me in what I would deem to be inappropriate ways. If they were my lover and we were alone at home, such touch would be one thing. In a yoga class — nada.

So when I go to yoga classes more recently, I've made it gently and clearly known to the teacher / leader that I do not want hands-on adjustments during the class. Sure, sometimes they get upset that I make that request, but it doesn't matter—it's my body, it's my choice.

VERBAL CUES vs. HANDS-ON ADJUSTMENTS

After I was certified to teach yoga, something within me realized that I would be getting in the way of my student-participants' own explorations of their own selves if I was walking around the room and using my hands or just my fingertips to make even the slightest hints of adjustments, that student-participants would become sensitive to my presence instead of sensitive to their own body and their own sensations.

Quickly, I learned the wisdom of staying put and out of the way when working with anyone who has experienced trauma. (Anymore, this is pretty much all of us, in some sad way.)

And indeed standing over someone creates a power-dynamic. If I'm standing over you as you sit or even lie on the ground, how would you feel as I look down at you?

So I try to keep my eyes at the same level as my students—a move that seeks to remember that we are co-learners with one another, that there is as little of a power-dynamic as possible.

And sure there are times when we as teachers and yoga-leaders do indeed need to get up . . . to close a door that was opened and not shut by a late-arriver, to adjust the temperature in the room, etc. And anytime I do get up to do that, I try to as simply as possible explain what I'm about to do when I get up so that people do not jump or freeze at my movements through our shared space—so that they can anticipate my moving around the room has nothing to do with them individually, that they are free to explore in their own safe ways for themselves without worrying that I'm seeing something that they are doing 'wrong' and then getting up to correct.

If I see someone doing something that I think will be not so helpful or even painful for their body during any movement classes I share, I offer a general verbal cue to the whole group, something to be sensitive to in this shape or this move. Almost never do I even call out the person's name so that they do not feel picked on—unless it's a last resort and the person didn't take the hint and I think the shape they've chosen is going to be problematic for them.

A lot of people really enjoy some simple presence during savasana—like having the teacher-leader come around and place their hands on them as they relax on the ground. A lot of teachers I know use oil / aromatherapy. Hopefully, the teacher-leader has received permission from everybody about touch and oil, and has announced clearly where they will touch, etc.!

We do not use oils / aromatherapy at VITALITY because we've found a lot of people are allergic to smells or the smells exacerbate their asthma—even with the so-called 'purest' brands. I use aromatherapy quite a bit in my personal life and recommend it highly for anyone who has no allergies to them. But as for using them in the room at VITALITY, we never do because the smells linger. A lot of us like the smells, for sure! A lot of us have allergic reactions to them—and we want to choose to do things at VITALITY that honor every person, not just the majority and not just a few.

I GET OUT OF THE WAY...INVITING PARTICIPANTS TO TOUCH

As for hands-on work in yoga trainings and classes, I like to invite anyone who wants to to pair up with one another (with someone they trust) and assist one another very simply in savasana. Very simply.

I encourage the pair to check in and make sure touching feet or ankles is okay with one another—and ONLY feet and ankles—and I remind everyone that they can change their mind later and no one will be offended. 'It's YOUR experience,' I remind people. Sometimes people feel more comfortable and at ease with a blanket covering their feet. Great. Give yourself what you need.

I encourage the one in savasana to find a way to relax using any props and any position they choose for themselves. And if it's alright with this person to receive a light touch on their feet (directly on their feet or over the blanket, as both are comfortable) in savasana, I encourage the person assisting to find a way to sit comfortably and close to the savasana-person's feet. It's important that this assistant be comfortable, to build a little nest for themself where they can be as still and calm as possible. If the assistant is tense, that tension can be communicated even with the lightest touch!

With that touch, with that very light yet comfortable connection—hands of one on the feet or ankles or blanket of the other—I might offer a few words to assist one another in coming back to noticing their own natural breath. And then I shut up for a good stretch of minutes—5? 10? 15?—and let them have their experience.

It's not massage. It's not time to get up and try to re-arrange the person's body. It's just sit there and breathe and relax and sense what happens with such light touch.

When the time is right, I invite them to switch roles silently, so as not to stir up a lot of thoughts with a bunch of words.

Quite amazing what happens with presence, with touch—in some safe place of each person's body—in an experience like this.

THE SIMPLE POWER OF HEALING TOUCH

It's what nurse Janet Mentgen discovered in hospital settings with her patients. It's what medical doctor Brugh Joy discovered with his patients. After studying with Brugh Joy and a number of other healers—medical and non-medical types—Janet Mentgen founded Healing Touch Program®. Something happens with the smallest nudge—in this case the smallest touch. And it doesn't even need to be a touch! Even having one's hands just off the person's body seems to make a difference too.

There is something incredible to this Nature, this human body, when we give Nature a chance . . . !

And we don't need some ceremony to pass on the skills to be this Nature, we don't need to pass energy from some gifted teacher to another to be able to offer Healing Touch . . . as seems to be the case in reiki (which is a wonderful practice, a wonderful certification I've enjoyed, for sure).

Healing Touch is the democracy of energy-sharing . . . the recognition that we all have the gift and power to make a difference when we show up.

To bring us back to our conversation before about 'hands-on' in yoga classes . . . when Nature meets Nature—in this case, person meets person with touch or even without touch in savasana in a yoga class—incredible things can happen. Especially when we're attentive to staying out of the way of the person relaxing in savasana—one reason I recommend feet instead of head or hands or anything else as the place to touch on the person in savasana.

As for adjusting people's bodies <u>when I'm the teacher-leader</u> either while participants are moving or while they are resting still in savasana in a yoga class . . . I try to stay out of people's way and never do that myself. For a lot of reasons.

To hot yoga, or not to hot yoga . . . ?

My house every summer is hot yoga...no A/C!

I get the charge from it, from the warmth, the sweat, all of it.

I also get the importance of being in our environment, meeting it, of moving and breathing and resting in the environment in which we spend most of our time each day.

Sure, hot yoga can acclimate us to a greater range of environments. Much like saunas do in winter. I often meditate in saunas.

But deep stretches in hot environments? Are you sure you want to <u>stretch</u> those deep ligaments that deeply? They are what keep you upright in gravity! Do you want those places of stability AND flexibility—your joints—to become loose and overcooked-noodle-like?

Inviting ligaments to lengthen, to find their length, well, that's an entirely different thing, isn't it?

People who think that yoga is about stretching, in my humble opinion, do not really understand what this is all about.

The fitness craze in the US has taken on hot yoga as a sibling, and what a gift that yoga is finding a home in so many new people's lives.

My sister teaches hot yoga, and I enjoy it when I take her classes. For sure.

But to do this every day? I'm not so sure.

To nude yoga, or not to nude yoga . . .?

I've participated in many nude yoga classes over the years.

Some of them have a 'back-to-nature' vibe that I quite enjoy.

The freedom of feeling the air with your whole being. Even your asshole, your armpits, your genitalia, your whole self. How often do you notice your whole self? without any need for shame or embarrassment or whatever? Honestly, this is the biblical tradition that a lot of people would rather forget—what the prophets (ecstatic-visionary-healers) were doing on the hillsides 3000 years ago. The whole story is referenced in 1 Samuel of the Bible—though so few read it and wonder about it.

Perhaps what Samuel and his gang were doing is pretty close to what the most ancient yogins were doing too . . . perched there on the edge of the Indus River, who knows?!

The wind has its wild and wonderful ways.

It can be lovely.

I've participated in nude yoga classes that were closer to sex too ("okay, let's all stand here in the circle and put your genitalia in the circle" — actual quote) and not my cup of tea.

But one thing that has interested me quite a bit is when I do yoga at home or in a nude yoga class . . . there is a freedom to more than being naked. Clothes can hold any human body in shapes, and even loose clothing can prevent anybody from moving in all the helpful ways that a person might want to move. Clothes act as an outer fascia, an outer binding. Sometimes that might feel protective and helpful, at other times less helpful and actually restrictive. Move around a bit in clothes and you might sense it too.

To be free of clothes and to move with the breeze — well, it can be pretty sweet. Especially — and most importantly! — when the teacher stays on their own mat and verbally cues the class and keeps their hands to themselves, no matter how loving their hands are.

To 'ida' and 'pingala' or not, to right side first or left side first or not worry about it all because there's more than 'masculine' and 'feminine' anyway . . . ?

The ancient wisdom of yoga and tai chi is that the right side of the body (with the left hemisphere of the brain) is masculine — pingala.

And then the left side of the body (and right hemisphere of the brain) is feminine—ida.

And the wisdom has often been to do the right side of two-sided shapes first before the left side, the doing 'both' that is the process of welcoming the divine marriage of masculine and feminine within ourselves. (Those who KNOW themselves, of course, know there is no right-side of a shape or left-side of a shape . . . there is only one's whole body in this shape, one's whole body in another shape.)

I've said much about the divine marriage throughout this text. I like the idea very much, find it very helpful. Beautiful even.

All that being said, what if ida and pingala and the divine marriage do not exist, are conceptions of our imaginations—much like 'leg' is—as a leg does not exist without a heart pumping blood and nutrients to it and drawing wastes away from it and a leg does not move without a nervous system that coordinates something finding the ground below so that something can move forward or back or up or down. What if focusing on 'anatomical parts' like leg or 'energetic parts' like ida and pingala cloud us from knowing something else, from glimpsing the whole, THE ALL . . . huh? what if . . . ?

Even the 'divine marriage' that I so love might make me think that there is something I need <u>to do</u> to make the whole happen, that I need to do this and this and this—as in unite masculine and feminine or whatever—to make THE ALL come about.

THE ALL, the infinite, cannot be divided. Otherwise it's not the infinite, after all.

There's nothing that anyone needs to <u>do</u> to make THE ALL come about. It's always there . . . THE ALL.

Are there things we do to wake ourselves up to the reality of the indivisible ALL? Sure.

'NEW' WAYS HAVE ALWAYS BEEN AROUND

In the 21st century, we're just beginning to wake up to the reality that has always been with us—that there might be more than 'masculine' and 'feminine' gender-characteristics, more than 'male' and 'female' gender, more than 'man' and 'woman.' This reality—of third genders or more genders than male and female—has most certainly been with us since the beginnings of human creation on this earth. Even the most ancient Vedic / yoga texts reference this third gender possibility.

Some cultures even revere 'third gender' people as the shamans, as the ones who know more than two possibilities and contain then all possibilities, sometimes even in their genitalia.

So I'm not all that convinced of the need to do right side first to honor the masculine and then left side second to honor the feminine.

I am more interested in THE ALL.

It's a big, big life . . . what labels or categories could possibly embrace THE ALL?

To kundalini yoga or big-set pranayama, or not . . . ?

A number of my teachers encouraged me a great deal with pranayama, and I am grateful to have worked up to big, long sets of pranayama of some significant level for a number of years. Everything I've done and experienced, I'm sure, has been to the benefit of where I am this very moment.

And some friends teach transformational breath and kundalini classes which I enjoy when I take them every now and then.

Everything can be a nudge, a helpful nudge.

It's the every-day thing that I wonder about.

FUN & DIFFERENT DRILLS IN SPORTS

When I was coaching golf and swimming, we put a lot of time and attention on drills—on doing things out of the ordinary in the same sport to encourage a new feel for the club / golf-swing or feel in the pool. For instance, in golf, to hit one hundred yard shots with a 6-iron and a much-shortened swing. (Someone of my size and experience would normally hit a 6-iron about 180 yards.). Or we'd go out and play a round with just a few clubs to nudge ourselves out of habits that might be limiting us.

In swim-coaching, we would do a lot of drill-work early in the practice to promote a feel for catching the water . . . the athletes I coached were fond of these 24 x 25 sets, as we called them. It was a set I had inherited from other coaches—gratefully. By the end of that set each day, these beginner competitive swimmers had an amazing feel for the water. And if they lost that feel as we did the challenging main-set later, all I had to do was remind about one thing and something within each swimmer's whole stroke 'remembered' and improved.

That's what a drill does. That's was a nudge does. We find our natural rhythm again with that technique, with the tool and then we can let it go to go after the bigger things—full swings that are different every time on the golf course (different ground, different distances, different conditions, different hole placements, different wind) and competitive swimming with the wave generated by all swimmers, a wave that's different in every lane too.

THE NUDGES OF YOGA-PRACTICE

I suspect that's the purpose of pranayama, of asana . . . to do something that nudges us out of our doldrums and into realizing THE ALL. Probably true of every limb, yes? Having compassion for and responding nonviolently to an oppressor—as the first limb (yamas) invites—would nudge me out of my habitual reaction toward violence (in word or deed or thought) and into a new possibility.

Maybe all those pranayama sets and kundalini classes prepared me for the rigors of vipassana meditation that I enjoy now a great deal and have found the teaching there to be the culmination of most of my fields of study.

Some people find lots of pranayama and kundalini yoga helpful for them. Good for them.

Some people like myself find smaller nudges like vipassana meditation helpful. Good for us.

Even when I let go of all those pranayama sets and such—all those things that are bigger than 'nudges' in my opinion—and when I sit in meditation for long spells of time and do nothing in particular with my breath other than to watch it and its natural rhythm, I'm amazed that a big breath comes out of nowhere . . .

as if something within me, some deeper intelligence, knows what is needed, knows to nudge me, my breath, in a certain direction, in a certain way, and then . . .

something new comes about within me.

Ruthy Alon points out that a yawn will do the same thing, will nudge us out of our pattern and into some new awareness, an awakening. Pets know that too, right? They get up from a nap and stretch and yawn.

It might not take much to know health, to remember wholeness . . . THE ALL. Maybe just a nudge.

Sense what works for you, friend. And if you're wise, let what nudges you be small and slow and gentle.

To heal, or not to heal . . . ?

Healing is not curing. Healing includes the 'things' we do to remember it's all one whole . . . THE ALL . . . such is healing, 'wholing.'

Anyone who tells me they know what they are doing to heal me or someone . . . I run from them!

Healing might be as simple as being in touch with the natural world that welcomes healing. Worked for Florence Nightingale, yeah?

And let's not forget that a human being is an example of 'the natural world'—so when a human touches another human, in ways that relax and calm both people, as I invited a few pages earlier, should we be surprised when healing or even curing happens?

To ritual, or not to ritual . . . ?

I grew up Catholic, with an appreciation for the Mass and for ritual and how it indeed could usher us through crises and hard times.

I've also appreciated the beauty of puja...the flowers, the bows, the water, all the elements prescribed in Vedic / yogic practice aimed toward devotion (bhakti).

Maybe there is indeed a time for them, for it ALL.

However . . . if you're following somebody else's script instead of what arises in the moment, how can you ever know THE ALL in this particular moment?

It's much like sex....sex that seems scripted, roled, assigned, or that falls into a predictable pattern is much different from real lovemaking, love-enjoying, real meeting one another in the moment, responding to invitations to sensation, yes?

Yoga teachers sometimes read or call out a bunch of shapes and expect something to happen in a class. And yes, it can, something can happen in a class like this. However it might be more in the 'how' than it is in the 'what,' right?

I really don't think there is any 'magic' that happens by doing a bunch of movements or asanas with little awareness. I'll be quite bold, at least to some, and say there is no 'magic' to any of the yoga-shapes in themselves. This will wrankle a lot of my dear friends!

The 'magic' happens when I tune in to myself with all my senses, most often by moving slowly so I can take it all in. Later, moving more quickly might be nice too . . . though if I really want to welcome some change in my body or in my life, moving slowly—on mat and off—seems to be the most helpful thing for me and the students with whom I've been honored to learn together.

I sense. I choose what's best for me and my world right now.

Rituals just might take me out of sensation and into trying to remember what comes next.

To lotus, or not to lotus . . . ?

When I first began yoga, lotus was the goal for a lot of teachers and students. Maybe it was just the trend at the time. A number of my early teachers (NOT Larry and Amber!) made two goals (!) for me of being able to get my feet flat on the ground in downward-facing-dog and of sitting in full lotus—goals to which I didn't really consent. Today, we know that such a way as this of expressing downward-facing-dog is not only less dynamic and less available to respond to the moment—trying to get my feet flat on the mat in downdog actually causes a whole lot of grief and pain in most human bodies, from neck to low back to heels to ankles to toes. The more recent 'slightly bent knees are wise and available knees' we sometimes hear in yoga classes seems very wise to me in downward-facing-dog, in a lot of things!

When I was studying tai chi before yoga about twenty five years ago, I remember reading and hearing often that sitting in lotus was much less energetically helpful than standing and 'holding the ball'—the first move in many styles of martial arts training a beginner learns, standing with feet shoulder width, arms in front of one's chest as if holding a beach ball, knees slightly bent. Students are encouraged to learn to rest (!) in this shape, and even and eventually up to 1-2 hours at a time!

I've had some wild and helpful experiences 'holding the ball'—for sure!

IF YOU GOTTA SIT...

In any case, I used to sit half-lotus in yoga classes—at the invitation of my early yoga teachers—and could feel ligaments being pulled in ways that were not so helpful to walking, living, doing whatever I needed or wanted to do, on my yoga mat or off.

Finding a comfortable seat—ankles crossed and hips on a high or low cushion, or sitting on the front of a chair with feet on the ground for support, or whatever—is way different and way more important than just pushing oneself into lotus.

As they teach in vipassana meditation, it's not the shape of your body that leads to enlightenment, it's the attention to sensation and noticing the impermanence of everything and the equanimity that comes with such attention to the world within oneself and oneself alone.

Again, score one for Gautama who tried all the teachings of yoga and did not find enlightenment—but who found a new way. Did he use some of the yoga teachings he'd been taught? Of course. Did he have an experience—enlightenment!—that re-ordered some of the teachings and even led to letting go of some teachings that once seemed so important? Sure did.

Bring Gautama's realizations to movement practices like tai chi and yoga and even the weight room or pavement or pool (or anything) and the helpful sparks might just start flying!

To 'flat back, straight spine' . . . or to 'relaxed long back, naturally-curved and movement-informed spine'?

If your back has no curves to it, you must be dead.

So let that knowledge of yourself, of your body, inform the way you consider thinking about your spine, talking about your spine, and invite your yoga-leaders to do the same.

Sense those beautiful curves to your spine. Sense the ways they change as you move, even as you breathe.

Incredible. Amazing this human body!

What can we say instead of 'flat back' that is more true to who we are as human-creatures doing anything, including making yoga-shapes?

What is it we really want our students or ourselves to experience when we say 'flat back'?

Maybe 'find length' or 'gently take the crown of your head away from your tailbone until you feel a slight lengthening in your spine' or a million other possibilities . . . !

Consider studying Ruthy Alon's Movement Intelligence® to find ways of finding length and tallness without a muscular cost, i.e. without that 'pull your belly to your spine' cue that can get a lot of people into self-limiting trouble in yoga and in a lot of movement classes. Ruthy's onto something!

To pose / posture, or not to pose / posture?

The Sanskrit word 'asana' all too often gets translated as 'pose' in English—and to our loss!

What comes to mind when you say 'pose' to yourself?

How is the word 'pose' used in your life, in our larger culture?

'Posture' might be even more harmful. Do you really want to be a 'post'? Or if someone is posturing when they talk, what does that insinuate?

In this book, I've opted for the word 'shape'—hopefully with the realization that no shape is static, that you are constantly moving in one single asana, when you breathe, when you sense yourself and decide you need to move something within you to have more support—heck, I'd even argue that sensing yourself changes the shape even before you decide you need to move!

I like the word 'shape' for now—though my hope is that someone will come up with something better the more and more we all dig ourselves and one another out of the limitations of the 'pose' and 'posture' coffin.

To willpower through your cravings, or find another way . . . ?

I've willpowered my way through MANY cravings—sugar, alcohol / stopping at the bar for a beer or two when I was lonely, sex. I've set up millions of self-improvement plans and projects to make me 'a better person.'

Blah, blah, blah.

None of them ever worked.

Curiously to me, when I let go the need for getting rid of any habit in my life and simply loved myself, the cravings for whatever was ruling my world that week lessened.

Loving one's own self is probably the most difficult thing we can take on. And the most important.

Can you love the tangled mess that you are?

There's a reason that Jesus suggested we love our enemies. Maybe he didn't know the whole mimesis phenomenon that we played with in an earlier invitation—that we tend to have the same qualities that we can't stand or even hate in others. Maybe he did understand that. Being alone in the desert can teach us such things quickly . . . that our enemies are just like us, that we ourselves are flawed just as they are, that love could be the answer for our enemies and for one's own self.

Whatever is the case, when we love our enemies, when we find some way of offering love to a person who annoys us or even greatly angers us, that love for the other person can come back to us. When we love our 'enemies' we indeed are in some deep way loving those qualities in ourselves that we can't stand either.

There are a lot of opportunities that involve giving up our addictions to smoking and drinking and drugs and sex and food and more . . . and the opportunity that has helped me the most was vipassana meditation. Check it out: dhamma.org.

To experiment, or not to experiment?

Do you think the ancient yogins of the Indus River Valley—the very first generation of people moving and breathing and resting—were following some special protocol about how or when to move, how or when to breathe, how or when to rest, how or when or what to eat, how or when to have sex or not?

Surely not.

The next generations of yoga-practitioners after these first-experimenters were more than likely the ones writing down what they saw their grandparents doing. And then as those first-experimenters died out, the grand experiment of sensing for oneself and figuring out for oneself died too, and the game became one of following what someone else said, following what the later generations saw the first-experimenters doing, following prescribed words either in person or by reading a text or memorizing some formulation within a text (or what would soon become a text, if indeed these things were first orally passed down, as they more than likely were).

THE BRILLIANCE OF LARRY SCHULTZ

I love the story Larry Schultz often shared of how he developed The Rocket. Larry studied seven years with Pattabhi Jois and Austin's Stan Hafner, a protege of Jois. I had the pleasure of taking a class with Stan a few years ago, he's brilliant and creative and fun and wisely experimental in his teaching—loved it! While Larry was studying with Jois those seven years, Larry started wondering why everything that Jois had taught him was so regimented—same moves, same order, every day. Jois had said too—as he told everyone it seems in *Guruji*, the book about him—that all the moves and shapes of the secondary series and third series were off limits until primary series was accomplished. This really bothered Larry. It would bother me too.

Secondary series has some leg-splits and Larry found that after seven years of yoga, seven years of studying primary series, his attempts at the splits were very feeble—as he told me when I visited him in Sonoma at Nauliland. "Why didn't you start me on this years ago?" he asked Jois. "Primary series first," Jois is said to have responded.

Larry eventually left Austin, TX and his studies with Jois and moved to the Bay Area and began teaching yoga and soon received a phone call from what turned out to be the Grateful Dead who would invite Larry to join them on tour that year.

Larry's only responsibility was to stay in his hotel room each day until the Dead came to him for their yoga class.

You never knew when sound-check would actually end, so Larry would stay in his room and practice yoga until they showed up. He practiced what he had learned from Jois – Larry even honored his teacher Jois by crafting a yoga manual for primary series and dedicating it to Jois at the urging of the Grateful Dead. And then in all those hotel-hours of doing yoga and waiting for the Grateful Dead to show up for their class, Larry became curious. He started noticing his hands and feet would sometimes end up in the same places, sometimes in different places— all with the same shape each day. Say like downward-facing-dog. He began to trace his hands and feet on his mat and notice the distances from each other, the symmetry and asymmetry of where his hands were or his feet were. And he simply became curious about these symmetries and asymmetries.

And he noticed that doing his standing asanas as Jois had instructed were difficult and painful not only for him but especially for his balance-challenged students. So he tried having his feet in arrangements different from Jois's teaching and found it was a lot easier for him and his students.

He began experimenting with changing the primary series that he had learned from Jois and found that his students enjoyed the variety each day—of doing something similar and in the same basic order but different standing shapes added in or subtracted out of the standing portion of the series, same with the seated and floor portions of the series. He noticed his students needed some core strength, so he added in some extra ab-strengtheners. He wanted the class to be more playful so he added in more inversions and was expert at breaking down complex inversions into small pieces so that everyone could get a taste of them and build up each day toward having the strength and self-awareness to be upside down in a variety of shapes and ways. (His student Amber Jean Espelage from whom I learned a great deal is an expert at building up little steps toward complex and fun inversions—perhaps even taking Larry's excellent teaching a step further into the future of yoga.)

Though he was despised by many for changing the primary series, Larry can easily be credited with beginning much of the yoga that is practiced in most yoga studios today . . . free-form vinyasa-style, power yoga, on and on . . . all these different styles that emerged from what Pattabhi Jois learned from Krishnamacharya as he taught twelve-year-old boys in Mysore, India.

KRISHNAMACHARYA'S PLAYFUL WISDOM

Indeed, research is now showing that Krishnamacharya was experimenting big-time in creating ashtanga-vinyasa yoga in the first place. According to N.E. Sjoman's excellent *The Yoga Tradition of the Mysore Palace* (1999), Krishnamacharya was simply trying to meet his class of 12-year-old boys where they were. And these boys knew British gymnastics, even studied gymnastics in the same room as they were learning yoga. So Krishnamacharya combined the yoga-shapes he knew (and that might have been pictured on the wall of the palace as Sjoman has in his book) with the hop-around fun of gymnastics and—voilà—ashtanga-vinyasa yoga was born.

Going all the way back to the roots of yoga in the Indus River Valley 3000 - 5000 years ago, it's all an experiment, right? Yoga always has been. If we're wise, it always will be.

It takes courage to experiment, and yet it is the first thing we knew how to do as babies . . . to play, to try things out, to discover what works, to find the easiest way.

The challenge comes when we listen to gurus, people who have or at least think they have found the best way.

But any 'guru' worth their salt will invite you into your own experience to discover what works best and avoid prescribing any one way as the only right way.

Might you end up doing the very thing that the guru would have told you to do had the guru prescribed something instead of invited you to find your own way through an experience?

Quite possibly.

And yet the path is much different when we figure it out on our own, when we sense and learn ourselves, when we make 'mistakes' this way, and then try something different that way.

Truly, for anyone who is committed to real learning, there are no mistakes. Feldenkrais says the same thing. Thomas Edison too when interviewed about the creation of the light bulb.

THANK 'THE ALL,' THE AGE OF THE GURUS IS OVER!

In my humble opinion, the age of the gurus is over—and we'd be wise to note that the greatest yogin of the modern era, Krishnamacharya, is said to have shunned the title 'guru,' though his students—Pattabhi Jois and BKS Iyengar among them—seemed to accept the title of guru from their devoted students. And they very clearly knew a heck of a lot less than their teacher, Krishnamacharya, though he got them started on their learning journey in such helpful ways!

Throughout this book and my other writings, I explore just how problematic hierarchical relationships are for real growth in any group—families, schools, businesses, governments, whatever. I would venture to say that the guru-model and hierarchical-relationship we have inherited from the past few millennia could be the biggest thing we need to shake off and begin again—maybe for the first time—RELATIONSHIP.

When there is a power-dynamic among people—of someone having more power than another—trouble Arises, and discovery-inspired learning has a difficult time emerging because we're always trying to figure out if those who are 'wiser' than us approve of our growth, if we're on the right track, etc.

So in the classrooms where I've been an active participant / co-leader, I've opted to reimagine square-relationships and triangle-relationships (hierarchy-based 'relationship') as circle-relationships . . . as all of us sitting together in a circle, each one of us with our varied and wonderful gifts and questions and insights. Sure, someone in the circle might have something to say that's important for you—maybe even the wisest person in the circle or the wisest person in the world. Though it's up to you to test out their wisdom, to test out what they say that you think is helpful and find out if it is indeed helpful for you. And if it is, great! If it's not, great!

And let's not forget that someone who has a lot less experience than you at something might just have the exact idea you need. Some of the best yoga classes I've taken have been led by new teachers.

And that's the wisdom of all of us being in a circle together. Sure, the wisest in the circle, the one with the most experience, might be the person to lead an experience or a conversation about something, and also maybe not. As long as this wise person is open and permeable to the ideas of anyone in the circle and can even let ideas that they think are even wrong be part of the conversation and even say gently, "Hmm, I haven't thought of it that way," or "I'm not sure, maybe that's true, I've found it in the past to be not so helpful for me or anyone I've known, but maybe I'm now ready to try out what you're saying, I'll have to think about that and test it out, thanks for bringing that up," the learning potential for everyone grows.

Of course, if someone brings up something dangerous or potentially harmful, I think it's very fair for the person with some experience to point this out to the group, to gently question it, without a lot of fanfare, perhaps with something like, "Yeah, I've done thousands of upward-facing-dogs in my lifetime and have found they really messed up my shoulders, even with the best alignment cues. You know, doing one up-dog with some awareness every now and then, for me anyway, probably could be very helpful and feel good. For sure. But my days of doing 70 of them in the morning and 70 of them in the afternoon as part of some ashtanga-based sequence are over—and probably were when I was just a teenage kid too! Hahaha. We all need to find our way though, right?"

There are gentle ways to invite everyone in the circle to find their own way. The ways that we speak make a huge difference, right?

All that being said, though, blindly following anyone—no matter their title or credentials or charisma—is a recipe for disaster.

To practice religion, to be devoted to the divine, or not . . . ?

Bhakti or worship / devotion to gods/goddesses/God (no matter the religion) is a wonderful beginning. Stay here your whole life though and you'll never know the experience of the One, THE ALL, you revere—and that experience is what the revered ones beckon us to know.

Once we get a whiff of THE ALL, things seem to change quickly . . . a paradigm shift is upon us . . .

some become a creature that follows no rules . . .

why? because they don't even need any rules
because of their ultimate respect for ALL creatures
because rules are usually created as barriers to protect creatures
and when someone already does that based on their experience of THE ALL...

what need is there for rules or laws?

Someone who gets a whiff often of THE ALL
has no need for rituals,
no need for any prescribed disciplines of any kind,

no need for sacred space because IT'S ALL sacred,
not even any need for 'sacred' ancient stories
(although I love them dearly!!!) . . .

why?

because such an enlightened person—one who knows THE ALL—freely
chooses what's best every day

something that is <u>sensible</u> for all relationships, for the world!

I bow at every altar, to every creature, to every breath of the wind. It's
all THE ALL, after all, right?

To know the 'other,' or not . . . ?

Who is it who might challenge you to know a completely different view
of reality?

Consider taking the person out for coffee. Let that person talk, let that
person tell their story without a lot of interrupting from you, except to
ask a question every now and then to clarify.

I taught high school boys for 17 years. I am a boy. Every man is at heart.

Then I got an invite to teach for a short stint at a girls school . . . invited
by three wonderful former colleagues from the boys school who were
now running the girls school.

My world was so positively thrown for a loop.

These young women's stories were different. Their challenges. Their relationships. Their views of boys and their stories of the sexual shenanigans
of adolescence and the expectations their boy-peers had for them, their
hopes for life, their dreams.

There were tampons in the single-stall bathrooms that anyone could use by oneself. There weren't any in the single-stall bathrooms in the boys' school. This alone made me re-think the hospitality—or lack of it—we had offered at VITALITY for seven years.

I grew up with a mom and a sister and plenty of female relatives and best friends. I wasn't clueless. But I realized I was entirely clueless in so many ways.

I had never had the wonderful opportunity to just listen to young women for hours upon hours every day. As if it were my job—because it was! For eight great weeks of this maternity-coverage stint!

In listening to these young women, I began to realize some of my assumptions about life—and how wrong I had been, how much of THE ALL I had missed by these assumptions that held me from knowing a larger world.

The brightest young women in these classes were far more insightful than the brightest young men I had taught, especially regarding insights into ancient stories. And that's not to put down the young men—they were incredibly insightful!

My world was opened up—THE ALL grew for me.

If you're like me and finally learn to listen just a bit more . . . you'll know the grandness of THE ALL . . . and fast!

To kill your yoga-practice, or not to kill your yoga-practice?

"The goal is to obliterate the ego—absolutely destroy it."
"I killed my yoga class today—check!"
"Eradicate the enemies of good practice—that's the goal."
"Kill your mind."

"Get rid of enemies within yourself, anything that gets in the way of your equanimity."

Even some of the greatest meditation teachers say such things! Then there's the 'fight this disease' or 'battle this condition' or 'fight climate change' or 'start a war on this social condition' or 'fight this team' or 'resist this group' or whatever . . . all this fight-talk!

When we use violent images and violent language—even when talking about 'improving' ourselves—we might be missing the very wisdom of THE ALL.

After all, THE ALL, the infinite, God, by whatever name, includes all possibilities, right? Dare you destroy some aspect of THE ALL? Are you wise enough to decide what has to go and what gets to stay?

If it's in THE ALL, if it's in your life, maybe it's there to teach something. Instead of killing it, ask it why it's there—you know, in meditation. Maybe in person. Have a conversation, a slow one. Love it. Kiss it. Perhaps the 'enemy' you see is you. Jesus thought the best action would be to love the enemy. Gautama too.

Sure, what is helpful for you might be poison to another. For sure. So all is gift to anyone who has the eyes to see, ears to hear, and hearts to feel. ALL is gift, choose what is helpful for you.

There's a reflection earlier about loving enemies, right? That love transforms. And hate and indeed even having enemies only pours gasoline on the fire as it blows up in front of you and all around you and all you touch.

Anytime I find myself thinking I have an enemy, I realize I need to sit down and meditate (whatever that might mean to me today) and see what Arises within my own self that's needing love. Enemies on the 'outside' of myself indicate that something 'inside' myself needs love, something inside me is begging for love.

But some things and some people are just horrible, right?

Even the nastiest presidents and politicians and most unethical CEOs are humans trying to figure it out just like I'm trying to figure it out. I've said and done some things in my own life that still give me pause. Probably you too.

Such looking within and loving some aspect of me that's crying out like a baby and needing tender love does not mean then that the presidents and politicians and CEOs and family and friends who hurt me are left off the hook. I can still stand my ground and my authenticity and call them out, seek healing, invite change. Though I might do it more cleverly and helpfully and lovingly if I befriend first whatever needs love within me.

The greatest challenge of the 21st century, in my opinion, is to love the ALL of a person and at the same time be able to nonviolently call someone, to invite toward growth and communal-transformation someone who is attempting to hold power over you or me or anyone or any creature. 'Power-Offenders' do not act alone. They are created by society, by our community. So to hold one person accountable and invite that person to grow is really—if we are wise—to invite the whole community to grow along with this person so the offense has less chance to happen again. With anyone.

Imagine a prison system that is attempting such growth as this!

Well, my friends, it's happening. Check it out: *New York Times* "What We Learned From German Prisons" - August 6, 2015. Love like this is so needed.

As for obliterating egos, such popular-speak in meditation and yoga circles—whatever is 'my ego' or whatever that means—maybe my need to try to control things through obliteration would benefit from some love.

Maybe we all and ALL THAT IS—THE ALL—could benefit from love.

To karma / reincarnate / past life, or not . . . ?

One area about which I very much disagree with Gautama and the yogic and Buddhist literature is some of their specific thinking regarding reincarnation and past lives.

Do we reincarnate? Do we come back? Does the wheel of 'karma' exist? Does what we habitually do in this life—especially the very last thing we do in this life—manifest what happens in the next?

How am I to know?

I do find it rather strange that with my very first steps in the sweet little town of Galway, Ireland I knew I had been there before. Curiously though, in this skin, I had never been there!

Early Christians had some sense of reincarnation and past lives, and medieval Christians too, especially a group known as the Cathars in what we today call southern France. They are a rather curious group, very much influenced by and influencing the troubadour music of love that seems to have shaped much of our modern consciousness across the world, in my opinion.

The Roman Catholic Church eventually had all the Cathars killed—as the Catholic monk and abbot and crusade-leader Arnauld Amalric was said to have announced to his Catholic Crusaders who were leery about killing what might be innocent people: Kill them all. God will know his own and sort them out.

Another day, another genocide. All through the centuries.

The history of people in hierarchical power—religious, government, corporate, all—is very difficult to digest.

And not just hierarchies in big institutions! I have used hierarchical power in my roles as teacher and mentor and coach and brother and lover and all. Not to kill . . . but to get my way, to try to make people see that I'm right, my way is right. This is far from relationship. This is far from discovering THE ALL together, far from working / playing out real relationship with one another.

And yet there are moments too in my life where there is a <u>meeting</u> someone, allowing one another to be as we are, dancing one another into life without stepping on each other's toes or dropping one another on a dip or pulling one another in so close that's its difficult to breathe.

These are beautiful moments when we meet another human being. Even for a split-second, a recognition of eyes meeting and knowing THE ALL with and through one another.

But what to do with these moments of horror and sadness that happen in the life of our world—slavery and unequal relationship in all its ugly forms over the millennia?

We all have much to sit with in our meditation—much to be with to watch it transform before our eyes as Gautama reminds us. At least I hope my past foibles transform as I meditate!

And maybe that's just it. Maybe that's all the world needs to become a freer place, a home for us all to work out our destinies, all nearly eight billion of us human-creatures with the seemingly infinite non-human creatures with whom we live.

A RENEWED PEEK AT REINCARNATION

As for reincarnation? Does the framework of 'past lives' or 'multiple lives in multiple skins/bodies over the millennia' provide some help trying to sort out our troubled history as human beings together on this planet? Do we require multiple lifetimes to work out our destinies?

I'm very intrigued by Brian Weiss, MD. His book *Many Lives, Many Masters* (1988) tells the story how he, raised Jewish, a medical doctor practicing psychiatry, stumbled upon the reality of reincarnation, though in a very different form . . . one that does not have your 'karma' in one life dictating what happens for you in the next life . . . at least not without your own personal choosing the next life under the direction of 'ascended masters' who help you to choose the future circumstances to live the life you want in the future and are playfully curious about . . . all of these lifetimes as a way to better know THE ALL and all possibilities. At least as many possibilities as one 'person' would like to try on and choose.

Weiss' experiences suggest that we might be bully in one life and bullied in another, father to a child in one life and then in the next life the one who was child becomes the father . . . role reversals as the lifetimes unfold, as people travel together from life to life. That the 'husband' in one life might be the 'wife' in the next life or 'transgendered' or whomever . . . that we take on multiple roles to better know THE ALL, at least as I'd say what Weiss is guessing at in his book.

It's the wildest story, Brian Weiss' and his patient's, and so much of it rang true to me to whatever it is I know about life and the universe. Read it yourself and decide for yourself.

WHAT TO DO ABOUT GAUTAMA'S TEACHINGS ON KARMA'S WHEEL? CAN WE STEP OFF?

Some might worry then that the meditation techniques that Gautama perfected and passed on to stop the wheel of incarnation might then be worthless—that there's then no need to meditate and clear our karmic-path if indeed there is no karma that we need to somehow 'burn up' through all of our yogic practices.

Actually, my experience is that Gautama's technique helps me to live a better life not so much out of fear of what might become in the next life as to enjoy the very heart of life in this life—to be in love with THE ALL, in all the ways THE ALL comes to me, within and Within, to discover relationship in its as-close-as-possible-to-equal form.

That's why I think it helps to have a balanced view of every human being . . . to be able to say things like 'this person offered these great gifts to human-life and also destroyed human-life in these ways....' And to say it all without judgement, without the need to only say one side of the story and forget to say the rest.

We humans are a tangled mess—each one of us.

To expect to find a person who is not all tangled up in some way is ridiculous.

Maybe this is why Gautama and Jesus and all the teachers we hail as important remind us to have compassion and love for one another, even our enemies.

The enemy in this life might be your lover in the next life!

Maybe this reincarnation / past-life possibility is the only thing that makes sense with all the traumas we cause one another. That we're all trying to work it out, play it out with one another, that we are indeed players on a stage with one another for a short time, as Shakespeare imagines.

THE ALL . . . and its infinite possibilities.

Discover for yourself, friend. THE ALL includes you, after all.

To date one's students, or not . . . ?

Do I think it's wise for yoga-teachers to date their current students?

No.

Students seek out teachers for an experience of knowing themselves and the world/universe.

Teachers who are wise offer hospitality for the students to discover—in each student's own individual way, in each student's own individual time—that all they really need is within their own individual self . . . indeed, that THE ALL is within.

For a teacher to complicate this learning through dating, inappropriate touch, a romantic relationship, etc. is, well, complicated and unfair to the student.

I give students space to discover what they wish to discover, and hope my teachers do the same for me.

Sometimes we project something, some aspect of life we're trying to work out, onto our teachers. I know I have, and still catch myself doing it, even after all these years and all these teachers. Even with a muted and equal-minded power-dynamic as we try to have at VITALITY, for a teacher to suggest having a romantic/sexual relationship with a student or a teacher who lets a student entwine their projections with sexual-relationship is not fair to students in their discovery of what it is they showed up to learn about yoga or self-care or life.

I've known teachers who have met their eventual spouses at classes they've offered, and I've admired the intelligent ways they've negotiated those teacher-student 'contracts' together that have been fair to both of them and fair to the whole class too. These teacher-student contracts don't last forever. For sure. Though I do think some time needs to pass between the learning/certification process before a romantic relationship or a relationship that has the potential to blossom into a sexual relationship can come to be.

With teacher-student contracts—written or verbal or understood—there's a power-dynamic, right? If I'm the one signing a certificate or accepting donations for the class, I assume there must be a power-dynamic, an unequal one that happens between teacher and student . . . even as circular as we try to invite with all of us being co-learners together at VITALITY.

I try to do the best, try to be the most authentic I can be. And I hope I always do and am.

To celebrate Pattabhi and teachers
who are brilliant and help a lot of people
and
who hurt even just one person,
or to reject these teachers entirely?

I wrote this on MLK weekend as I was putting the final edits on this book—the day after the viral media storm about the students and demonstrators clashing on the steps of the Lincoln Memorial on January 19, 2019.

MLK

perhaps one of the most brilliant people
to walk this land
to walk the entire earth

and he was not sexually faithful to his wife
broke the trust of their relationship
hurt her

Ava DuVernay's beautiful film SELMA pointed it out so clearly and wisely

what are we to do with MLK?
what are we to do knowing all we do?

shall we be judge and jury and decide to ban him?
ban his day?
his teaching?
his books?
roll back the freedoms that he helped us all realize in this grand experiment with democracy?
(while the world holds its breath and waits and hopes USA-democracy will work)

I find it unwise to pick up any stones to hurl at anyone
they always come back around

on the globe of earth
on which we live
this big rock
its center molten, fire

so what to do?
what to do when someone—anyone—does something that is awful or
disturbing or whatever like this?

might I suggest we be with it?
might I suggest we be with this person? as a whole?

might I suggest we be with all of your very own self, my very own self?

sure, gratitude might arise with all that you recognize as 'gift' and
'goodness'

sure, sadness and anger might arise with all that you recognize as
'shameful' and 'embarrassing' and 'badness'

what to do then?

we humans are complicated beings, individuals
nearly none of us ever completely enlightened and free
yet we have glimpses
people like MLK and Gandhi, many more glimpses than me

when I be with what is 'good' and 'what is 'bad' within myself
when I be with my whole self
soon
if I stay here awhile
I know love

and when I be with the 'good' and the 'bad' of MLK and Gandhi and
just about anybody
I know love too

love doesn't offer itself as a reward for 'good' behavior

love offers itself as itself (for all behavior)
as love

and love after awhile changes things, perspectives, people
and sometimes the 'bad' habit begins to dissolve
and then it's all good ;)
though we don't know how it happens
it happens
life's mystery

just below the spot where MLK gave us his Dream
— and what a Dream it is and will be —
some teens and a man and a crowd confronted one another
perhaps in ways that forgot the Dream spun out
on the stairs above them
not
all
that
long
ago

there are things in the viral-videos of that confrontation that seem 'bad'
and 'good' to me
things where love did not yet happen
things that have viraled out hate among us all
things where none of us 'met' one another as we are —
the 'good' and the 'bad'

I wonder
what would happen
if we sat down
in love
with all involved
these boys
their parents
their chaperones
the man, his friends
the crowd

the ones said to be jeering in the crowd

I wonder
what would happen
if we sat down with them all
with my own brokenness
and yours
and let both 'bad' and 'good' be
and let love swim among us all
in me
in you
in all the 'players' of the confrontation
in all the viral surety

God knows

Pattabhi Jois helped spread yoga all over the world, inspired many, helped many, AND he hurt many people too. There are even photos of him—photos!—offering in his yoga classes hands-on adjustments and full-body adjustments that are physically dangerous and entirely inappropriate with his genitals on top of his students' genitals or his hands on top of his students' genitals. Some of his students have written about the pain he caused them and how he ruined yoga for them. Some people have written in *Guruji* too that Pattabhi's touching them—even their genitals—was helpful.

What a complex mess—he seems to traumatize some people with the same touch as he frees other people! It sure would have been nice if Pattabhi had simply asked his students if he could touch them and been clear about where he was asking to touch them and especially why. But it seems he didn't ask. And it seems that he didn't wait to hear whether a student wanted to be touched or not.

It would have been even better if Pattabhi had taught by voice alone and kept his hands to himself.

On top of all this, Pattabhi was so sure that his multiple series of yoga-asana were <u>the way</u> to experience yoga—whether he or Krishnamacharya created these series or evolved them from an ancient text they were said to have found. Whether we trust the *Yoga Korunta* story or not about how Pattabhi and Krishnamacharya found 'ashtanga yoga' in this no-longer-existing book, it seems that Pattabhi named or at least dedicated his teaching to Patanjali's 'ashtanga'...the eight limbs. (Better than naming it after one's own self, I suppose, as Mr. Iyengar and many more 'gurus' of the 20th century have done!) If Pattabhi had only practiced what he (and Patanjali) preached! Yamas! Niyamas! Even yoga-asana! But it appears he didn't, it appears he could have done a lot better. Perhaps we all can.

Pattabhi, like most human beings I know and try to love, could be invited to grow. A lot. Just as I need to grow a lot more.

THE ALL is vast. Growth is never finished for any of us in an infinite universe.

Not to let Pattabhi off the hook without some reconciliation between Pattabhi and those who claim they were injured or traumatized by him and his hands-on adjustments . . . I'm sure it's not only Pattabhi who is a tangled mess with his teachings by word and deed. Perhaps we all are 'entangled' to one another with things we say and do, and things we neglect to say and do. I find it difficult to point out others' faulty splinters when I have plenty of faulty beams in my own eyes . . . as Jesus wisely invites us all to realize. Perhaps that's just one more problem with having 'gurus'—we expect more of them when they are simply human beings, with gifts and with problems, like the rest of us.

I'm sure there are things that I've said or invited either here or in life that have freed people to know THE ALL —

and I'm sure there are things I've said or invited here or in life that have tangled people up and prevented people from knowing THE ALL.

HOW TO UNTANGLE SUCH MESSES?

Messes of any sort don't just go away or untangle themselves by doing nothing or ignoring them.

With a guy like Pattabhi Jois, I think it would be most helpful to say, "Pattabhi Jois helped spread yoga around the world and many helpful teachings about yoga that have helped a lot of people, and his actions—especially his hands-on adjustments that often involved touching people's genitals—caused a great deal of grief and pain and trauma for some people too. We can learn a lot from Pattabhi—both in what to do to be helpful and what not to do." We can honor his gifts and name his harmful actions. All in the same breath. All with the reality that he, like anyone, is tremendous gift and painful problem—all at once! Gift and problem do not cancel one another out, and yet the gift does not let the problem off the hook either.

If Pattabhi were living, healing could be easier. He could explain what he was doing, and maybe more honestly why he did what he did. Perhaps we then could use the wisdom within the ancient yoga tradition to bring about positive change in the teacher-student relationships that he seems to have messed up greatly with his trauma-inducing teaching methods. Perhaps forgiveness and reconciliation could come about. Perhaps it still can—even with being on different sides of the veil of life.

For those of us still on this side of the veil of life . . . we do not have many great right-in-front-of-our-faces models of reconciliation between offender and offended. The courtroom is rarely a place where reconciliation happens, unfortunately. US prisons are far from places of reconciliation either. I felt traumatized just waiting in line to visit a friend in prison—and I didn't have to live there! Tuberculosis cure-pioneer Paul Farmer details his visits to prisons around the world in the amazing book Tracy Kidder wrote about him, *Mountains Beyond Mountains* (2004). It's absolutely harrowing to me that we on this side of prison bars would do these things to any human being—no matter what these offenders have done.

In my humble opinion, I think our world would be much improved—especially the very subtle psychology of every single person, in prison or out—if prisons were places for reconciliation instead of even more violence.

Germany's recent prison-reforms give me great hope. (*New York Times* "What We Learned From German Prisons" - August 6, 2015) If reconciliation can be invited for 'the least of these' in society—serious offenders—perhaps it's possible for us all. I do hope so, and I'm encouraged that some people from both sides of the US political 'aisle' are agreeing that what's happening in German prisons might be needed and possible in the US as well.

A NEW WAY FORWARD FOR TEACHERS

There are plenty of stories about the 'gurus' of yoga and the geniuses of lots of brilliant endeavors of the 20th century saying and doing inappropriate things, even awful things.

I do not condone them or their sad, dangerous behavior.

I do not want to look past the gifts they've offered either.

The four people I've raised up as helpful teachers in this book—Tirumalai Krishnamacharya, Moshe Feldenkrais, Ruthy Alon, Marion Woodman—I'm sure all have their incredible gifts they've offered our world and our world's ever-growing wisdom for living. I'm sure too they have their not-so-helpful things. One of our Feldenkrais teachers who knew Moshe Feldenkrais intimately shared with us stories about him about how he was not always so loving, even with people who tried to love him.

Life is complicated. Very.

Perhaps love is the answer.

Love does not look past or let people off the hook for their bad behavior. Nor does it hang them on the hook either.

Vipassana meditation helped me a great deal to find equanimity with the people who hurt me in years past. Gautama's 'techniques' are quite intriguing to me. I marvel at how helpful they have been for me, for many, in allowing a path to emerge within all the daily-wreckage of human, relational life.

And love does not prevent us from standing tall in our own authenticity and personal experience and calling out someone—teacher, lover, friend, anyone—clearly and intelligently and helpfully to stop offending behavior and invite change. I do think it's helpful when doing this to recognize that I'm flawed too—and that mutual compassion might help us both! The earlier discussion on ahimsa and the cleverness and equanimity of nonviolence might offer something to help (re)imagine our situations where the power-balance is off and to welcome a new way forward in relationship. In my opinion, clever nonviolence invited out of love is the only thing that works in the short and long runs of life.

To vipassana, or not to vipassana . . . ?

95% of this book was written before the silent vipassana meditation retreat I took at the end of 2018, and so much of what was written before that vipassana retreat was confirmed for me as a result of that retreat. I VERY HIGHLY recommend sitting a vipassana retreat—dhamma.org

Just be sure to arrive to the retreat knowing what you're getting into—about 120 one-hour meditations over 10 silent days, the whole experience offered for donation, by volunteers who have experienced the retreat themselves and are giving back so generously—and come with a good seat you've tried and tested many times! :)

I had a groundswell of stuff get gently sifted upward and outward from me during these 120 meditations . . . much like a river that finds some stuckness just below the surface and somehow, without any apparent effort from the river or the stuck-stuff, it just goes and goes and goes on, floats downriver to become something helpful for some other creature.

There were places in my body that felt softer, emptier, ready to welcome some newness, like layers had been peeled off, had been removed.

Try as hard as I did with asana after asana for years, so much of the stuckness within me moved without any effort but the nudge of vipassana meditation.

S.N. Goenka is a genius. And it's not like he set out at age three to be a meditation guide. He was a successful businessman in Burma (Myanmar). And Hindu at that.

Gautama's teachings / Buddha / Buddhism were not welcomed as friends to a lot of Hindus through the centuries!

How Goenka, a Hindu, comes to be the one to take Gautama's meditation techniques back to India is a great gift to me—to know how life works in the long view, even over thousands of years. How sediment like this—centuries of argument and pain and loss and nonacceptance between Gautama's followers and the Vedic/Hindu followers—can be picked up by the river in some moment just when it's right and be recreated and suddenly, positively enlivened again! And not just for one another . . . but for the whole world, it seems.

This is a very great time to be alive!

I invite you to learn more of Goenka's story and his teacher, Sayagyi U Ba Khin (1899 - 1971), and how they both came to vipassana meditation in quite surprising ways. *The Clock of Vipassana Has Struck* (1999, compiled and edited by Pierluigi Confalonieri) tells much of their stories.

VISION: THE WHOLE WORLD IN THESE HANDS

With all the gunk of life below the surface that came up within me during the retreat, I was surprised that the only moment when tears came to me was when I had some vision of how Gautama's teaching—rejected by most Hindu & yogic scholars—eventually became the foundation, in my vision anyway, for tai chi and qigong. (Some scholars do think that some of Gautama's teachings did indeed find their way into Patanjali's Sutras.).

Tai chi masters are known for 'holding the ball' (standing, feet shoulder width, arms extended at chest level and holding an imaginary ball of energy, THE Universe, in their arms) for one or two hours a day. Without intentional movement. With the smallest breath even—breath that wouldn't disturb a feather beneath the nose of the practitioner.

I had some friends long ago who used to do this very thing—hold the ball for an hour or two every day.

The story I heard long ago in my tai chi and qigong training was that this was the entire first or second year of training for a ten year old. Stand, hold the ball for an hour. Every day for a year.

Vipassana meditation gave me a window into understanding this training and this phenomenon as indeed possible.

What a gift vipassana is now rooted again in India, that the conversation between yoga and Gautama's teachings can come around again—hopefully this time with happier results that help the whole world.

My hope is that this book aids in that conversation. And that we all might know THE ALL.

And you too!

To tantra, or not to tantra . . . ?

Tantra and meditation—in its infinite guises—and yoga all developed together. I'd throw in tai chi / qigong too.

There is no separation.

Indeed, there was no separation during the creations of these seemingly separate studies either—as people most likely responded to Nature as they discovered their own Nature. There were no names. There was no 'now this is yoga' and 'this is tantra' and 'this is meditation.'

Though we humans are awfully good at separating things out. All too often for marketing purposes...and to make a buck.

When it first came out, I read Douglas Veenhoff's most fascinating *White Lama: The Life of Tantric Yogi Theos Bernard, Tibet's Lost Emissary to the New World* (2011). Most fascinating. I'm quite intrigued that N.E. Sjoman refers to Theos Bernard so often in his excellent *The Yoga Tradition of the Mysore Palace* (1999), which I've alluded to throughout this book. Bernard wrote a book on hatha yoga—I have yet to read that except for references in *White Lama*.

A few friends tried to get me interested in tantra shortly after I had read about Theos Bernard. I picked up and read quite a few pieces of books, heard a few talks. It was fascinating for me to discover what people had uncovered for themselves through tantric imagination and practice—and what people had developed for themselves through the centuries.

Very complicated cosmologies and ceremonies and practices. For sure.

The whole invitation by my friends reminded me a bit of my Catholic friends who left behind their Christian roots because they had tired of the cramped-quarters of Christian doctrine . . . only then to plunge themselves head-first into another tradition—Buddhism, Hinduism, Islam, Judaism, etc.—to absorb a whole new doctrine that is just as confining, in my opinion.

NATURE AS A WISE(R) TEACHER

My question, though, as I've tried to point in this book is . . . would you rather have a personal EXPERIENCE of THE ALL or a deep study of other people's experiences?

Each of these traditions—Christianity, Buddhism, Hinduism, Islam, Judaism, and sure many more—has a deep well of EXPERIENCE to which interested people are invited. And if you look carefully enough, each of these traditions invites participants to engage with nature in interesting ways.

Maybe it's Nature that is the true initiator. More deeply and particularly . . . the wind.

It's no secret that most ancient languages do not differentiate much between wind and breath and spirit and air. Perhaps for good reason.

Maybe that's the helpful point of these traditions and their scriptures / writings—not so much the constricting doctrine and complicated cosmologies as the invitation to EXPERIENCE.

Sure, I delve very deeply into ancient people's experiences through biblical translation and such, and my own cursory studies of the yoga classics. Maybe that's what my friends were inviting by trying to get me interested in tantra—though they had no interest in the ancient languages out of which tantra sprung.

I think it's more important to have personal, right-now EXPERIENCES of Nature—indeed of yourself as Nature—than to take on someone else's cosmology and doctrine and try to have these ancient teachers' experiences from hundreds or thousands of years ago. That's why I have parsed out Patanjali's Sutras and *The Bhagavad Gita* as I have done in this book—to invite EXPERIENCES that might help us to know a taste of what they were inviting . . . and yet to invite you to trust more YOUR OWN experiences than theirs.

In my humble opinion . . . for what it's worth . . .

continue experiencing and sensing Nature . . .
and THE ALL will take care of itself
and lead you
without your need to know anything.

To marry, or not to marry . . . ?

Within your own self. Absolutely yes.

The invitation of bringing 'masculine' and 'feminine' and 'something more' (shape-shifting 3rd+ possibilities) within oneself that is the heart of yoga and Jungian psychology is really not a game of gender or gender-attributes.

It is about allowing <u>differences</u> or <u>complements</u> within oneself to dance with one another, to allow not a single one of them to dominate.

No 'masculine' domination—whatever masculine means to you.

No 'feminine' domination—whatever feminine means to you.

Not 3rd+ 'something mores' dominating—whatever they might mean to you.

This is the teaching about the gunas as well, right? To allow rajas, tamas, and sattva to all be in harmony together within oneself.

When I can recognize differences within myself —
perhaps even contradictions —
and when I allow them all to be
within myself
without trying to root out any of them
and when I offer them all LOVE
THE ALL is revealed
within me
and what was once so different
can be recognized as ONE,
from one and the same Universe.

The tangled mess of contradictions that I AM can be seen for WHAT I AM . . . of the same tangled, beautiful mess that is THE ALL, the infinite universe and then some.

And when I know THE ALL within me—with my contradicting and competing and complementing energies and impulses and all—it's a heck of a lot easier to meet someone else with all their contradictory and competing and complementing energies and impulses and all. And I can love them too, for ALL they are. And something happens—some mystery. Transformation.

And marriage is possible. Within and WITHIN.

Indeed, you are the center of the infinite 'universe' —
though the world
or anyone
or anything
or any system
(including the solar system)
does not revolve around you!

To seek purity, or not to seek purity . . . ?

I've noticed that every time in my life I seek purity—whether by following some specific diet or movement-regimen or thinking or philosophy or relationship—that something goes haywire in my life.

It's as if Nature—which is far from pure—has a way of inviting me, reminding me that all is good in THE ALL, that nothing is impure or profane or whatever.

Sure, some things might not be good for me in large doses—perhaps even in any dose at all.

As always, what's poison for me might actually be the saving grace for you!

I'm reminded of that in a lot of ways. I'm reminded of that often when we try to silence people with whom we do not agree—or when we refuse to listen to people who have even done terrible things.

In my experience, it's people with whom I disagree or people whom I've decided must be 'worthless' because they have opinions very different from mine—it's these people who have the most to teach me.

For that reason, I'm very grateful to live in Cincinnati—a city with people of VASTLY different political persuasions. Bumping into people who hold very different ideas from me has helped me to grow. It's not easy though. It's probably one reason why meditation & yoga are so needed in my life . . . to help me discover my own biases and assumptions, to encourage me to know and practice equanimity, to calm myself when I'm feeling chafed by someone else's very different ideas so that I might listen to them with some hope of understanding their viewpoint, of knowing THE ALL.

Listening doesn't mean I need to agree! For sure! Though I'd be wise to at least wonder about what the person said, to turn it over in my imagination, in myself.

THE ALL includes all possibilities, after all, right?

THE ALL doesn't then demand that I take on and then advocate the viewpoints of people with whom I would ordinarily disagree. Instead, my encounters with THE ALL might remind me in the future to take in someone's 'impure' idea that I might better appreciate them for who they are, and realize I alone am not THE ALL, at least not ALL of it.

After all, can THE ALL be impure?

To memorize and learn other people's movement/ meditation sequences, or not . . . ?

When I was studying tai chi and qigong, we memorized the whole Secret Yang format . . . Seven Principle Exercises (Qigong), Heaven Form, Earth Form, (Hu)Man Form. We learned Vince Lasorso's fast forms that he created from the Heaven Form—one of my favorite things I've learned in all the things I've studied. Tolo-Naa taught us the Bagua Mother Form and later tuina, which has a self-care regimen that we've redeveloped a bit and share as Chair Yoga at VITALITY. Tolo-Naa also offered during that same tuina–weekend I've mentioned before a workshop on Shackle Hands—a special set of about 40 moves that each one of us was asked to then demonstrate in front of the entire group after only having experienced it a few times just an hour before!

Amazingly, we all could do that when we asked it of ourselves.

I do think there was a wisdom in memorizing these forms.

When I learned yoga in my first yoga certification program with Amber Jean Espelage and Larry Schultz, we learned modified primary series, primary series, Rocket 1, Rocket 2. While each of these series is different from each other, there was a solid backbone that ran through them all (modified primary) and each time one taught Rocket 1, for instance, it was similar to the last one and different too. But essentially we were mastering one series—modified primary—and riffing on it in all the yoga classes we taught, no matter what the class was called.

In Healing Touch Program®, Janet Mentgen advised her students to learn a Healing Touch technique and not deviate from it in any way until you've practiced it 100 times—so that you can learn and know the intention and experience of that particular technique before you go changing it. Whatever one might think they know after trying a technique a few or even a dozen times will be vastly different—right?—from how someone would experience it after 100 times.

In Movement Intelligence® and Feldenkrais Method®, we're invited to know and try to practice the processes / lessons step-by-step, without changing anything except to modify something only to meet our students where they are.

SO . . . LEARN A SEQUENCE??

Sometimes yoga-teacher interns moving toward certification get all bent out of shape about being invited to learn to teach a small set of asanas very well before creating their own versions.

I used to be more 'free-for-all' in inviting yoga-teacher interns create their very own classes near the very beginning of the training. Though—my fault entirely—I didn't find they knew a whole lot of depth in what they were so freely creating. When I started asking students to learn a series of asanas VERY WELL and to be able to teach that series in that particular order and with some knowledge of how to invite their students into these shapes and all that could be sensed in each shape, these yoga-teacher interns then seemed to become richer teachers who had some deep knowledge of that original series and then also an ability to create their own series on their own from that deep knowledge and study of the initial memorized series.

I'm sure that it's from that original tai chi and qigong teaching where we learned to step into someone else's 'ancient' creations with these forms and moves that I came to be able to memorize many other series of moves/rests in the other holistic disciplines I've studied. If my first studies had been more 'free-for-all'—who knows!—maybe I wouldn't be able to learn other series of moves/rests, appreciate their wisdom as they are, and then create riffs on them to meet my student wherever they are in that moment.

And yet . . . the wisdom of free-form!

As wise as it is, I think, for us to study other people's movement-rest series and processes and lessons,

as wise as it is, I think, to step into someone else's shoes and wonder for awhile why this follows this follows this . . .

I find it incredibly valuable to be free of forms and step-by-step processes and just explore what feels good in moving and resting . . .

as a baby explores and wonders and plays . . .

as humans dance without any preconceived expectations about how to move.

Maybe there's wisdom in entertaining both invitations every day (every hour?) . . . to follow a series of movements/rests created by someone else and to make up our own.

Seriously . . . to come back to this: are we really to offer love to our enemies???

I find life to be very strange.

Awhile back, I had a great mentor who had helped me tremendously in bringing forward all I could be as a mentor to others.

It's almost as if this person put into order and perfect perspective all that I had known before and all that I would know.

That is until he began talking about how he didn't like gay people, didn't think they should be around.

I was stunned, couldn't believe what I was hearing. How could he say this? Didn't he know me? Was he saying this to shun me or to try to make me change?

I couldn't find the words to defend myself, my choices—if being gay or my loving another man is somehow really a choice? I was much younger then, and probably would have openly and wisely and cleverly confronted him today if he had said the same things to me now.

He even seemed to be conspiring against me behind my back to others.

I was furious.

I passive-aggressively channelled my anger toward him—I got publicly mad at him about something that needed to be confronted about our work, something that was entirely unrelated and, in the scheme of life, not that big of a deal at all.

And then the next day I slipped down my concrete steps at home and was in terrible, terrible pain. Fortunately, I didn't hit my head. I did wrench my back very badly.

Went to the ER, took a half-day off work (I never had done that), tried to take care of myself.

The Universe conspires in strange ways. I went to the grocery still in a lot of pain and gingerly picked up what I needed and—lo and behold— when I returned with my groceries, someone had pulled their car up right next to my driver's side door. There was no way to get in that door, so I would have to climb through the passenger-side and with my back all twisted and in pain find a way into the driver's seat to start the car and pull away. I considered waiting it out, waiting for the driver of the other car to come back. But it was very, very cold.

So I went through the passenger-side and got in the driver's seat by screaming and screaming out the pain of my wrenched back, the pain of having to wrench it even more to get into my car, the pain of trying to find a way through it all. HOW COULD ALL THIS SHIT KEEP HAPPENING TO ME?

I got home and cried.

And I sat there. For awhile.

My tears had stalled me, helped me to find my seat in that moment.

And some perspective began emerging about him, about this mentor, about our relationship, about how he might indeed be trying to work through his own homophobia about himself by projecting it onto me, how I didn't need to wrap myself up in the mad messiness of it all. That I could defend myself and all LGBTQ+ people in some even-keeled, equanimous way. That I could step aside when his insults and insensitive words came at me . . . much like I had in first grade when this bully had tried to punch me hard in the gut and I stepped aside and he hit the brick wall instead of me and broke his wrist—and how we later become good friends.

Something shifted within me as I considered this man, this mentor, and his own internalized homophobia. Some compassion. A flood of compassion.

It didn't let him off the hook for his insensitivities toward me or any of the LGBTQ+ people in his life that he also seemed to slight at any chance he could.

I made it a point, even in my younger self, to be ready the next time he expressed his homophobia to remember my roots and my ability to stand tall in my own authenticity to offer some loving response to him, some response that might awaken him to all he is. This, after all, is the hallmark of nonviolence, of ahimsa . . . to be ready to respond in some loving and mutually-awakening way to any oppressor . . . to let the heart of the Universe speak through you the wisdom for that moment.

I tried to be able to hold in one hand all that he had so helpfully taught me through the years, and in the other hand all the ways he had hurt me. Gratitude and anger, compassion and hate—all these seemingly conflicting emotions ran through me, one right after the other. It was overwhelming, just how quickly it changed, my feelings for him changed. I found some peace.

This was a 'loving my enemy' I had not had the opportunity to experience before.

I knew I would never be the human being I am without this man in my life as a mentor. Maybe my authentic self had some calming effect on him, some small way of encouraging him to be more honest with his own feelings that he had not dealt with for—who knows? decades? That's not say that he was/is gay or anything like that—though like just about every human being I know, I think he had some unresolved feelings about same-sex attraction in his own life-experience that he had not dealt with and it came out as dislike or disrespect toward LGBTQ+ people. My memories raced through all the comments he had made over the years, his own fears quite evident. Yeah, maybe that was indeed it, I thought to myself.

Time passed. Things between us sometimes got better. Things between us sometimes got worse. We found ways to work together helpfully for all involved with our work. I learned what I could from him and at the same time made sure I wasn't projecting onto him some hoped-for 'guru-ness' that he could fulfill as a mentor. I tried to remember he was human, that I am human—that we are rich creatures trying to figure out this life together.

I went to a chiropractor or two to help with my back that had troubled me when I fell down those stairs. Years later, long after we no longer worked together, on a leisurely drive back from the chiropractor and just as I was thinking of this mentor and all that he was for me—both as a pain and as a tremendous help—I noticed a car in front of me driving VERY slowly. And I noticed the license plate. And just how queer is the Universe? It was my mentor's car, my mentor driving.

The Universe is a very strange place.

There's a long road to our conflicts. Trust Brian Weiss' experience and maybe what you know yourself and it's not just this lifetime but LIFETIMES of working things out—to know THE ALL in all its incredible ways.

Even more strangely, I don't think I would have pursued the richness of Movement Intelligence® and Feldenkrais Method® without having injured my back on those stairs in my anger toward my mentor.

All of this by leaning into that wisdom from Jesus and Gautama—two wise human teachers—to love my enemies.

To separate body & mind & spirit, or not . . . ?

Can you?

To talk about 'the body'
or to talk about 'your body'?

Each person's body is very different . . . so why talk about some platonic-ideal of 'body'?

My Feldenkrais teachers pointed out in my own teaching that I often talked about "our body" . . . as in, "let's move our body to the left." And as they wisely said—though I was angry at first!—"there is no 'our body'"—at least not when talking about how one's body moves or lives or breathes or whatever. And they're right, right?

Whenever I hear people talk about '<u>the body</u>' I wonder what in the world they mean. 'The body is an amazing thing! The body is very resilient!' Seems too nebulous to me. I mean, whose body are they talking about? To say instead . . . "Human beings are amazing creatures! Human bodies can be very resilient in all these incredible ways, (followed by examples)" . . . seems more accurate and more inviting of noticing my own body in those statements.

How we speak about ourselves—you and me—matters, yes?

Just as much as when I hear yoga teachers say, "grab your right knee and pull it into your chest" . . . instead of something like "find your right knee and bring it gently in the direction of your chest—only do what's easy." What happens in <u>your</u> body as you say these two invitations out loud . . . ?

Are there really seams & contradictions & strange agreements in the ancient yoga writings?

So maybe you're wondering why I have said that there are big disagreements in the ancient yoga writings . . . or why I continue to say that there are seams—or places where there are inconsistencies in yoga-philosophy, and thus the possibility either of another writer—within Patanjali's Sutras or *The Bhagavad Gita* or *The Dhammapada*?

Perhaps you might discover for yourself.

Read them, one at a time, slowly and with a pen and simply mark places that are interesting for you. I recommend reading them in the order above. Then read them again, this time a bit more quickly, with a different colored pen.

Make notes of where texts agree with one another, where they disagree. For example, I simply write in the margin of the Gita 'Patanjali' if the Gita seems to agree with what Patanjali is saying. Or 'not Patanjali' if the text is vastly different.

You'll notice the seams within a text too, places where a competing voice is introduced, probably a later voice trying to reinterpret the original teaching for a later time.

Not so obvious to you? Try reading Genesis (Bible). It's a hodge-podge of voices. A story begins, and then begins again just a little differently a few lines later. And then there's a cut-away from the action to put it all into a larger context, often as a genealogy or family tree. And then back to the first story-author, then maybe to the second story-author. (The Noah / Flood story is especially like this.)

After doing this with Genesis, consider going back to a text like the Gita. The seams become more apparent—probably even more apparent if we were to read it in Sanskrit.

One easy example is the teachings on the gunas in chapters 14 and 18 of the Gita. Do they quite match?

An exercise such as this—textual-analysis—might even improve your own sensitivity as a whole, with all of your bodily sensations.

It sure has mine. Sometimes even my own 21st century assumptions about life and the ways of the world become apparent when I read ancient texts with such curiosity.

Compare *The Dhammapada*'s teaching about the brahmins—the highest caste of ancient India—with what the Gita teaches, what Patanjali assumes. Gautama and his students are wily ones—and wise.

Movement and rest . . . movement and rest . . . even through the centuries of philosophical conversations about THE ALL!

'The language of the nervous system is noticing differences' . . . the nonjudgmental, curiosity-inducing rally-cry of Feldenkrais Method® and most slow, somatic opportunities . . . can be an invitation for one's whole life!

To get upset and throw the baby out with the bathwater here if something bothered you, or not . . . ?

I welcome professional teachers at VITALITY to share their wisdom and viewpoint with the yoga teacher trainings I lead. Very often—as in every time—these teachers say things that I completely agree with . . . maybe 80% of what they say . . . and they say things that I know from my own experience and study not to be true to life . . . maybe 20% of the time.

Should I ban them because they said something that bothers me?

Of course not.

I celebrate the areas where we are in agreement—and wonder too if maybe we're both wrong.

And I challenge myself to wonder about those few things I found troublesome—who knows, maybe I'm missing something!

We grow through dialogue, conversation, wondering out loud together and letting each other off the hook if we make mistakes as we try to make sense of life in all its fullness. And often, when someone offends us, we can grow through humor and gently teasing one another into realizing our mistaken idea, our missing THE ALL. Jesus was onto this with his Hebrew/Aramaic form of Patanjali's ahimsa, his clever nonviolence that disrupts and disarms oppressors, from within the oppressor's own imagination . . . that we might all begin again with one another.

We grow with one another as we keep the conversation going and give each other space to mess up and keep the conversation going to know more intimately THE ALL as it unfurls and unfolds before us.

If my 'style'—like these blasted single quotation marks—bothers you and yet I said something that seems to help you in welcoming a new vision of THE ALL, then welcome whatever you can!

All of my teachers have bothered me. Greatly. And yet they've all helped me too to know THE ALL.

To a (re)new(ed) world, friends!

So get going.

And I will too.

Let's discover for ourselves what is possible with moving and breathing and resting within one's own body, with sensation as the guide, our common invitation . . .

how might we meet differently the world, THE ALL, within and Within, as a result of moving and breathing and resting—all with sensation-mindedness?

how might we fall in love with one's own self and with one another, with the sensations—all of them—that are alive within us, without any grand need for external additions besides the natural rhythm of one's breath, of how breath breathes us on and on and onward?

The most important thing any of us can do is 'practice' . . . which in my opinion is to say 'play' . . . let's have fun with it, let it be wonderful. Do what feels right, be who you'd like to be, as I'll do and be as I'd like to do and be, in ways that respect each other in every way imaginable.

May we have the courage to let our net be wide with what 'yoga' is . . . after all, it always has been. Study the history of yoga and it's clear to see—even with the little tidbits I've sprinkled throughout this book—that yoga has always been permeable.

Ideas compete, they rub up against each other, sometimes bristle each other. Ideas collide, and some of one ends up with the other and same for the other. We can see that with Patanjali's Sutras and *The Bhagavad Gita*. They seem to be in conversation with one another, pushing each other, revising ideas and conceptions of the way IT IS, the many ways to know THE ALL through moving and breathing and resting and living. *The Dhammapada* too.

Some might say that what I have done here is cultural (mis)appropriation, that I have 'stolen' the ideas of India and reshaped them in my own way. Maybe I have. And yet I hope that as we all come to know THE ALL, we exchange and share ideas, and that the most helpful ideas rise to the surface of within and Within—that we might all grow together. Indeed, there is no separation, right?

And too, before 'India' became India after throwing off British Rule in 1947 / 1950, and before the British enacted their hierarchical rule over that land, 'India' was a vast land of many principalities, sometimes getting along together, sometimes not. *The Bhagavad Gita*—a sliver of the epic *Mahabharata*—is in some ways the mythic story of these collisions between Indian principalities and rulers (even within singular families) that happen over and over and over again—and what to do about them. As *The Bhagavad Gita* reminds, it's not just ideas that bump into each other and collide and morph and change one another—it's politics too, power and class/status enacted within our own families too. Most ancient texts—including and especially the Bible—are political statements after all. They try to understand power.

With the complexities of the political-history of India, the very origins of what we call yoga—from the Indus River Valley—indeed might not have even begun in what is today India. The Indus River winds through not only India but Pakistan and Tibet / China too. Are we to assume that all ancient yoga practitioners were exclusively in the India-portion of the Indus River Valley 3000 - 5000 years ago? Did not one wander up or down river into another land, another territory?

And then there's the important reality that Krishnamacharya had to leave India to find the yoga that became what he later shared—he had to go to Tibet to meet Ramamohana Brahmachari, Krishnamacharya's cave-dwelling, house-holder teacher for seven years.

Yoga was never simply held within the borders of India. And it certainly is not now in the 21st century. Yoga has become a world-wide endeavor.

Maybe whatever has THE ALL in mind cannot be contained—not in any one movement-breathing-resting discipline, not within any one religion, not within any one philosophy.

Indeed, maybe yoga—the glimpse of THE infinite ALL that we seek—is our key to helping humanity thrive on a planet that we humans seem hell-bent on destroying. I marvel at the ways that I have been involved in this destruction every day—often without even thinking about the destruction I do in my own little wrecking-bits every day.

Maybe yoga is our way to awaken to THE ALL—I do hope so.

So let's be human and wise and not get all in a huff about cultural (mis) appropriation when the very idea, the very goal—if there is one—is to become aware of THE ALL, the undivided, infinite ALL which has no borders, excludes no one, includes all things and people and possibilities. And it wasn't just Hindu / Vedic influence that has influenced the ongoing, ever-ever-developing traditions of yoga—even modern yoga crafted by Krishnamacharya for those twelve-year-old boys in the jump-around, acrobatic style we call vinyasa (a word that Krishnamacharya was said to coin himself). As was discussed earlier through N.E. Sjoman's research, ashtanga-vinyasa was born through a combining of British gymnastics and yoga-asana in the 20th century! less than 100 years ago! even our beloved sun salutations!

Maybe yoga has always been a permeable, borrowing type of endeavor—and it makes sense when it's THE ALL we're after with yoga, right?

The teachings of Gautama—begun in India—were soon challenged and forced out of India for centuries, for millennia. (Except perhaps a few of the teachings rubbing off on Patanjali.) It would take a Hindu (Goenka) to bring Gautama's techniques back to India.

Life is rather strange as we look backwards . . . without the British grabbing India into its empire-hold, Krishnamacharya might have never been exposed to British gymnastics that fueled his curiosity about how to help rambunctious 12-year-olds learn and appreciate the incredible helpfulness that is yoga . . . and without Britain and India colliding—all too often in violent and non-helpful ways—yoga might not have become what it is today with the playfulness and tailor-it-to-the-person style Krishnamacharya espoused . . . and so very many of us might not have ever known the depths of yoga that drew me and many first through the hop-a-lot playfulness of the ashtanga-vinyasa sequence.

I of course wish no violence and no empire upon anyone! I sit here in tears and great sadness about what my own country has done for centuries and unconscionably continues to do to the world and the environment and the earth's people. May the nudge that is yoga be a way to bring us all to an awakening that helps us all to realize the all-too-many ways we hold power over people—that we might live with the realization of THE ALL in mind in all pursuits.

Perhaps through reading and participating with this book your concept of THE ALL is expanded, perhaps especially with the contributions of VITAL-friends who have shared their stories about moving and breathing and resting together, of sharing life together.

Perhaps especially your own experiences have become a guide for you.

Let us have the courage to let the walls within and the walls outside us to fall, to tumble in their own ways, in their own time.

I imagine a world with no boundaries, no borders—a world of all humans and all creatures living together in love, in ever deepening love for and with one another. To know the world is round—that what I say and do and even how I move and breathe and rest has some effect on people on the other side of the world, on the other side of this round globe that is our planet.

The first person I know of who conceived of a world without boundaries or borders was Paul, the letter-writer of the Christian scriptures. Paul often gets a bad rap. He is credited with encouraging fixed gender-roles in the early churches just like they were fixed in the Roman Empire—some of 'Paul's' letters say as much, that nasty 'wives be submissive to your husbands' crap. Yet today, as scripture scholars examine the seams within those letters, we're all beginning to realize that those gender-role passages were interpolated or added into his letters (or even whole letters were written in Paul's name) to soften Paul's mighty sting for a new world and a new way forward he imagined—a world with no particular roles, a world with circular communities who invite within and Within a greater realization of THE ALL. Paul wrote to people on the edges of society—often the lowest rungs of the empire—to reveal and remind that the cruel and terribly violent Roman Empire was not the end of the story—that indeed there would be a day when empires crush themselves and all humans would bow down with Jesus (imagine it! not all humans bowing down <u>to</u> Jesus!) before THE ALL, before God—perhaps with the recognition that we are THE ALL, all of us and each one of us, but we alone are not all of THE ALL.

And some of these walls that might need to tumble for THE ALL to have its day are the ones that say 'this is yoga' and 'this is not yoga.' How wise we would be to let yoga be yoga—whatever it is that assists us in knowing THE ALL . . . especially with the asana-craze that has engulfed our world where people think you need to be able to tie yourself in knots and do handstands and a million plank-updog-downdog vinyasas and look a certain way clothed or unclothed to achieve 'yoga,' to be able to say that you are doing yoga.

Yoga's not just about being able to touch your toes, right? Though yoga-practice might be helpful to increasing flexibility to touch your toes more easily, or the flexibility of realizing touching one's toes while standing is not the most important thing in life.

Yoga's not about having a body fit for the cover of a magazine, right? At least until we recognize through yoga-practice that ALL bodies are beautiful because they are of THE ALL, of life.

Yoga does not require a quiet mind, right? Though yoga-practice might be helpful in finding a quieter mind, a calmer self or in realizing how simply to love myself when my thoughts are all over the place.

Hopefully this book invites people to realize yoga is vast, much bigger than a bunch of hopping around . . . that yoga is THE ALL.

Don't get me wrong—I love hopping around! Though now I realize there's way more to it than that, this pursuit of a bigger, deeper glimpse of THE ALL.

Some yoga-friends with whom I study Feldenkrais Method® in New York City and I joke that we do our yoga at Feldenkrais class. That we awaken to THE ALL through the slow, clever movements and simple rest of Feldenkrais' genius method.

And so can you awaken to THE ALL with tai chi or qigong, or ballet, or cycling, or sailing, or dancing, or cooking or cake-making classes or any darn thing where you are invited or you invite yourself to become aware of what you are doing, how you are doing it, of being curiously and playfully attentive to the sensations that arise within you and you respond accordingly with what feels appropriate of the whole, of THE ALL . . . presence . . . relationship that is alive to the possibilities, ALL of them.

Such awakening to THE ALL could happen anywhere, anytime.

It could happen in your lover's bed or a bed where you are alone and not happy about it. It could happen as you meander a forest or even a busy city street. It could happen as you read a book. It could happen as you do the laundry or the dishes. It could happen when you are so happy you can barely stand it. It could happen when you are majorly depressed.

THE ALL arrives much like the wind . . . without any announcement but itself.

For those who have eyes to see and ears to hear and hearts to feel, THE ALL invites us all at every moment . . . the deep consciousness of life that is ALL and in ALL.

We began our time together with this book wondering about the roots of the word 'hatha' . . . to strike, to have an effect upon.

Have you discovered through your own experiences that it doesn't take much to know THE ALL? No acrobatics needed. Perhaps just a nudge, a hint, a gentle poke, as one would playfully poke a baby in the ribs to get a cute laugh from the baby.

Maybe this renewed look into hatha yoga—from within the yogic tradition and outside it—helps to relax a little bit any convictions about the way you think yoga SHOULD BE...or the way humans SHOULD BE...or whatever silliness from which I all too often find myself clinging and suffering.

Hopefully this book is contributing to a larger and more harmonizing view of what yoga is and can be—especially among all the competing voices within 'yoga' and all who play with moving and breathing and resting.

Could it all be so simple as simply noticing? Consciousness? Could such awareness of sensation be the way to renew the whole world?

May you be nudged.
May we all be nudged.
May we sense all there is with that gentle nudge . . .
and may you find the soil that's best for you —

somewhere in the middle of vast space that is THE ALL —

the soil where you can grow in your own unique way with your special limbs and bends and leaves that dance in the breeze and your roots that twist and twine and celebrate you and what you are about as a unique creation just as every tree is so, so very different

every tree, every creature, every creation its own beautiful mystery to appreciate

that such appreciation radiates and falls us into the spell of love

that we all once knew and can know again and again and again

yes, let it be so

as IT IS . . .

to a new world, friends! to a new world . . . !

In great gratitude for my teachers . . .

who pointed out a few things I might have never noticed or sensed and then left me alone to figure it out for myself because they knew that anyone and everyone can . . . any teacher worth their salt simply and with as few words as possible helps us listen to the Inner Teacher, the voice inside our very own self that invites us more deeply into life, the gentlest nudge...

Guided Meditation
First experiences with St. Ignatius Grade School Youth Group leaders

Meditation
St. Xavier High School Health & Religion Teachers, especially Dave Eby & Ron Stegman (Religion)

Qigong, Tai Chi, Tuina, & Bagua
Vincent Lasorso + Victor, Steve, Helen (White Willow, Cincinnati) & Nganga Mfundishi Tolo-Naa (QuieScience - national)

Yoga
Amber Jean (Yoga Ah! - Cincinnati) & Larry Schultz (It's Yoga - San Francisco)
Becky Morrissey (Sangha Yoga - Loveland, OH) & Lila Lolling (EcoYoga Life)

Sekhem-Seichim Reiki & SKHM
Anne Steffen (Cincinnati)

Healing Touch Program®
1: Daniel Snyder (Cincinnati)
2: Charlette Lev Gordon (Cincinnati)
3: M. Anne Boyd (Asheville, NC)
4: Mary Ann Geoffrey (national teacher)
5: Sharon Scandrett Hibdon (national teacher)
ongoing studies: Mary Duennes, Lynn Placek, Cynthia Hutchison (national teachers)

Movement Intelligence®
Cynthia Allen (Future Life Now - Cincinnati) &
Ruthy Alon (program founder - Tel Aviv, Israel)

Feldenkrais Method®
David Zemach-Bersin, educational director at the Feldenkrais
Institute of New York, with Sheryl Field, Anastasi Siotas, Carol
Kress, Aliza Stewart, Deborah Bowes, Raz Ori, Elizabeth Beringer,
and many more

The Bengston Energy Healing Method®
Dr. William Bengston & Margaret Nies

Vipassana Meditation
S.N. Goenka & his international assistant teachers at the Bay Area
Vipassana Center (California)

and the best teachers of them all . . .
the students in my classes at St. Xavier High School & St. Ursula
Academy & the people who come to teach and learn together
at VITALITY Cincinnati . . . Larry Schultz's last words to me,
"You'll realize you don't really know much of anything until you start
teaching, and then your students will teach you the most through
their questions." So true!

To deepen your discovery...

some recommended resources

I learn something in every single yoga or moving-breathing-resting class I take—no matter if the teacher is teaching their first class or has been at it for decades.

Sometimes it's even just the particular cadence or tenor of someone's voice that helps me to finally hear something that my teachers have been inviting me to for decades.

Invitation to sensation is a rich endeavor, and so important and so great when we are human beings in the same space with one another, in friendship with one another, sharing the same air with one another.

Sometimes I do all that the teacher-leader invites me to do in the class, sometimes I pick and choose among the invitations and just rest as everyone else explores—especially if I know a teacher-leader's invitation is going to harm me.

Relationship in all ways is key, right?

These books are wonderful invitations too:

'Classical' Yoga Teachings

Patanjali's Yoga Sutras . . . I've enjoyed Barbara Stoler Miller's translation *Yoga: Discipline of Freedom...The Yoga Sutra Attributed to Patanjali.* (New York: Bantam, 1995).

The Bhagavad Gita . . . I've enjoyed the translation by Swami Prabhavananda & Christopher Isherwood (*The Song of God.* New York: Mentor, 1944). Their contextual essays explaining where this relatively short Gita story rests in the larger *Mahabharata* are quite helpful. I've also benefited from Sri Swami Satchidananda's *The Living Gita* with its commentary set nearly line-by-line between the Gita's verses (Yogaville, VA: Integral Yoga Publications, 1988). Recently found my way to Barbara Stoler Miller's translation too (New York: Bantam, 1986).

Whatever translation you choose—and there are many more!—consider reading The Gita along with and at about the same time as Steven Pressfield's *The Legend of Bagger Vance* (New York: Avon, 1995) . . . do so and you too will know all things! :)

The Dhammapada . . . like these classics above, there are MANY translations available. I've recently enjoyed the translation by Gil Fronsdal. (Boulder: Shambhala, 2005).

Hatha Yoga Pradipika . . . while not so much a 'classical' yoga text as a text of the medieval period, I've found it helpful to see where some of the collisions of the ever-unfolding yoga tradition get resolved by Svatmarama in his own interesting ways. I've read often Brian Dana Akers' translation (Woodstock, NY: YogaVidya.com, 2002).

Dr. Jason Birch's work with Sanskrit has inspired me to begin my own studies. His important article: "Meaning of 'hatha' in Early Hathayoga" Jason Birch. Journal of the American Oriental Society 131.4 (2011) - easily found at https://www.academia.edu/1539699/Meaning_of_haha_in_Early_Hahayoga

Sanskrit Glossary of Yogic Terms. Swami Yogakanti. (Bihar, India: Yoga Publications Trust, 2007). I've appreciated this resource a great deal. To get a deeper take on the word 'rishi / rishika' and all the references Swami Yogakanti suggests, I checked out a number of references, including Wiktionary, which relates the rishi-poetry back to the Proto-Indo-Iranian concept of flowing or pouring (shape-shifting!). Know something of poetry and this makes a great deal of sense!

More on Tirumalai Krishnamacharya . . .

Krishnamacharya: His Life and Teachings. A.G. Mohan with Ganesh Mohan. Boston: Shambhala, 2010.

The Yoga of the Yogi: The Legacy of T. Krishnamacharya. Kausthub Desikachar. New York: North Point Press, 2005. (written by Krishnamacharya's grandson)

The Yoga Tradition of the Mysore Palace. N.E. Sjoman. (New Delhi: Abhinav Publications, 1999). Brilliant, including his take on why we fell for gurus in the 20th century.

Yoga books written by Krishnamacharya's long-time students . . .
much, much different from the yoga-asana offered
by Pattabhi Jois and BKS Iyengar

The Viniyoga of Yoga: applying yoga for healthy living. TVK Desikachar with Kausthub Desikachar & Frans Moors. (Chennai: Krishnamacharya Yoga Mandiram, 2001). A wonderfully revealing book about how to tailor yoga practice to individuals.

Yoga for Body, Breath, and Mind: A Guide to Personal Reintegration. A.G. Mohan. Forward by Shri T. Krishnamacharya. (Boston: Shambhala, 2002). Mohan studied with Krishnamacharya weekly for eighteen years at the end of Krishnamacharya's life.

Yoga for Americans: A Complete 6 Weeks' Course for Home Practice. Indra Devi. (Englewood Cliffs, NJ: Prentice-Hall, 1959). The actress-turned-yoga teacher, thanks to her courage to seek training from Krishnamacharya!

Resources that might help us all to realize the age
of the gurus is over, if it ever was . . .
YOU be the light and stop giving your power away to 'gurus'! :)

The Science of Yoga: The Risks and the Rewards. William J Broad. (New York: Simon & Schuster, 2012). We use this book in our VITALITY 300-hour yoga teacher training. It's that good and frees us, as we hope this book you've read here does, of our attachments to the way yoga SHOULD be. One of the best collections of the academic research on yoga available.

Breath of the Gods: A Journey Into the Origins of Modern Yoga (documentary-movie) by Jan Schmidt-Garre (2012). Explores the teachings of Krishnamacharya, especially through his 'star' pupils Pattabhi Jois & BKS Iyengar.

Ashtanga: Ashtanga Yoga As Taught By Shri K Pattabhi Jois. Larry Schultz. (San Francisco: Nauli Press, 1997). My first yoga manual, and one of the first created for yoga teacher trainings—at the insistence of the Grateful Dead!

First There is a Mountain: A Yoga Romance. Elizabeth Kadetsky. (New York: Little, Brown and Company, 2004). Kadetsky talks about her studies with BKS Iyengar and his family.

The Prophetic Imagination. Walter Brueggemann. (Minneapolis: Fortress, 1978). What the prophets are up to is quite surprising . . . ! Just wait until my translation of I Samuel (from the Hebrew) is released later this year (I hope) . . . the invitation to find IT ALL in the breeze . . . !

The Gospel of Jesus: According to the Jesus Seminar. Robert W Funk, Arthur J Dewey & the Jesus Seminar. (Salem, OR: Polebridge, 2015—be sure to check out the new and improved Second Edition). What Jesus was up to is quite surprising . . . !

The Authentic Letters of Paul: A New Reading of Paul's Rhetoric and Meaning. Arthur J Dewey, Roy W Hoover, Lane C McGaughy,

Daryl D Schmidt. (Salem, OR: Polebridge, 2010). What people think goes back to Paul and what doesn't will surprise you . . . ! Perhaps Paul is indeed the first person to imagine a world without borders, all under the rule of THE ALL, God.

More on Moshe Feldenkrais . . .

The Brain's Way of Healing: Remarkable Discoveries and Recoveries from the Frontiers of Neuroplasticity. Norman Doidge, MD. (New York: Viking, 2015). Chapters 5 & 6 are about Feldenkrais . . . a great place to start.

Embodied Wisdom: The Collected Papers of Moshe Feldenkrais. Moshe Feldenkrais. (San Diego: Somatic Resources, 2010). If you're looking for Feldenkrais' clear and resonant voice, begin here!

The Elusive Obvious (or Basic Feldenkrais). Moshe Feldenkrais. (Capitola, CA: Meta, 1981).

Making Connections: Hasidic Roots and Resonance in the Teachings of Moshe Feldenkrais. David Kaetz. (Metchosin: River Centre, 2007). I am delighted to have met and chatted with David Kaetz, one of the brighter minds in our world today.

Moshe Feldenkrais: A Life in Movement. Mark Reese. (San Rafael, CA: ReeseKress Somatics Press, 2015). It's a thick biography . . . and the first half reads like a novel because Feldenkrais' life-story is so fantastic!

More on Marion Woodman . . .

Dancing in the Flames: The Dark Goddess in the Transformation of Consciousness. Marion Woodman & Elinor Dickson. (Boston: Shambhala, 1997).

Bone: Dying into Life. Marion Woodman. (New York: Penguin, 2001).

Leaving My Father's House: A Journey to Conscious Femininity. Marion Woodman, with Kate Danson, Mary Hamilton, Rita Greer Allen. (Boston: Shambhala, 1993).

The Pregnant Virgin: A Process of Psychological Transformation. Marion Woodman. (Toronto: Inner City, 1985).

or . . . instead of a whole book you might enjoy little dollops of Marion Woodman's writing . . . *Coming Home to Myself: Reflections for Nurturing a Woman's Body & Soul.* Marion Woodman & Jill Mellick. (San Francisco: Conari, 1998).

More on Ruthy Alon . . .

Her best written work, in my opinion, is the Bones for Life® Manual . . . *Movement Intelligence: Bones for Life: The Movement Answer for Bones Strength and Weight Bearing Posture.* Three Manuals used in certifying Bones for Life Teachers. 2014.

Or purchase her recordings. I was honored to attend and then be invited to create a detailed index for her *Movement Intelligence: Solutions for Optimal Mobility 2 - part 2* (New York City: 2017). Reach out to Feldenkrais Access at info@feldenkraisaccess.com for details about this particular recording.

Or take a workshop with her: movementintelligence.com

Or take a class in the US with her certified teachers: movement intelligence.org

Or join us at VITALITY...in person, or online with Future Life Now's Cynthia Allen:
vitalitycincinnati.org

Check out his QuieScience Sacred Science Temple (quiet science) at <u>myqsst.com</u>. I couldn't have asked for better teachers and human-initiators in the healing arts when I was in my early 20s than I found with Tolo-Naa and Vince Lasorso (White Willow - Cincinnati) and the people with whom they surrounded themselves and allowed / authorized to teach me. Gratitude!

My experiences with both of these teachers were more experience-rich. During that time, though, I read three great books:

Tao Te Ching. Translated by Stephen Mitchell. (New York: HarperCollins, 1988).

Chronicles of Tao: The Secret Life of a Taoist Master. Deng Ming-Dao. (New York: HarperOne, 1993).

Book of Ki: Co-ordinating Mind and Body in Daily Life. Koichi Tohei. (Tokyo: Japan Publications, 1976). What Tohei is up to with 'immovability' is incredibly interesting to me. Vince Lasorso is a master at Tohei's immovability ideas. While I disagree that Mind and Body are ever separate, I completely agree with the idea of finding ways to remind ourselves of the oneness of body-mind-spirit—that we are a 'unity' unto our own self. And yet a permeable one . . . breath, spirit.

Curious & inspiring resources to consider . . .

Song of Myself. Walt Whitman. I like the lovely little version edited by Stephen Mitchell. (Boston: Shambhala, 1993). Whitman might know more about yoga than any of us yoga teachers today, though I don't think he studied any of it, unlike his contemporary Henry David Thoreau who read *The Bhagavad Gita* and maybe more. No need for all the 'information' <u>about</u> yoga when you can find it in your own experience of Nature!

The Holographic Universe. Michael Talbot. (New York: Harper, 1991). Traces the fascinating research of physicist David Bohm and neuro-physiologist Karl Pribram and finds Carl Jung and so many in the middle of it.

The Brain's Way of Healing: Remarkable Discoveries and Recoveries from the Frontiers of Neuroplasticity. Norman Doidge, M.D. New York: Viking, 2015. Incredible.

Healing and the Mind. Bill Moyers et al. (New York: Doubleday, 1993). Bill Moyers interviews many medical professionals about what medical professionals are using holistically in their hospital practices. The interview with Jon Kabat-Zinn was an inspiration for me personally and in envisioning VITALITY . . . as Kabat-Zinn began a 'Stress Reduction Clinic' in a major hospital with much success. In the 1980's!!

Many Lives, Many Masters. Brian J Weiss, M.D. (New York: Simon & Schuster, 1988). A psychiatrist tells the story of discovering the veil between this life and the next(s) very thin for himself and his patients. It will have you re-thinking whatever it is you're so sure of about past lives . . . no matter what you think you know now.

Infinite Mind: Science of the Human Vibrations of Consciousness. Valerie V. Hunt. (Malibu, CA: Malibu Publishing, 1989 & 1996). Like Brian Weiss, another researcher who didn't go looking for anything like this through her university-lab experiments and stumbled upon a remarkable discovery . . . the human energy field.

The Spell of the Sensuous: Perception and Language in a More-Than-Human World. David Abram. (New York: Vintage, 1996). I'm so grateful I found this book, which helped me appreciate language again . . . as sound.

The Energy Cure: Unraveling the Mysteries of Hands-On Healing. William Bengston, PhD. (Boulder, CO: Sounds True, 2010). Many of us have benefitted from Bengston's work/play a great deal at VITALITY . . . from cancer cures to new jobs to worldwide adventure to . . . who knows what goodness is next. Quite a good guy too.

Healing Touch Program®—take a class, we recommend our yoga teacher trainers do, best explanation of chakras and energy for beginners to advanced practitioners out there . . . and it's wonderful collection of MANY different healing approaches, not just founder Janet Mentgen's approach, which is wonderful in itself. Even the most 'advanced healer' will find a gem or two in this program. healingtouchprogram.com

Joy's Way: A Map for the Transformational Journey & An Introduction to the Potential for Healing with Body Energies. W Brugh Joy, M.D. (New York: Penguin/Putnam, 1979). The story of how a United States medical doctor left his practice because he found that hands-on healing work and even people being heart-centered in a group together without any touch transformed more lives than his medical practice.

Vipassana Meditation as taught by S.N. Goenka: dhamma.org. I helped a young man find his way from LaGuardia airport to Penn Station to get to New Jersey and on the subway he helped me find vipassana. It only took me 15 months to get there on retreat. :)

To learn more about Ignatius Loyola, SJ, and his brother from a different mother Pedro Arrupe, SJ, mentioned earlier . . . *Ignatian Humanism: A Dynamic Spirituality for the 21st Century.* Ronald Modras. (Chicago: Jesuit Way / Loyola Press, 2004).

Stride Toward Freedom: The Montgomery Story. Dr. Martin Luther King, Jr. (New York: Harper & Row, 1958). The very best work on nonviolence, written before MLK was on the international stage.

Neuroplasticity. Moheb Costandi. (Cambridge, MA: MIT Press, 2016). A delightful little book that surveys the history, biology, and practicality of this new medical / scientific field.

RECIPES

Conversations around food
are always better!

At just about every VITALITY function, we have food. Most of it 'healthy.' As much as possible from local growers.

One time the bell peppers from Our Harvest were so big, so beautiful, multi-colorful, and so delicious we refused to cut them up and served them like apples!

We learn something of each other when we share food together. We learn about the food-preparers' likes, their interests, their style, their taste. We come to appreciate that person in a new way, in gratitude for offering food. There is power in a group, in friends coming together. And THE ALL is no quick fix . . . we need sustenance for the journey of letting it unfold for us.

We offer you a few recipes we've enjoyed and hope that through sharing food among friends you too can come to know life in all its fullness . . . that we are indeed the apples of the eyes of one another . . .

Apples, Red Lentils, & Your Favorite Things!

cup of dry red lentils, rinsed
2 cups of water or veggie broth or your favorite stock
3 small apples diced, with cores removed and composted
today I added dried sage from VITALITY-grad Aprilann Pandora's Eden Urban Gardens, a couple dashes of ginger, cinnamon, red pepper flakes, salt and a cap-full of apple cider vinegar with the Mother
your favorite greens, veggies, meat, etc.
sea-salt to taste

Combine the lentils and water/broth and a dash of salt in a pot and warm on the stovetop. About half-way through their cooking add the remaining ingredients.

Simmer for 30 minutes or so until the lentils break up and enjoy!

Would be lovely over some of your favorite white rice—so easy to digest :)

Persian-style Pomegranate-Apple-Walnut Sauce

3 medium-sized pomegranates
2 small apples
3 cups of walnuts
at least 1 tablespoon of maple syrup
dashes of ginger, cinnamon, turmeric, & coriander...all to taste

I had a sauce similar to this at a Persian restaurant that a friend took me to in San Francisco as I told him all about my vipassana experience. It was amazing, and richer than the one I made at home . . . true of vipassana too!

Cut each pomegranate in half and then use a fork to dig out the interior—the arils that contain the seed—and put the arils/seeds in a blender (discard the rind) with the two apples (cores removed, peel could be removed too) and add the rest of the ingredients above. Mix until smooth, preferably very smooth.

Studying this sauce, which goes by the name of Fesenjan in Persian, many recipe contributors suggest blending the pomegranate seeds just long enough to separate the juice from the seed and then to strain the juice from the seed-remnants and keep only the juice for the sauce. Boo! I prefer to keep it all—and the fiber! Health!

Pomegranates can be bitter or very sweet, depending on many factors. (They all stain light colored material, etc. so be smart!) You might need to add more or less maple syrup to sweeten the sauce as you like. If you'd like it to be thicker, add more walnuts. I added apples to this version to stretch the pomegranates a bit, as they are pretty expensive in Cincinnati, though a nice treat!

The sauce is delicious raw like this or warmed in a pot on the stovetop.

And it's very versatile as a dip for anything (raw veggies or fruit or spread it on bread), as a sauce with warmed vegetables or greens over rice and lentils, with meat if you're a meat-eater, whatever.

Make it festive and fancy and garnish it all with fresh herbs!

Sweet Salad with Apples

3-4 medium sized apples
8 ounces of raisins
4 ounces of maple syrup
1 medium sized orange
1 teaspoon of apple cider vinegar
3-4 dashes of cinnamon, or to taste
8 ounces of almonds
16 ounces/big container of salad greens

Chop apples into tiny little pieces and place them in a bowl. Add raisins, maple syrup, apple cider vinegar, cinnamon. Cut in half and de-seed the orange, then squeeze out the juice on top of everything in the bowl. We like to include the pulp too for flavor/texture. Mix everything very well, cover, and chill for awhile if possible.

Put almonds into food processor and grind them down to powder.

When ready to serve, mix salad greens into the apples+. Once everything is well mixed and all salad greens are wet, pour almonds onto the top of the salad, add one dash of cinnamon on top, and serve.

* sometimes we add a can or two or drained and rinsed chickpeas to the salad for an extra protein kick

Caramel Apple Pudding
with Chilled Coconut 'Cream'

12 ounce can of coconut milk—chill it in the refrigerator one night before
2 medium-sized apples, cores removed, peel them if you prefer
about 25 large pitted dates (I used Medjool)
8 ounces of almond butter (or peanut butter)
1/2 teaspoon vanilla extract
1/2 teaspoon of salt (more or less to taste, maybe a lot less if the nut butter is salted)
tablespoon of maple syrup (more or less, to taste)
1/2 cup of water

Boil water. Put pitted dates in a glass/metal bowl, smash them down and cover with the boiled water. Cover and let sit for about an hour.

In processor, empty entire can of coconut milk after it has chilled in the refrigerator overnight. Add vanilla extract and whip until thick.

Drain most of the coconut milk-whip into a separate bowl and return it to the refrigerator.

DO NOT CLEAN THE PROCESSOR! :) Put remaining ingredients— including the water with the dates—into processor and mix thoroughly.

Chill again. Or serve warmed on the stovetop.

Serve with chilled coconut cream as a topping, maybe with a dash of cinnamon or ginger for extra flavor or decoration. Delicious!

About the artists . . .
creations here & the stories they invite

Parrish Monk *created the inspiring painting on the front cover of this book, and covers for two earlier VITALITY buzz & books . . . the front cover of* Sweet Lady J *and the second edition back cover of* A New Setting of Ignatius' Spiritual Exercises.

In addition to being a husband and father of three boys, Parrish is a self-taught, full-time visual artist and artisan living in Northern Kentucky where he also works as a part-time adult educator and college professor teaching math and business management courses to adult learners. Parrish is passionate about using his creativity to help empower others and support other artists, artisans, organizations and small businesses through his non-profit artist collaborative and business incubator.

Parrish was fortunate to meet VITALITY members like Brian Shircliff early on in his art career in 2013 and while Parrish no longer practices yoga-asana, Parrish has enjoyed the mutual support and shared vision of helping people to heal and become their better selves as practiced by VITALITY and its members.

Diana Avergon *created the inspiring print for the back cover of this book. She and her husband* **Eugene Avergon** *are committed to art, both as artists and art education publishers. Eugene's focus is on sculpture, while Diana's is on printmaking, in which they each hold advanced degrees. They have been incredibly generous supporters of VITALITY through many donations of original art for inspiring decoration at VITALITY and for VITALITY's many auctions raising funds for their mission.*

Julie Lucas *created the images throughout the body of this book, in addition to VITALITY's logos. She is an industrial designer with an intuitive design sense and an inclination to wonder. Through the art of* *listening and inquiry, she amplifies intentions and brings story to life. She has been a supporter of VITALITY from its beginnings – see more of her creations at* <u>withinwonder.com</u>.

Julie's images tell the story of growth, of yoga, of THE ALL:

- a whole apple
- an apple split in thirds

. . . the story of creation alluded to in <u>The Bhagavad Gita</u>, *the three gunas: rajas, tamas, sattva.*

- a human planting a small apple-seed in the earth - EARTH
- the rain assisting the apple-seed to grow - WATER
- the sun assisting the apple-seedling to grow - FIRE
- the wind assisting the apple-plant to grow deeper roots - AIR
- the moon and the sun watching over the small apple-tree growing and differentiating leaves from branches from trunk and roots rooting down even more through all the space upward, downward, outward - SPACE / ETHER

. . . the five elements of life, of creation, in Yogic & Buddhist philosophy . . . how life grows with the elements, how life is enriched by the elements.

- the two-panels: fully-grown, abundant fruit-bearing tree among all life, all creation, and with Patanjali's Eight Limbs as guides to knowing THE ALL, all life, all creation.

VITALITY began small, three of us at Healing Touch Program's Level 4 who dreamed about making Healing Touch affordable for all. Quickly, we gathered an important group of people from all walks of life who wanted to make that a reality. Self-care was very important to all of us — the 'good news' we wanted to share. We chose Healing Touch, yoga, journaling, meditation and recently added Movement Intelligence® & Feldenkrais Method® because they are all gentle, holistic modalities that can be learned easily and practiced by people in their own homes, with family and friends, often with very little equipment needed.

And that is how we work at VITALITY. Through these self-care modalities, we invite growth with one person who shares it with another person and another person, and before you know it, there is a holistically-minded person in every home in Cincinnati, Northern Kentucky, and all over the world who can share what they know and listen to and learn from one another's experiences.

In a most important sense, then, it's relationship that is vital. Perhaps these 'modalities' are simply ways of opening to one another, of being fully alive to one another . . . to see and hear and sense the wholeness — THE ALL—of one another.

VITALITY was founded in 2010 as a 501(c)3 charitable/educational organization. We rent a small space in Norwood, the center of Cincinnati.

All of our programs welcome everyone and are donation-based . . . from a handful of change to a check.

Since beginning VITALITY's Yoga/Healing Touch Internship—which certifies 200-hour yoga teachers—our graduates have shared yoga and Healing Touch-inspired meditations all over the country—even as far as South Africa!

Our Yoga/Healing Touch Intern-Graduates have shared their gifts in college yoga clubs, among high school faculty/staff, in recreation centers and gyms among all ages, in fields, at traditional yoga studios owned by themselves or friends, at businesses and research labs, in garden centers, in restaurants and tea houses, in parks, in food pantries, in churches and places of worship, in coffee shops, in community rooms, in food courts, in senior centers, in board rooms, in art galleries, among grade school & junior high faculty/staff, on farms, in barns, in fields, in prisons, in hospitals, in health centers, at resorts, in factories, in centers for the blind, in their own homes, in apartment community rooms, in recovery centers, at farmers markets, at breweries and bourbon distilleries, at food co-ops, at pre-schools, at orphanages, at homeless shelters, for hospital networks, in classrooms, at cancer recovery centers, in auditoria, at nature centers, in garages, in grocery stores . . . in just about any place you could imagine.

And what's even better, these graduates create their own brands, their own versions of moving-breathing-resting that are not VITALITY's brand. Graduates create small businesses to help themselves and their families thrive holistically and financially by meeting their class-participants where they are.

Some graduates share their holistic-gifts for a living, as full-time or part-time jobs; others volunteer as they are able; others share with family and friends as they feel most comfortable. Nearly all of our graduates offer at least some classes by donation (as we do at VITALITY) or on a sliding-scale.

One day, VITALITY hopes to have its own energy-self-sufficient building, retreat-house, and publishing center that will gather funds not only to keep VITALITY Cincinnati growing but will also provide seed-money & micro-lending for graduates and groups of people like VITALITY around the world committed to deepening the growth of humanity on this planet through:

- organic community gardening and healthy-eating gatherings where relationship and ideas are born;

- places for the study of gentle movement, meditation, contemplation, nonviolence's cleverness . . . where people gather to imagine a new world, a citizenship of the world-over where we recognize our planetary intraconnectedness . . . where we might cleverly, non-violently, joyfully, freely, responsibly, and abundantly live together on our earth for many more generations as we discover and live out our common human life together;

- small communities that use earth-friendly energy-sources and seek the joy of self-sufficiency, minding the relationships between and among all that lives.

We welcome you to join us and share your gifts, especially the most important gift of your presence.

VITALITY

buzz & books

(re)discovering roots

vitalitycincinnati.org

available through vitalitycincinnati.org,
Amazon, and your local bookstore!

A New Setting of the Spiritual Exercises: Hearing, Seeing, Feeling Old Stories in New Ways
(2015, 2nd Edition coming in 2019)

Brian J. Shircliff offers a very different take on Ignatius' notebooks that gave birth to Ignatian Spirituality through the Spiritual Exercises, and yet this 'new setting' is very true to the spirit of Ignatius. Authors Dan Price, Tamilla Cordeiro, Brian Geeding, Maureen Sullivan-Mahoney, Bridget Rice, Mike Eck, Carol T. Yeazell, Shelia Barnes, Theresa Popelar, Richard Bollman SJ, Bailey Dixon, Melanie Moon, Jalisa Holifield, and Elizabeth J. Winters Waite contribute their personal lifestories to the book . . . the book's true richness. An interview with Jean Marie Stross, Dan Price, and Richard Bollman, S.J. offers a context to this new setting of the Exercises, part of a larger re-imagining of the Exercises in Cincinnati and around the world.

Sweet Lady J...Mother, Muse & Root of Nearly Everything: The 3000-year-old Campfire Stories of Biblical Genesis Giving Birth to Judaism, Christianity, Islam, Nonviolence & Neuroplasticity (2017)

With an original and lively translation from the Hebrew text into English, Brian J. Shircliff takes us on a journey into the first strand of the Bible.

Coming in 2019 . . .

Richard Bollman, S.J. **Selected Homilies: allowing life experience to open up the ways and the Word of God**

Brian J. Shircliff **The Naked Path of Prophet: a translation of 1 Samuel & invitation to the prophetic ecstatic-visionary-healing lifestyle of Jesus, of many**

VITALITY authors **Inviting Eve to Speak**

About the lead author

Brian J. Shircliff *is one of the original founding members of VITALITY in 2010.*

He taught religion and coached golf & swimming at St. Xavier High School (1997 - 2013) & taught religion at St. Ursula Academy (2018). Thanks to his own excellent teachers, from the very beginning of his own teaching career, Brian realized that providing opportunities for people to share with one another stories and insights from texts and life was the very best way of education . . . a discovering together, a 'leading out' to new horizons. Everything is new again, or can be, every day through each of our rich perspectives shaped by imagination and sensation.

He is fascinated by the impossible and incredibly important opportunity of trying to imagine or even guess at the human experiences that gave rise to ancient stories and traditions by reading the ancient texts and artifacts we have inherited . . . the inner basements within us ALL.

He directs programs at VITALITY and is excited to see graduates beginning their own small businesses through yoga, meditation, gardening, herbalism, sustainability, Movement Intelligence, Healing Touch and more that they go on to invent.

He is grateful to Amy Fogelson, Jodi Shircliff, and Carol T. Yeazell for reading and offering valuable feed back on this book.

Brian was surprised this book arrived as it did . . . more of a theological-philosophical conversation and invitation to experience. He'd love your feedback . . . reach out to him through **vitalitycincinnati.org**.

walk my life
in shoes
and my feet never meet the ground
and my life is all 'up there'
hifallutin
nowhere
toes-stick
brain-sick
stuck-fast
nothin

walk my life
barefoot or shoed
on hard surfaces
concrete, hardwood, godforbidden linoleum
and everything starts too soon to hurt
nothing gives
but me
and when I have to give too much
i can't meet you
with anything to give
tangled mess of humanity that I am

walk my life
barefoot
naked feet
on the soft surface of the earth
blanketed just right
with leaves and grass and wet
and my feet shape the muddy earth
and the muddy earth me
through my feet
each shoulder rises differently with each step
as my foot gives with the muddy earth
my ribs spring back to life like a child

and all so suddenly THE ALL
it's so rich
i linger here
even in bare feet
the hawk flies so ridiculously high overhead
the wind blows my face to follow it
my heart beats a different rhythm
nature's drum within all creatures
nature meeting nature
something warms inside
the sexiness of the muddy earth
it gives and receives
true life, THE ALL

do you really think
you're wiser than
the wind?
than Old Breezy?
the wind laughs at you.
and loves you.
even if you don't

a little nudge
every day
and before i know it
i've traveled
the galaxy
nearly ALL
the way
and back
again

anew

some days
the wisest thing I do
is sit and listen
to the neighborhood hawk
whose cry speaks for the world

CPSIA information can be obtained
at www.ICGtesting.com
Printed in the USA
FFHW011934070919
54785701-60455FF